YALE ORIENTAL SERIES

RESEARCHES

VOLUME XIII

PART I

(All Published)

PUBLISHED ON THE FOUNDATION
ESTABLISHED BY THE
KINGSLEY TRUST ASSOCIATION

AMS PRESS
NEW YORK

YALE ORIENTAL SERIES · RESEARCHES · VOLUME XIII–1

PERSONAL NAMES
FROM
CUNEIFORM INSCRIPTIONS
OF
CAPPADOCIA

BY

FERRIS J. STEPHENS, PH.D.

ASSISTANT PROFESSOR OF ASSYRIOLOGY IN YALE UNIVERSITY

NEW HAVEN · YALE UNIVERSITY PRESS

LONDON · HUMPHREY MILFORD · OXFORD UNIVERSITY PRESS

MDCCCCXXVIII

Library of Congress Cataloging in Publication Data

Stephens, Ferris J. 1893–
Personal names from cuneiform inscriptions of Cappadocia.

Reprint of the 1928 ed. published by Yale University Press, New Haven, which was issued as v. 13-1 of Researches of the Yale oriental series.
1. Names, Personal—Cappadocian. 2. Cuneiform inscriptions, Cappadocian. I. Title. II. Series: Yale oriental series: Researches; v. 13-1.
PJ3591.Z8 1980 929.4′093934 78-63557
ISBN 0-404-60283-5

International Standard Book Number
Complete Set: 0-404-60270-3
Volume 13: 0-404-60283-5

Reprinted by arrangement with Yale University Press, from the edition of 1928, New Haven. Trim size has been altered (original: 17.5 × 24.5 cm). Text area is unchanged.

MANUFACTURED
IN THE UNITED STATES OF AMERICA

TO THE MEMORY OF

ALBERT T. CLAY

MY ILLUSTRIOUS TEACHER

AND ESTEEMED FRIEND

CONTENTS

ABBREVIATIONS

ADB — Johns, C. H. W., *An Assyrian Doomsday Book*, Band XVII, *Assyriologische Bibliothek*, 1901.

Babyl. — *Babyloniaca.*

BE III(1) — Myhrman, David W., *Sumerian Administrative Documents .... from the Temple Archives of Nippur*, Vol. III, Part 1, *The Babylonian Expedition of the University of Pennsylvania, Series A: Cuneiform Texts.* 1910.

BE VI(2) — Poebel, Arno, *Babylonian Legal and Business Documents from the Time of the First Dynasty of Babylon*, Vol. VI, Part 2, *The Babylonian Expedition of the University of Pennsylvania, Series A: Cuneiform Texts.* 1909.

Bezold — Bezold, Carl, *Babylonisch-Assyrisches Glossar.* 1926.

Bi. — Biblical.

BIN II — Nies, James B., and Keiser, Clarence E., *Historical Religious and Economic Texts and Antiquities*, Vol. II, *Babylonian Inscriptions in the Collection of James B. Nies.* 1920.

BIN IV — Clay, Albert T., *Letters and Transactions from Cappadocia*, Vol. IV, *Babylonian Inscriptions in the Collection of James B. Nies.* 1927.

CCT I — Smith, Sidney, *Cuneiform Texts from Cappadocian Tablets in the British Museum*, Part I. 1921.

CCT II — Smith, Sidney, *ibid.*, Part II. 1924.

CCT III — Smith, Sidney, *ibid.*, Part III. 1925.

CCT IV — Smith, Sidney, *ibid.*, Part IV. 1927.

Chantre — Chantre, E., *Mission en Cappadoce.* 1898.

Clay, *Empire* — Clay, Albert T., *The Empire of the Amorites*, Vol. VI, *Yale Oriental Series, Researches.* 1919.

Clay, *Traditions* — Clay, Albert T., *The Origin of Biblical Traditions*, Vol. XII, *Yale Oriental Series, Researches.* 1923.

CPN — Clay, Albert T., *Personal Names of the Cassite Period*, Vol. I, *Yale Oriental Series, Researches.* 1912.

CTK — Contenau, G., *Les Tablettes de Kerkouk et les Origines de la Civilization Assyrienne, Babyloniaca*, Vol. IX, Parts 2–4.

DmlPan	Deimel, Anton, *Pantheon Babylonicum.* 1914.
DmlWTF	Deimel, Anton, *Wirtschaftstexte aus Fara*, 45 *Wissenschaftliche Veröffentlichung der Deutschen Orient-Gesellschaft.* 1924.
Gol.	Golénischeff, W., *Vingt-quatre Tablettes Cappadociennes.* 1891.
GTK	Gadd, C. J., *Tablets from Kerkuk, RA*, Vol. XXIII, No. 2–4.
HPN	Huber, P. Engelbert, *Die Personennamen in den Keilschrifturkunden aus der Zeit der Könige von Ur und Nisin*, Band XXI, *Assyriologische Bibliothek.* 1907.
HSS III	Hussey, Mary I., *Sumerian Tablets in the Harvard Semitic Museum*, Part I, Vol. III, *Harvard Semitic Series.* 1912.
HSS IV	Hussey, Mary I., *ibid.*, Part II. 1915.
JSOR	*Journal of the Society of Oriental Research.*
KTS	Lewy, Julius, *Die Altassyrischen Texte vom Kültepe bei Kaisarije, Keilschrifttexte in den Antiken Museen zu Stambul.* 1926.
LC	Thureau-Dangin, Fr., *Lettres et Contrats de l'Époque de la Première Dynastie Babylonienne, Musée du Louvre, Départment des Antiquités Orientales.* 1910.
LgrTemps	Legrain, L., *Le Temps des Rois d'Ur*, 199 Fascicule, *Bibliothèque de l'École des Hautes Études .... Sciences Philologiques et Historiques.*
Liv.	Pinches, Theophilus G., *The Cappadocian Tablets Belonging to the Liverpool Institute of Archaeology, Annals of Archaeology and Anthropology*, Vol. I, No. 3.
LTC IV	Contenau, G., *Tablettes Cappadociennes*, Vol. IV, *Musée du Louvre, Départment des Antiquités Orientales, Textes Cunéiformes.* 1920.
M-A	Muss-Arnolt, W., *A Concise Dictionary of the Assyrian Language.* 1905.
MVAG	*Mitteilungen der Vorderasiatischen Gesellschaft.*
NBC	Stephens, Ferris J., Collations from unpublished Cappadocian tablets in the Babylonian Collection of James B. Nies.
NBPN	Tallqvist, Knut L., *Neubabylonisches Namenbuch*, Vol. XXXII, No. 2, *Acta Societatis Scientiarum Fennicae.* 1905.
OLZ	*Orientalistische Literatur-Zeitung.*
PSBA	*Proceedings of the Society of Biblical Archaeology.*
RA	*Revue d'Assyriologie et d'Archéologie Orientale.*
RPN	Ranke, Hermann, *Early Babylonian Personal Names*, Vol. III, *The Babylonian Expedition of the University of Pennsylvania, Series D: Researches and Treatises.* 1905.
RT	*Recueil de Travaux Relatifs a la Philologie et a l'Archéologie.*

SATK	Lewy, Julius, *Studien zu den altassyrischen Texten aus Kappadokien.* 1922.
SCTP	Stephens, Ferris J., *The Cappadocian Tablets in the University of Pennsylvania Museum, JSOR,* XI, 101–136.
SPN	Sundwall, Joh., *Die einheimischen Namen der Lyker nebst einem Verzeichnisse kleinasiatischer Namenstämme,* elftes Beiheft, *KLIO.* 1913.
TAPN	Tallqvist, Knut L., *Assyrian Personal Names,* Vol. XLIII, No. 1, *Acta Societatis Scientiarum Fennicae.* 1914.
TbD	Genouillac, H. de, *Tablettes de Dréhem, Musée du Louvre, Départment des Antiquités Orientales.*
TrD	Genouillac, H. de, *La Trouvaille de Dréhem.* 1911.
TTC	Contenau, G., *Trente Tablettes Cappadociennes.* 1919.
UDT	Nies, James B., *Ur Dynasty Tablets,* Band XXV, *Assyriologische Bibliothek.* 1920.
UMBS XI (2)	Chiera, Edward, *Lists of Akkadian Personal Names,* Vol. XI, No. 2, *University of Pennsylvania, the University Museum, Publications of the Babylonian Section.* 1916.
YBT IV	Keiser, Clarence E., *Selected Temple Documents of the Ur Dynasty,* Vol. IV, *Yale Oriental Series, Babylonian Texts.* 1919.
YBT V	Grice, Ettalene M., *Records from Ur and Larsa,* Vol. V, *Yale Oriental Series, Babylonian Texts.* 1919.
YBT VI	Dougherty, R. P., *Records from Erech Time of Nabonidus,* Vol. VI, *Yale Oriental Series, Babylonian Texts.* 1920.
ZA	*Zeitschrift für Assyriologie.*

INTRODUCTION

The number of published cuneiform tablets from Cappadocia has increased very rapidly in the last decade. The result has been that the attention of Assyriologists has been directed to the problems raised by these tablets. A people hitherto unknown to history have now to be considered in the effort to reconstruct the early history of Asia Minor. One very useful factor in the reconstruction of the history of any people is the study of their personal names. It is therefore the purpose of the present work to present for the study of scholars a complete list of the personal names found in the Cappadocian tablets, together with a glossary of the elements contained in the names.

The first attempt at collecting Cappadocian personal names was made by W. Golénischeff, in *Vingt-Quatre Tablettes Cappadociennes,* 1891. A more complete list of the names of the same tablets was published by F. Delitzsch in *Beiträge zur Entzifferung und Erklärung der Kappadokischen Keilschrifttafeln: Abhandlung der philologisch-historischen Classe der Königlich Sächsischen Gesellschaft der Wissenschaften,* XIV 4. Leipzig, 1893. Dr. Georges Contenau in his *Trente Tablettes Cappadociennes* has collected all the names of the Cappadocian tablets which were published at that time. But the texts published since Contenau's list was made number a great many more than those which his list includes. With more material it has been possible to correct the reading of many of the names and to add new ones. The aggregate of published texts has now reached the point, however, when each new lot brings fewer new names, and less new light on the reading of old ones. Though the writer is aware that not a few Cappadocian tablets remain unpublished in the various museums of the world, it is his belief that the list here presented contains almost the entire number of personal names which were in use among the people represented by these business documents.

Attention is now directed to a few points of interest with reference to the reading and interpretation of some of the names.

THE GOD *Al*

Johns, *ADB*, p. 15, says that the name of a god in Harran was pronounced *Al, Alla,* and not *Ilu,* or *El.* The element *A-li* is of common occurrence in the names of the first dynasty of Babylon. To be compared with these in

Cappadocian names is the very common *A-lá-ḫu-um,* also *A-lá-bu-um,* *Al-be-li,* and *A-al-ṭâbu.* Surely the divine element in these names is *Al.* At the same time the names in which the divine element was *El* or *Ilu* are very numerous, as may be seen by consulting the lists. It is evident, then that all the Semites of Cappadocia did not pronounce this divine name in the same way.

THE ELEMENT *EL.ŠÚ.GAL*

THIS element occurs once in the name *Buzur-EL.ŠÚ.GAL,* where, from the analogy of other names compounded with the element *Buzur,* it must represent a deity. *ŠÚ.GAL* is a deity known in Cassite names (*CPN,* p. 207). *El* is here used in the same way as in the names *El-Amurru, El-Shaddai,* etc. (cf. Clay, *Empire,* p. 167). The Cappadocian name *Ì-lí-ŠÚ.GAN* is also to be compared. Weidner has shown (*Boghazköi Studien,* 6, p. 77, note 1) that *l* and *n* are frequently interchanged as in *Nur-Dagal* for *Nur-Dagan.* In view of this fact, and the Cappadocian use of the sign *NI* with the value *lí* as often as *ni,* it is not impossible that they wrote *ŠÚ.GAN* for *ŠÚ.GAL.*

THE ELEMENTS *BĀ.ŠÁ* AND *MAN*

THESE two elements are very common in Cappadocian names. Ungnad showed (*OLZ* 24, pp. 15, 16) that each is to be read *Puzur* in Assyrian names. The same will hold true in Cappadocian. The spelling *Buzur* has been adopted in this list because of the universal use on the part of the Cappadocians of *b* for *p.* The following facts prove that the two ideograms are but variant ways of writing the same name. The name of the son of *Ì-lí-a-lim* is written *BĀ.ŠÁ-A-na* (*CCT* II, 47b:3), and *MAN-A-na* (*BIN* IV, 185:8). The text *CCT* IV, 16b, where the name *BĀ.ŠÁ-Ištar* and *MAN-Ištar* each occur several times, might lead one to suppose that they were not variant spellings of the same name (cf. *CCT* IV, p. 3), but further consideration must reverse the decision. The document is a letter of *ŠÚ-Ištar* addressed to *Ga-ta-tim, BĀ.ŠÁ-Ištar* and *BĀ.ŠÁ-Ištar.* Here we evidently have two individuals with the same name who are later distinguished and addressed separately as *MAN-Ištar* (line 5), and *MAN-Ištar,* son of *Im-tí-lim* (line 14). Now unless the *MAN-Ištar* of line 5 is identical with one of the *BĀ.ŠÁ-Ištars* of the formal salutation of the letter, and the *MAN-Ištar* of line 14 is identical with the other, those portions of the letter (line 5ff, line 14ff) are addressed to individuals not mentioned in the formal salutation, which is a procedure unparalleled in Cappadocian letters. There are, however, numerous examples of letters in which a number of individuals are named in the salutation, and then certain ones of them singled out for particular messages (e.g. *CCT* IV, 8b, 9b, 14a, 14b, 20a, 21a, 27b, 49a, *BIN* IV, 17, 20, 41, 47, 55, 57, 69, etc.). The conclusion is, then, that *BĀ.ŠÁ* and *MAN* are but variant ways of writing the same name element. There is no Cappadocian evidence for the pronunciation of the element, but it may be safely read *Buzur*, for *Puzur* in Assyrian.

THE GODS *Sin* AND *ZU*

The God *Sin* is evidently spelled phonetically in Cappadocian (*zu-in*, *zu-en*) though in a few instances it is written ideographically (*EN-ZU*). The evidence from the Cappadocian inscriptions is not yet convincing that the God *ZU*, which appears rather often, is also a variant way of writing *Sin*. It is to be noted, however, that the father of *ŠÚ-A-nim* is *En-na-ZU*, and the son of *ŠÚ-A-nim* is *E-na-Sin*(*zu-in*). If it is the same *ŠÚ-A-nim* in each case, then *En-na-ZU* was the grandfather of *E-na-Sin*. Remembering the habit of naming a child after its grandfather, numerous examples of which may be found, it is possible that these two names are the same and thus *ZU* would here be written for *Sin*, but the evidence is slight.

THE CAPPADOCIAN SIGN 

It has long been recognized that this sign had the values *dī*, *ti*, *ṭi*, in Cappadocian, but there has been some question as to whether or not it also had the value *din* (cf. *OLZ*, 1925, p. 230). Consequently the names which involve the sign have been variously read, as *I-din-A-šír*, *I-di-A-šír*, *A-šír-i-din*, *A-šír-i-di*, etc. The following facts show that the name element *i-*, is to be read *i-din*, doubtless for Assyrian *iddin*, due to the well known Cappadocian habit of failing to double consonants. The names *A-šur-i-dī-in*, *E-dī-in-A-šír*, *I-dī-in-a-be-im*, *I-dī-in-Ištar*, show that the name element *i-din* (*iddin*) was in use. Moreover the same individual's name is sometimes written both ways, e.g. the name of the son of *ŠÚ-Ištar*, is written *I-dī-in-a-be-im* (*CCT* I, 22b:10), and *I-din-a-be-im* (*BIN* IV, 197:15); the name of the father of *I-din-a-bu-um* (evidently another *I-din-a-bu-um*) is written *I-dī-in-Ištar* (*BIN* IV, 61:39), and *I-din-Ištar* (*CCT* II, 10:69); the name of one of the writers of the letter *CCT* IV, 31a is written *A-šur-i-dī-in* (line 2) and *A-šur-i-din* (line 36). The first and second examples might conceivably be mere coincidences, but this can hardly apply to the third example. The three together sufficiently establish the point. The sign in question is made by the scribes in three or four variant ways, but any of the variants may be used for any of the values *dī*, *din*, *tî*, *ṭi*.

THE PREFIX *Mâr*

The large number of names of the Cassite period in Babylon which are prefixed by the element *TUR* or *Mâr*, "son," is paralleled by a similar phenomenon in the Cappadocian names, with the difference that in the Cappadocian names only the element *Mâr*, and occasionally *Mârat*, "daughter," are found, while in the Cassite names many other prefixes are used (cf. *CPN*, p. 45). Apparently also, the purpose of the prefix is somewhat different from that of the Cassite usage. One is reminded of the Arabic *Ibn* so often used as a prefix in personal names. Possibly the Cappadocian who bore a name with the prefix *Mâr* had a name of his own, but for some reason he was better known as the son of his father; he was therefore referred to by his father's name, using the prefix *Mâr*. The extent to which the element was used in this sense is unique in cuneiform names.

SIGN VALUES PECULIAR TO CAPPADOCIAN

The system of accentuation used in the name and element lists here presented is that published as Vol. IX—Appendix, *Yale Oriental Series, Researches*, by C. E. Keiser. There are, however, three sign values in common use in Cappadocian tablets which do not appear in Keiser's list, and for which the writer has adopted an accentuation in accordance with the system of Keiser. The Assyrian form of the signs with their Cappadocian values and the writer's accents are given below.

 *šál.*

 *dūr.*

 *dī, tî*

It seems that the sign *ni*, *lí*, was sometimes written for *NIN;* cf. the elements *Ni-tî, Ni-ra-aḫ;* and possibly *Ni-mar* is for *Nin-mar* (cf. *^{d}Nin-mar-ki*, *DmlPan*, p. 216).

CONCLUSION

An examination of the Name and Element Lists will show the reader that there was a mixture of many races among the people who wrote these documents. A very large percentage of the names are pure Semitic, and an almost equally large number are non-Semitic. Of the Semitic names many are distinctly West Semitic, others are early Babylonian, and still others are Assyrian. It is perhaps not necessary to conclude that because the deity whose name was used more than any other in names was Ashur, that therefore the majority of the names are those of Assyrians. The original home of Ashur may not have been Assyria; both Assyrians and Cappadocians may have adopted his cult from some other source. Among the non-Semitic names there are strong resemblances to Hittite, Subaraean, and even Aryan and Greek names. In such a population there must have been considerable syncretizing of religious cults. The following names may give evidence of such a process: *A-šír-ur-ḫi, Ištar-lá-ba, Ḫa-lá-be-im, Ku-bu-lim, Šá-ra-Sin, Zu-na-nim, Zu-ta-A-šír*. Eastern Asia Minor may be thought of as an ancient "melting pot" of races. It is a fair conclusion that among these races the Semites dominated. Not only is the language of our documents purely Semitic, but almost without exception the names of persons in official positions are Semitic.

The list here given combines all the names of the published texts, together with collations made by the writer from over 200 unpublished tablets in the Babylonian Collection of James B. Nies at Yale. Names to which any distinguishing mark was found to be added in the text, such as the name of a son, or father, or office are listed as separate individuals. Where no distinguishing mark was given all the references are thrown together, though it is quite evident in many cases that many different individuals with the same name are to be found in one list of references. For example, under the name *A-šur-ma-lik*, which was a favorite name, there will be found listed 45 different individuals each distinguished in some way, with a correspondingly long list of occurrences of the name in which individuals cannot be separated.

The List of Elements has been arranged according to Semitic roots even though a great number of elements are non-Semitic. One of the chief aims of the list is to index the second and third elements of names for the purpose of study. All comments upon the names have been purposely omitted from the List of Names and reserved for the List of Elements. It is quite possible that some of the non-Semitic names have been wrongly divided, but the effort has been to group those with similar elements.

LIST OF PERSONAL NAMES

Abbreviations: b., brother; d., daughter; f., father; gf., grandfather; gs., grandson; h., husband; s., son; w., wife.

Determinative: ^{d}, *dingir*, god.

Feminine names which are known to be such are indicated by ^{f}.

A-ba, f. of *A-bu-um-Ili*, *BIN* IV, 25:23.

A-ba-a-a, *BIN* IV, 80:1; *CCT* IV, 8a:2.

A-ba-ba-a-a, *ḫamuštum*, *BIN* IV, 210:5.

A-ba-be-a, s. of *Za-zi-a*, *TTC*, 19:18.

A-ba-el, *SCTP*, 5:4.

A-ba-nim/ni-im, *BIN* IV, 218:4; *NBC*, 3799:5.

A-ba-ta-na-nu(-um), *CCT* III, 34b:2; *CCT* IV, 8a:3.

A-ba-zi-a-šú, f. of *Da-nim*, *LTC* IV, 99:5.

^{d}*Ab-ba-ni*, f. of *La-ki-bi-im*, *BIN* IV, 113:21.

A-be..., f. of *A-šur-i-din*, *NBC*, 3775:6.

A-bi-a, *A-be-a*,

1. s. of *ŠÚ-Da-gan/ga-an*, *CCT* I, 5a:15; *LTC* IV, 86:12.
2. f. of *Buzur-A-šír*, *CCT* I, 10a:27.
3. f. of *En-na-nim*, *CCT* I, 40c:12.
4. f. of *I-ku...*, *NBC*, 3795:3.
5. *KTS*, 57b:3.

A-bi-a-a,

1. s. of *En-na-nim*, *KTS*, 50a:13.
2. f. of *Ú-zu-a*, *CCT* II, 9:27.
3. *SCTP*, 6:7.

A-bi/e-a-nim, *CCT* III, 18a:14; *KTS*, 21a:25, 29.

A-be-Î-lí, *CCT* I, 23:34; *LTC* IV, 109:8.

A-be-lá, *A-bi-la*, *BIN* IV, 66:2; *TTC*, 12:13; *Chantre*, 4:13.

^{f}*A-be-i-lá*, *CCT* IV, 23a:6.

A-be-ma-ni, *CCT* I, 41b:2.

A-bi-na-ir, (for *A-bi-na-zi-ir*) *KTS*, 37b:4.

A-be-na-zi-ir, *LTC* IV, 43:20.

A-be-zu-ra, *LTC* IV, 87:10.

Áb-si-e-ni, *CCT* I, 20b:5.

Áb-šá-lim, *CCT* III, 14:3, 32; *KTS*, 50a:3; *TTC*, 3:9.

^{f}*Áb-šá-lim*, *BIN* IV, 68:2; *CCT* IV, 13b:2; *KTS*, 2a:2; *TTC*, 19:2.

A-bu-di, f. of *E-na-nim*, *CCT* II, 10:47.

A-bu-um-Ili, *A-bu-um-me-lim*,

1. s. of *A-ba*, *BIN* IV, 25:23.
2. *ḫamuštum*, *CCT* I, 6b:6.
3. *CCT* III, 20:26; 28b:31; *CCT* IV, 13c:3; *Gol.*, 2:5.

A-bu(-um)-šá-lim,
1. s. of *A-šur-e-mu-qi*, *Babyl.* II, 40, line 22.
2. s. of *A-ta-a*, *KTS*, 40:44.
3. f. of *Ku-ra-ra*, *BIN* IV, 94:6; *CCT* II, 9:25.
4. *BIN* IV, 11:2; 198:16; *NBC*, 3859R:8; *CCT* I, 16a:5; 22b:18; 25:30; 45:43; *LTC* IV, 42:2; 44:3, 18; *KTS*, 32a:4; 53c:5; *Liv.*, 4:3.

A-bu-zi-a..., *KTS*, 45b:19.

A-da..., f. of *I-ku-be-a*, *NBC*, 3712:3.

^{d}*Adad-a...*, *NBC*, 3767:LE.

A-da-da, (cf. *A-ta-ta*)
1. f. of *A-šur-rabi*, *LTC* IV, 82:25.
2. *dub-šar*, *CCT* II, 25:11; *LTC* IV, 70:25; *TTC*, 9:17.
3. *BIN* IV, 37:25, 30; *CCT* I, 37b:4; *CCT* II, 38:26; *CCT* III, 24:24; *CCT* IV, 37b:6; 42a:3; 44b:32; *LTC* IV, 6:13; *Chantre*, 10:20.

^{d}*Adad-ba-ni*,
1. *lîmu*, s. of *I-din-A-šír*, *KTS*, 45b:17.
2. s. of *A-gu-a*, *LTC* IV, 64:1.
3. s. of *Bu-da-tim*, *CCT* I, 35:32.
4. s. of *Ib-ni-*^{d}*Adad*, *KTS*, 49b:14.
5. s. of *Zi-lá-*^{d}*Adad*, *KTS*, 47b:17.
6. f. of *Du-du*, *LTC* IV, 81:16.
7. *lîmu*, *CCT* I, 4:44.
8. *BIN* IV, 27:13, 17; 48:3, 30; 65:47; 78:2; 162:39; 233:21; *CCT* II, 18:2; 37a:23; 49b:3, 11; *CCT* III, 39b:3; *CCT* IV, 41a:15; *LTC* IV, 43:2; 48:2, 13, 22; 55:24; 64:10; *KTS*, 26a:7, 21.

^{d}*Adad-be-lá-aḫ*, *CCT* I, 8a:15.

^{d}*Adad-damiq*,
1. s. of *Be-lá-aḫ-Ištar*, *LTC* IV, 67:4.
2. *CCT* I, 17b:15; *LTC* IV, 67:5.

^{d}*Adad-illat(at)*, *CCT* III, 10:11.

^{d}*Adad-iqbi*, *CCT* I, 30b:4; 48:1, 5, 6, 8, 12, 15, 17, 25, 28, 30; *KTS*, 6:29; 7a:3.

^{d}*Adad-ma-lik*, *Chantre*, 5:14.

^{d}*Adad-ra-be-tim*, *CCT* IV, 1a:3.

^{d}*Adad-rabi*,
1. s. of *A-šur-ma-lik*, *CCT* III, 50a:10.
2. *dub-šar*, *CCT* I, 8a:3.
3. *BIN* IV, 59: 2, 7, 11, 18; 123:9; 195:16; 203:1; *CCT* I, 5b:20; 29:32; *CCT* III, 38:12; *LTC* IV, 84:7; *KTS*, 50b:16.

^{d}*Adad-rê'ûm*, *BIN* IV, 192:4; *NBC*, 3771:2, 17; *CCT* I, 25:18.

^{d}*Adad-ri-a-ri*, *CCT* I, 50:22.

^{d}*Adad-ri-zi*, *KTS*, 19a:16.

^{d}*Adad-ta-ak-lá-ku*, f. of *A-šur-ma-lik*, *CCT* I, 20b:10.

^{d}*Adad-ta-ku-ul*, *SCTP*, 22:3.

^{d}*Adad-zi...*, *NBC*, 3788:26.

^{d}*Adad-zu-lu-li*,

1. s. of *ŠÚ-A-nim*, *KTS*, 48c:19.
2. *BIN* IV, 36:2; *NBC*, 3876:4; **CCT* III, 32:2, 16; 49b:4, 16, 25; **CCT* IV, 39b:2, 16; *KTS*, 48c:11.

A-da-làl, f. of *I-ku-bi-a*, *BIN* IV, 160:46.

A-da-ta, (cf. *A-da-da*) f. of *Ma-nim-kî-A-šur*, *BIN* IV, 89:20.

A-dī-a,
1. f. of *Bûr-Nu-nu*, *BIN* IV, 207:13; 207case:1.
2. f. of *Ištar-be-lá-aḫ*, *CCT* III, 26a:15.
3. *CCT* IV, 48b:8.

A-dī-A-šur, *CCT* I, 30a:12.

A-dī-da, *CCT* IV, 14b:1, 12; *LTC* IV, 81:55.

A-dī-lá-at,
1. f. of *A-lá-ḫu-um*, *BIN* IV, 145:7.
2. *CCT* I, 24a:25.

A-di-nim/nu, *CCT* I, 42a:17; 49a:7; *CCT* III, 39a:2.

A-dī-na, f. of *Aš-ku-tim*, *CCT* IV, 32a:2.

A-du..., *CCT* IV, 17a:23; *KTS*, 59a:4.

A-du(-ú), *NBC*, 1887:3, 7; *CCT* I, 43:2, 21, 28; 44:2; *CCT* IV, 44a:3, 6.

A-du-a/e, *KTS*, 3c:2; *TTC*, 26:2, 19.

A(d)-du-(a)aḫ-si, *CCT* I, 23:21; 39b:8.

A-du-da, *LTC* IV, 81:51; *KTS*, 50a:16; *TTC*, 21:11.

A-du-du, *NBC*, 3723R:2; *Chantre*, 9:2, 4.

A-ga-áb-si, *BIN* IV, 186:12; 186case:1.

A-ga-li-ú-ma-an, *CCT* I, 7a:3.

A-gi-a,
1. s. of *I-ku-nim*, *LTC* IV, 81:23.
2. f. of *Ì-lí-a-lim*, *KTS*, 47c:8.
3. f. of *Ì-lí-dan*, *LTC* IV, 81:32.
4. *CCT* I, 7a:18.

A-gu-a,
1. s. of *Buzur-A-šur*, *KTS*, 23:25.
2. s. of *Ṭâbu-A-šur*, *KTS*, 27b:25.
3. f. of ^{d}*Adad-ba-ni*, *LTC* IV, 64:2.
4. f. of *Mâr-A-gu-a*, *CCT* IV, 10b:26.
5. *BIN* IV, 144:7; *NBC*, 3767:4; *SCTP*, 6:7.

A-gu-za,
1. s. of *ŠÚ-A-nim*, *Babyl.* IV, 1:8.
2. *Babyl.* IV, 3:2, 9, 15, 16.

A-ḫa-a, *A-aḫ-a-a*,
1. f. of *I-din-A-šur*, *LTC* IV, 81:54.
2. *CCT* I, 40a:19.

A-ḫa-ḫa, *BIN* IV, 10:32; 140:6; *CCT* II, 32a:2; *CCT* IV, 31b:3; *LTC* IV, 21:36; *KTS*, 50a:8.

^{f}*A-ḫa-ḫa*,
1. d. of *Bu-šú-ki-in*, *LTC* IV, 79:9.
2. *CCT* I, 17b:11; *LTC* IV, 79:28.

A-ḫa-na-ar-si, *Chantre*, 16:3.

A-aḫ-A-šír, *CCT* I, 41b:3.

* Two not entirely identical autographed texts from the same tablet.

A-ḫa-tim, A-ḫa-tum, BIN IV, 183:4; *CCT* IV, 15a:1; *KTS,* 49c:17.

ᶠA-ḫa-tum, BIN IV, 153:3.

A-aḫ-Ili, Aḫ-Î-lí, NBC, 1887:2, 4; *CCT* II, 7:28; *CCT* III, 40b:2; *LTC* IV, 52:1.

A-aḫ-Ištar, CCT I, 43:11.

Aḫ-me,
1. f. of *En-na-Sin, CCT* I, 1a:31.
2. f. of *Mâr-Aḫ-me, BIN* IV, 177:2.

Aḫ-šá-lim,
1. s. of *Bu-zu-ta-a, CCT* I, 2:2, 13.
2. *BIN* IV, 26:4; 44:3; 121:3; 129:10; 151:25; 180:4; 223:3; *CCT* I, 40a:6; 44:4, 7; *CCT* II, 29:1; 37b:6; 40b:1; *CCT* IV, 16c:18; 17a:1; 33a:9; *LTC* IV, 38:1; 52:15; 53:3; 56:3; *KTS,* 32a:12; *SCTP,* 18:1, 4.

A-aḫ-ᵈŠamaš,
1. s. of *Be-lá-nim, NBC,* 3755:12.
2. *BIN* IV, 208:16; 208case:1; *CCT* II, 34:7.

A-aḫ-šú, CCT I, 37b:17.

A-a-aḫ-šú-nu, CCT I, 34a:12.

A-ḫu-qar, A-ḫu-wa-qar,
1. s. of *ŠÚ-Ištar, CCT* I, 4:3; *SCTP,* 24:18; *Babyl.* IV, 2:1.
2. s. of *Zu-ur-zu-ni, CCT* I, 36b:5.
3. s. of *Zu-ur-zu-ur, CCT* II, 5b:5.
4. f. of *A-šur-ma-lik, LTC* IV, 81:23; 88:3.
5. f. of *Ma-nu-kî-A-šír, CCT* I, 50:24.
6. f. of *ŠÚ-Ištar, LTC* IV, 99:9, 18.
7. *lîmu, CCT* I, 4:13.
8. *BIN* IV, 9:4, 29; 151:13, 18; 206:4; 206case:8; 210:3; 221:18; *NBC,* 3724:3; 3730:4, 19; 3864:3; 3905:29; *CCT* I, 8a:4; 48:35; *CCT* II, 11:2; *CCT* III, 20:10; 22a:1; *CCT* IV, 22b:3, 6; 23a:46; 24a:12; *LTC* IV, 23:9, 21, 23, 26, 31; 31:14; 88:5; 115:10.

A-ki-a-a,
1. f. of *I-din-A-šír, CCT* I, 32a:5.
2. f. of *I-ku-bi-a, CCT* II, 30:22.

A-ak-li-a,
1. s. of *ŠÚ-Ištar, LTC* IV 81:46.
2. *CCT* I, 31c:10.

Ak-ta-ma-tim, CCT I, 27a:8.

A-ku-a, A-ku-a-a,
1. s. of *Buzur. . .*, *BIN* IV, 112:43.
2. f. of *ŠÚ-Sin, BIN* IV, 187:23.
3. f. of *Ú-zur-šá-A-šur, BIN* IV, 105:25.
4. *LTC* IV, 64:8.

A-ku-tim, A-ku-tum,
1. f. of *Ri-a-a, KTS,* 47c:5.
2. *lîmu, BIN* IV, 160:32; *CCT* I, 2:9; 3:42; 11b:8; *KTS,* 44a:9.

3. *CCT* I, 6b:3.

A-ku-za,
1. *ḫamuštum*, *NBC*, 3713:3; *Gol.*, 7:8.
2. *KTS*, 13a:2; *Liv.*, 14a:6; 14b:3, 8.

A-lá-be-im, *A-la-bi-im*, *A-lá-bi-im*, *A-la-bu-um*, *A-lá-bu-um*,
1. s. of *A-šur-ma-lik*, *NBC*, 3911:6.
2. s. of *Lá-ta-ra-ak*, *CCT* II, 19b:5.
3. s. of *Ma-nu-a*, *BIN* IV, 74:2.
4. s. of *Šú-ḫa-ir-*^{d}*Adad*, *LTC* IV, 32:10.
5. f. of *I-ku-bi-a*, *BIN* IV, 42:8.
6. *BIN* IV, 42:6; 74:6; *CCT* I, 10a:2, 7; *CCT* II, 26a:12; 48:4, 11, 15; *CCT* III, 13:7; *CCT* IV, 42c:7; *LTC* IV, 32:15; *Liv.*, 15:6.

A-la-ḫa-am, *A-lá-ḫa-am*, *A-la-ḫi-im*, *A-lá-ḫi-im*, *A-la-ḫu-um*, *A-lá-ḫu-um*,
1. s. of *A-dī-lá-at*, *BIN* IV, 145:6.
2. s. of *E-na-aḫ-Ì-lí*, *LTC* IV, 82:2.
3. s. of *I-bi-zu-a*, *SCTP*, 18:2.
4. s. of *Ma-nu-a*, *LTC* IV, 37:7.
5. s. of *Nu-ur-Zu*, *LTC* IV, 81:7.
6. s. of *Zi-ku-ḫi-im*, *BIN* IV, 56:3.
7. f. of *A-šír-lá...*, *BIN* IV, 71:8.
8. f. of *A-šír-ma-lik*, *BIN* IV, 216:LE 2; *CCT* I, 14a:14.
9. f. of *A-šur-ták-lá-ku*, *BIN* IV, 127:14; *CCT* I, 2:3, 14; 3:55; 4:25; *CCT* II, 47a:25; *KTS*, 45a:8; 49a:13.
10. f. of *A-šír-ṭâbu*, *CCT* II, 9:28.
11. f. of *Ba-al-du-bu*, *CCT* I, 18a:22.
12. f. of *Buzur-A-šur*, *CCT* III, 38:6.
13. f. of *I-din-Sin*, *CCT* II, 10:72.
14. f. of *Kúr-ub-Ištar*, *NBC*, 3787:6; *CCT* I, 3:51.
15. f. of *ŠÚ-A-šur*, *CCT* II, 41a:16.
16. *lîmu*, *CCT* I, 8a:13.
17. *ḫamuštum*, *BIN* IV, 121:5.
18. *BIN* IV, 19:38; 27:3; 49:1; 51:25; 52:1, 19; 53:2; 54:4; 60:1; 64:23, 24; 146:27; 149:19; 219:2; *NBC*, 1643:1; 3863:2; *CCT I*, 12b:2, 6; 18b:2; 34a:25; 35:8, 13; 39a:2, 6, 18, 20; 41a:23; *CCT* II, 6:2, 5, 46; 7:7, 8, 21, 30; *CCT* III, 2a:1; 3b:28; 7b:1; 8a:22; 9:1; 14:2, 20; 31:29; 33a:4; 45b:1; *CCT* IV, 6c:17, 21; 14b:22, 27, 31; 21a:3, 11; 23a:16; *LTC* IV, 2:5, 7, 14; 4:1; 8:5; 12:1; 21:4; 46:5; 89:4; *KTS*, 2a:6; 9b:1; 10:1; 11:1; 12:1; 23:37; 60b:5; *TTC*, 22:2; *Gol.*, 16:2, 3; 21:6; 24:3, 7, 10; *Babyl.* VI, 3:2.

A-lá-ḫi-na-am, *A-lá-ḫi-ni*, *A-lá-ḫi-nim*, *BIN* IV, 45:25; 63:3,

13, 27; 157:29; *CCT* I, 33b:20; *CCT* II, 30:3, 31; *LTC* IV, 87:26.

Al-be-li, *CCT* II, 37b:28.

A-li-li, *KTS*, 21a:1; *Chantre*, 4:14.

A-al-ṭâbu, *A-al-ta-bu-a*,
1. s. of *Be-lá-aḫ-A-šír*, *Gol.*, 9:11.
2. s. of *Ištar-lá-ba*, *LTC* IV, 71:2, 6.
3. f. of *Bi-lá-aḫ-A-šur*, *CCT* II, 9:40; *KTS*, 16:13.
4. f. of *ŠÚ-Lá-ba-an*, *LTC* IV, 79:2.
5. *lîmu*, *CCT* I, 5b:19; *KTS*, 44b:17.
6. *BIN* IV, 12:5; 111:1, 2, 8, 14; *CCT* I, 38b:8; *CCT* IV, 8b:3; *LTC* IV, 71:12; 109:11.

A-lu-ud-ḫu-ḫa-ar-šá, *Chantre*, 2:5.

A-lu-uk-ri-im, *SCTP*, 5:3, 5.

Al-lu-uḫ-ru-um, *CCT* IV, 50b:20.

A-lu-lá-a, *BIN* IV, 160:25; 164:11, 20; *NBC*, 3779:2; *CCT* II, 13:20; **CCT* III, 49a:2; **CCT* IV, 47b:2; *SCTP*, 15:3.

A-lu-lu, *CCT* IV, 17a:5.

A-lu-wa-zi, *CCT* I, 10b:1.

A-ma-a, *Am-ma-a*,
1. f. of *A-šír-*^{d}*šamši(-ši)*, *BIN* IV, 91:7; 154:25; *NBC*, 3905:21.
2. f. of *I-ku-nim*, *KTS*, 46a:7; 46b:2.

Am-lá-ḫa-a, *CCT* I, 37a:11.

A-am-ri-a, *Am-ri-a*,
1. f. of *A-šur-ta*..., *NBC*, 3730:5.
2. f. of *En-na-nim*, *BIN* IV, 122:18.
3. f. of *Lu-lu*, *Liv.*, 17:5.
4. f. of *Mâr-Am-ri-a*, *BIN* IV, 38:7; 49:4.
5. *BIN* IV, 148:37; *CCT* II, 9:26; *CCT* III, 10:4; *KTS*, 3b:10; *SCTP*, 33:8.

A-mur..., *CCT* IV, 11b:1.

A-mur-^{d}...,
1. f. of *A-šír-i-me-tî*, *LTC* IV, 96:1.
2. *NBC*, 3749:8; *Chantre*, 7:1.

A-mu-ra, *A-mu-ra-a*,
1. s. of *Zu-ga-li-a*, *LTC* IV, 66:2.
2. f. of *A-šur-be-el-a-wa-tim*, *CCT* II, 19a:7; *LTC* IV, 43:22.
3. f. of *I-na-a*, *BIN* IV, 87:10; *CCT* I, 4:19.

A-mu-ra-am, *BIN* IV, 87:12; *NBC*, 1903:10; 1903R:12.

A-mur-A-šír, *A-mur-A-šur*, *A-mur-*^{d}*A-šur*,
1. s. of *A-mur-Ili*, *CCT* I, 21d:7.
2. s. of *Ili-rê'ûm*, *CCT* I, 12b:4.
3. s. of *I-tî-lim*, *SCTP*, 18:11.
4. s. of *ŠÚ-A-nim*, *LTC* IV, 90a:Seal B.
5. s. of *ŠÚ-Iš-ḫa-ra*, *KTS*, 43a:2.
6. s. of *ŠÚ-Ištar*, *LTC* IV, 26:15.
7. s. of *Za-li-ti*, *CCT* I, 26c:7.
8. s. of *Zi-ku-ur-Ì-*[*lí*], *CCT* III, 39a:9.
9. s. of *Zu-ga-li-a*, *BIN* IV,

* Two not entirely identical autographed texts from the same tablet.

8:33; 140:2; *CCT* I, 19a:16; *CCT* III, 45a:21.
10. f. of *El-ba-ni*, *BIN* IV, 112:41.
11. f. of *Ú-za-nim*, *KTS*, 49a:9.
12. *BIN* IV, 19:33, 36; 27:11; 50:2, 6, 12, 15; 103:27; 140:7; 148:32; 184:7; 224:3; 227:2; *NBC*, 3788:25; *CCT* I, 12b:8; 41a:25; *KTS*, 8c:5; 47a:4, 8; 58c:16; 60b:8; *SCTP*, 2:21; 15:20; 35:15; *TTC*, 14:24, 27; *Gol.*, 4:15; 23:2.

A-mu-ur-ba-ni, *CCT* I, 31c:4.

A-mur-Ili,
1. s. of *Amurru-ba-ni*, *LTC* IV, 71:17.
2. s. of *I-bi-zu-a*, *CCT* II, 8:20.
3. s. of *I-nu-ma-a*, *Gol.*, 9:6.
4. f. of *A-mur-A-šur*, *CCT* I, 21d:7.
5. f. of *A-mur-Ištar*, *CCT* I, 13a:18.
6. f. of *ŠÚ-be-lim*, *BIN* IV, 173:36; *TTC*, 25:16.
7. f. of *ŠÚ-Lá-ba-an*, *KTS*, 34a:24.
8. *BIN* IV, 3:3; 94:9; 101:1, 3, 11; 103:26; *NBC*, 3771:20; *CCT* I, 18a:7; 28a:4, 14; 44:1; *CCT* II, 8:2; 10:74; 26a:2; 46a:2; *CCT* IV, 17a:3, 13; 20b:2; 22b:5, 9, 15, 22, 26; 28a:2, 14, 15, 19, 22, 23, 25, 31; 28b:1; 50a:15; *LTC* IV, 13:9; 16:3, 26; 19:2, 43; 23:3; 25:2; 81:54; *KTS*, 4b:2; 15:2; 20:2; *TTC*, 28:2; 30:9.

A-mur-Ištar,
1. s. of *A-mur-Ili*, *CCT* I, 13a:18.
2. s. of *Da-da*, *CCT* II, 8:23.
3. s. of *I-din-Sin*, *BIN* IV, 25:24.
4. s. of *Me-šú-rabi*, *KTS*, 58c:4.
5. f. of *A-šír-na-da*, *LTC* IV, 71:7.
6. f. of *A-ta-ta*, *CCT* I, 4:38.
7. f. of *Mâr-A-mur-Ištar*, *BIN* IV, 6:30; *KTS*, 5a:7.
8. *ḫamuštum*, *Chantre*, 4:6.
9. *BIN* IV, 3:2; 26:13; 50:4, 7, 22, 27; 53:2; 87:6; 89:13; 113:1, 9, 16; 119:3; 144:9; 152:3, 13; 172:4; 199:3; 213:5; *NBC*, 1643:5; 3780:2; 3802:19; 3850R:1; 3863:14; 3903:1; 3915:16; 4049:2; *CCT* I, 20a:18; 21d:13; *CCT* II, 6:34; 10:71; 12b:7; 23:2; 25:16, 38; 28:8; 40b:1; 49a:2; *CCT* III, 1:3; 2a:2, 11, 25; *CCT* IV, 10b:2; 27a:20, 28; 34c:2; 41b:1, 20; 45a:2; 47a:1; *LTC* IV, 27:7; 55:2; 110:1, 11; *KTS*, 17:4, 25, 26; 18:2; 33a:1, 23; 42c:5, 6; *SCTP*, 42:3, 5; *TTC*, 30:22, 25, 33; *Liv.*, 4:3.

Amurru (*MAR.TU*), f. of *ᵈA-šír-GIŠ*, *Liv.*, 14b:seal, p. 69.

Amurru (*MAR.TU*)*-ba-ni*, *ᵈAmurru-*(*MAR.TU*)*-ba-ni*, *A-mu-ru-ba-ni*,
1. s. of *Ma-nu-um-ba-lim-A-šur*, *CCT* I, 22b:21.

2. f. of *A-mur-Ili*, *LTC* IV, 71:17.
3. f. of *Na-zi*, *CCT* I, 1a:14.
4. *BIN* IV, 120:3; *NBC*, 3770:9; 3903R:8; *LTC* IV, 54:13, 19; *KTS*, 57b:2; 60b:6.

ᵈAmurru(MAR.TU)-ki..., *ḫamuš-tum*, *Chantre*, 16:8.

A-mur-ᵈŠamaš,
1. s. of *A-šír-ma-lik*, *LTC* IV, 95:6, 8.
2. s. of *E-nu-a*, *KTS*, 31a:6.
3. s. of *Me-šar-rabi*, *BIN* IV, 24:4.
4. s. of *Me-šú-rabi*, *LTC* IV, 95:3, 22; 96:10.
5. *ḫamuštum*, *CCT* I, 8a:7.
6. *BIN* IV, 182:5; *NBC*, 3732:4; 3749:15, 17; *CCT* I, 13a:2; *CCT* III, 21a:3, 4; *LTC* IV, 17:2; 96:12, 17, 22; 109:12; 116:2; *Gol.*, 16:1, 10, 13, 16, 22; *PSBA* 1881, p. 34, lines 1, 4.

A-mur-šá-ra-za-a-na, *TTC*, 23:4.

A-mur-ᵈZu, f. of *A-šur-ma-lik*, *BIN* IV, 199:14.

ᵈA-na-da, *KTS*, 11:3.

A-na-aḫ-A-šur, *NBC*, 3873:3.

A-na-ḫi-el, *KTS*, 48b:14.

A-na-aḫ-Ī-lí,
1. f. of *Ba-ba-la-nim*, *Babyl.* IV, 1:5.
2. *BIN* IV, 23:33; 83:4, 9, 22, 30, 42, 50; *NBC*, 3927R:2; 4071:5, 7; *KTS*, 48b:1; *SCTP*, 16:7, 9; *Gol.*, 10:4; 20:15, 25; *Chantre*, 13:9.

A-na-ku-Ili, *CCT* I, 46a:4, 7, 12; 46b:1, 4, 8.

A-na-na, *BIN* IV, 165:1, 2, 3; *Liv.*, 8:14.

A-na-ni, *A-na-nim*, *A-na-nu-um*,
1. f. of *Kúr-ub-Ištar*, *LTC* IV, 110:33.
2. *BIN* IV, 5:3; 22:24; 49:19; 57:3; 204:2; *CCT* I, 15c:7; 18a:16; 25:5, 21; *CCT* II, 46a:1, 4; 50:5; *CCT* IV, 17a:18; 28b:29; *LTC* IV, 16:2, 8; 43:19; *KTS*, 5b:21; 19b:6, 20, 26.

A-na-aš, *BIN* IV, 209:5, 11; 209case:10.

A-ni-a, *Chantre*, 5:8.

A-ni-na, *A-ni-na-a*, *A-ni-nam*, *A-ni-nim*,
1. s. of *Si-a-im*, *CCT* I, 49a:1, 4.
2. s. of *Ú-zur-šá-A-šír*, LTC IV, 79:4.
3. f. of *A-šur...*, *CCT* IV, 33a:24.
4. f. of *Bu-uk-da-šú*, *NBC*, 3716:7.
5. f. of *En-um-A-šír*, *BIN* IV, 103:37; 105:2; *CCT* I, 9a:5, 15; 49b:2; *TTC*, 4:7.
6. f. of *Ištar-bi-lá-aḫ*, *CCT* II, 8:12.
7. f. of *Mâr-A-ni-nim*, *BIN* IV, 79:19; *CCT* III, 7b:9; 12b:4; 17a:19.
8. *BIN* IV, 169:8; *NBC*, 3873:1; *CCT* I, 16b:18, 20; 26b:12; *CCT* II, 32a:2; *CCT* III, 44b:2; *LTC* IV, 27:41; *KTS*, 48b:11; *Gol.*, 5:13.

A-ni-za-lá, *CCT* I, 45:2, 5, 20, 22.
A-nu-a, *LTC* IV, 87:48.
A-nu-an, *KTS*, 3c:3.
A-nu-nu-uš, *LTC* IV, 87:17.
A-ra-ar-ri-ḫi, *LTC* IV, 100:13, 18.
A-ra-wa,
1. f. of *Mâr-A-ra-wa*, *NBC*, 4004:18.
2. *BIN* IV, 195:5; *LTC* IV, 78:3.
A-ra-wa-ur-ḫi, *LTC* IV, 100:1.
A-ri-a, *CCT* III, 35a:22.
A-ri-lí, s. of *Be-lu-ba-ni*, *LTC* IV, 81:45.
Ar-nu-ma-an, *CCT* I, 33b:18.
Ar-si. . ., s. of *Dī-li*. . ., *LTC* IV, 119:7.
Ar-si-iḫ,
1. f. of *Mâr-Ar-si-iḫ*, *CCT* II, 41b:18.
2. *BIN* IV, 3:21; *CCT* II, 40b:6; *CCT* IV, 9b:3.
A-ru-ru, *BIN* IV, 189:3.
Ar-za-na-aḫ-šú,
1. f. of *Ri-en-šá*, *KTS*, 51a:11.
2. *LTC* IV, 87:57; *Gol.*, 5:12.
A-šír. . ., *A-šur*. . ., ^{d}*A-šír*. . .?
1. s. of *A-ni-nim*, *CCT* IV, 33a:23.
2. s. of *Be-lim-na-da*, *NBC*, 3796:2.
3. f. of *Buzur-A-šír*, *LTC* IV, 65:4.
4. f. of *Ì-lí-šá*. . ., *KTS*, 45a:seal.
5. *BIN* IV, 83:1; *NBC*, 1894:1; 3925:2; *CCT* I, 12a:10; *CCT* IV, 42b:1; *LTC* IV, 20:22; 114:8; 131:1; *SCTP*, 24:14; *Liv.*, 3:10; *Chantre*, 7:4, 5; 12:15; *Babyl.* VI, 10:5.
A-šur-a-ma-ru-um, *BIN* IV, 127:5.
A-šír-ba. . ., f. of *A-šír-ma-lik*, *SCTP*, 28:8.
A-šír-ba-ni, *A-šur-ba-ni*,
1. s. of *Ḫu-du-ur-lá*, *BIN* IV, 197:5.
2. s. of *Ku-ta-a*, *BIN* IV, 43:3; 108:22; 145:8.
3. s. of *ŠÚ-Sin*, *LTC* IV, 64:3.
4. f. of *Bi-lá-aḫ-Ištar*, *LTC* IV, 79:3.
5. f. of . . .*-i-A-šur*, *LTC* IV, 110:34.
6. f. of *Lu-zi-na*, *BIN* IV, 142:9.
7. f. of *Mâr-A-šur-ba-ni*, *CCT* IV, 26a:28.
8. *BIN* IV, 48:2, 8, 29; 187:2; 226:2; *NBC*, 3756:6; 3766:2; 3796:7; 3798:4, 7; 3908:1; 3937:9; *CCT* I, 17b:23; 24a:26; 31c:8; 32c:2; 41a:15; *CCT* III, 10:12; 21b:2; *CCT* IV, 12b:3; 17b:5; *LTC* IV, 28:1; 30:1; 86:4; 136:4; *KTS*, 3c:10; 22a:21; 29b:1; 60d:11; *Gol.*, 23:12; 23R:2.
A-šír-ba-aš-tí, *A-šur-ba-aš-tí*, *BIN* IV, 121:12; *CCT* I, 38a:15; *CCT* IV, 33a:6.
A-šír-be-el-a-wa-tim, *A-šír-bi-el-a-wa-tim*, *A-šur-be-el-a-wa-tim*, *A-šur-bi-el-a-wa-tim*, *A-šur-be-lá-wa-ti-ma*, *A-šur-bi-lá-wa-tim*,

1. s. of *A-mu-ra*, *CCT* II, 19a:6; *LTC* IV, 43:21.
2. s. of *Ì-lí-a*, *NBC*, 3765:4.
3. f. of *Be-lim-ba-ni*, *BIN* IV, 108:21; *CCT* I, 7b:2.
4. f. of *Ú-zur-šá-A-šur*, *BIN* IV, 24:13.
5. *ḫamuštum*, *NBC*, 3713:2; *Gol.*, 7:7; 8:7.
6. *BIN* IV, 81:3; 186:13; 186case:2; *NBC*, 3701:12; 3742:2; 3798:10; *CCT* I, 50:1, 4; *CCT* II, 19a:11, 14; *CCT* III, 10:1; *CCT* IV, 34a:5; *LTC* IV, 80:40; *KTS*, 9a:7; 37b:1; *Gol.*, 7:5; *Babyl.* II, p. 42, lines 3, 10.

A-šír-be-li, *A-šur-be-li*,
1. b. of *Ga-si-im*, *CCT* II, 30:8.
2. *BIN* IV, 189:20.

A-šur-be-el-lá-ma-zi, *NBC*, 3755:16.

A-šur-be-el-ma-al-ki-im, *A-šur-bi-el-ma-al-ki-im*, *BIN* IV, 224:2, 5, 26; *CCT* I, 24a:4, 10, 17, 27, 30; 27b:6; *CCT* II, 27:4; *CCT* III, 10:8, 28, 36.

A-šír-damiq, *A-šur-damiq*,
1. s. of *A-šur-ri-zi*, *CCT* II, 10:51.
2. *lîmu* (?), *KTS*, 57e:8.
3. *BIN* IV, 121:14; *CCT* I, 48:10, 14; *CCT* III, 15:3, 35; *CCT* IV, 28a:36; *KTS*, 19a:2; 44b:3; *SCTP*, 30:7.

A-šír-dan, *A-šír-da-ni*, *A-šur-dan*,
1. s. of *Az*, *BIN* IV, 225:9.
2. s. of *I-ku-be-a*, *BIN* IV, 161:6; *CCT* I, 16b:21.
3. f. of *A-ta-ta*, *BIN* IV, 138:10.
4. f. of *Buzur-A-šír*, *NBC*, 3755:5; 3755R:7.
5. f. of *I-din-a-bi-im*, *LTC* IV, 86:15; *CCT* I, 28a:16.
6. *BIN* IV, 19:34, 35; *NBC*, 3909:4; *CCT* I, 30a:4; *CCT* II, 10:73; *CCT* IV, 10a:6; *LTC* IV, 90a:1; 90b:15.

A-šír-du-kúl-tî, *A-šur-du-kúl-tî*, *A-šur-du-ku-ul-tî*,
1. s. of *Bi-la-aḫ-Ištar*, *NBC*, 1708:7.
2. *CCT* III, 45b:27; *CCT* IV, 40b:3; *LTC* IV, 45:2; *SCTP*, 25:4, 18.

A-šur-du-lu-bi, *Gol.*, 23R:9.

A-šur-du-ri,
1. s. of *Buzur-Ištar*, *NBC*, 1889:5; *LTC* IV, 81:7.
2. *NBC*, 1889:14; *CCT* II, 16b:10.

A-šur-du-ra-am, *BIN* IV, 134:4.

A-šír-e..., *A-šur-e...*, *KTS*, 3b:1; *SCTP*, 16:2.

A-šír-e-mu-qi, *A-šur-e-mu-qi*,
1. s. of *Ga-qa-da-nim*, f. of *Za-ḫa...*, *Gol.*, 9:4.
2. f. of *A-bu-šá-lim*, *Babyl.* II, 40, line 23.
3. f. of *ŠÚ-Ištar*, *BIN* IV, 197:4.
4. *BIN* IV, 20:3, 14, 23; *NBC*, 3873:2; *CCT* I, 1b:4; *CCT* II, 11a:16; *CCT* III, 39a:7; *CCT* IV, 10a:32; 35a:18; *LTC* IV, 116:8; *KTS*, 48a:4; *Gol.*, 21:7; *Liv.*, 15:9.

A-šír-e-na-am, *A-šur-e-nam*,
1. s. of *I-din-Sin*, *CCT* II, 35:41.
2. *NBC*, 3675:13; 3875:4; *CCT* I, 45:45; *KTS*, 60d:4.

A-šír-ga-si-id, *A-šur-ga-si-id*,
1. s. of *Ik-ra-a*, *LTC* IV, 81:29.
2. *CCT* I, 32b:3; *CCT* III, 6b:9; *CCT* IV, 13a:1.

A-šír-GIŠ(?), *ᵈA-šír-GIŠ*(?),
1. s. of *Amurru*(*MAR.TU*), *Liv.*, 14b:seal (p. 69).
2. f. of *I-din-ᵈAdad*, *Liv.*, 14a:18; 14b:1.

A-šur-i. . . , *NBC*, 3891:2.

A-šur-id. . . , *LTC* IV, 93:4.

A-šír-i-din, *A-šír-i-dī-in*, *A-šur-i-din*, *A-šur-i-dī-in*,
1. s. of *A-be*. . . , *NBC*, 3775:6.
2. s. of *A-šír-ma-lik*, gs. of *Lu-zi-na*, *NBC*, 3905:26.
3. s. of *Bu-za-zu*, *LC*, 239:8.
4. s. of *Ili-na-da*, *KTS*, 44a:3.
5. s. of *Ku-ku-lá-nim*, *CCT* II, 20:33; *LTC* IV, 81:9.
6. s. of *Mu-mu-lá-nim*, *CCT* I, 35:22; *SCTP*, 18:10.
7. s. of *ŠÚ-Ištar*, *CCT* I, 7b:21.
8. f. of *A-šur-na-da*, *BIN* IV, 119:7; 154:24.
9. f. of *Mâr-A-šír-i-din*, *CCT* II, 1:17.
10. f. of *Ṭâb-zi-lá-A-šír*, *BIN* IV, 103:38; *KTS*, 49a:11.
11. b. of *A-šur-ma-lik*, *CCT* IV, 45c:1.
12. *lîmu*, *KTS*, 44c:16.
13. *BIN* IV, 18:1; 53:1; 123:10; 160:48; *NBC*, 3772:18, 20, 22; 3909:1; *CCT* I, 12a:24; 16b:10; 25:5, 28; 31c:2; 39a:8; *CCT* III, 2b:1; 3b:1; 4:1; 5b:1; 6b:1; 8b:1; 29:3, 7; 48a:1; *CCT* IV, 1a:1; 1b:1; 2a:1; 2b:1; 10a:1; 16a:9, 17; 31a:2, 36; 45b:1; *LTC* IV, 2:1; 8:1; 12:19; 15:1; 16:2, 9; 18:1; 21:10; 29:1; 31:4, 23; 47:1; 80:19, 24; 88:9; *KTS*, 2b:1; 43b:3; 44b:3; 54b:5; *SCTP*, 38:5; *Liv.*, 15:10; *RT*, 31, p. 55:1.

A-šír-i-me-tî, *A-šur-i-me-tî*,
1. s. of *A-murᵈ*. . . , *LTC* IV, 96:1, 8.
2. s. of *E-lá-ni*, *NBC*, 3746:7.
3. s. of *El-ku-li*, *LTC* IV, 82:6.
4. s. of *En-na-nim*, *BIN* IV, 29:1; 173:2, 10, 19, 33; *CCT* III, 19b:18.
5. s. of *En-um-A-šur*, *LTC* IV, 66:1.
6. s. of *Ḫa-lá-be-im*, *BIN* IV, 200:1.
7. s. of *Idu-šá-Ištar*, *Babyl.* II, p. 42, line 7.
8. s. of *I-ku-a*, *CCT* I, 32a:11; *KTS*, 21b:26.
9. s. of *I-ku-bi-Ištar*, *BIN* IV, 28:13; 173:36; *KTS*, 43c:20.
10. s. of *Kúr-ub-Ištar*, *KTS*, 47c:3; Liv., 15:7.
11. s. of *ŠÚ-Ištar*, *CCT* I, 15b:18; *CCT* IV, 6b:9.
12. s. of *ŠÚ-Nu-nu*, *BIN* IV, 114:2.
13. f. of *Da-da-a*, *CCT* I, 2:22; *KTS*, 45a:2.
14. f. of *E-a-nim*, *KTS*, 47c:24.

15. f. of *I-din-A-šír*, *CCT* II, 8:17; *CCT* IV, 26a:31.
16. f. of *I-ku-be-a*, *KTS*, 44a:18.
17. f. of *Ku-lu-ma-a*, *CCT* I, 4:26.
18. f. of *Sin-damiq*, *BIN* IV, 211:21; 211case:3.
19. f. of *Ú-zur-šá-Ištar*, *CCT* II, 8:9.
20. *ḫamuštum*, *KTS*, 45b:7; *Babyl. II*, p. 38, line 5.
21. *lîmu*, *BIN* IV, 103:1; *CCT* I, 32b:13; *LTC* IV, 65:9; *Gol.*, 3:14.
22. *BIN* IV, 24:1; 25:22; 28:1; 33:1, 8, 21, 27; 50:3, 7; 64:32; 83:12, 15, 32, 47, 51; 87:11; 114:5, 9, 23, 30; 149:5, 18; 173:14, 37, 45; 184:5; 218:11; *NBC*, 1647:4; 1655:5, 9; 3732R:3; 3753:2; 3765:2; 3876:2; 4070:12; *CCT* I, 12a:5, 8, 16, 19; 20a:25; 26a:6; 38b:6; 39a:4; *CCT* II, 7:1; 10:68; 35:1; 36b:1; 41a:1; 43:2; 44a:1; 44b:1; 49b:2, 4; *CCT* III, 22b:2; 34b:11; 40c:4; 46:5, 16, 20; *CCT* IV, 7c:2; 18b:15; 19b:2, 4; 23a:44; 34a:3; *LTC* IV, 21:1; 30:29; 36:1; 95:1; 105:2; *KTS*, 21a:7, 18; 21b:3; 22a:1; 23:2; 25a:24; 34a:26; 35b:2; 48b:10; *SCTP*, 31:5; 41:6; *TTC*, 6:1, 28; 29:1; *Gol.*, 20:1.

A-šír-iqbi,
1. s. of *ŠÚ-Lá-ba-an*, *CCT* II, 8:8.
2. *BIN* IV, 56:5; 83:2, 21, 28; *CCT* II, 10:54.

A-šír-eš-ta-ki-el, *A-šír-iš-tí-gal*, *A-šur-eš-ta-ki-el*, *A-šur-eš-tí-gal*, *A-šur-iš-ta-gal*, *A-šur-iš-ta-ki-el*, *A-šur-iš-ta-ki-gal*, *A-šur-iš-tí-gal*,
1. s. of *A-šur-rê'ûm*, *CCT* I, 15a:15.
2. s. of *Zu-ga-li-a*, *CCT* IV, 21b:6.
3. f. of *Dan-A-šír*, *PSBA* 1881, p. 34, line 24.
4. *ḫamuštum*, *BIN* IV, 174:9; *LTC* IV, 65:7.
5. *NBC*, 1642:17; 3863:7; *CCT* II, 40b:2; *KTS*, 4a:20; 35a:3; 36a:14, 20; 60c:2; *Gol.*, 23R:10.

A-šír-i-ti, *A-šur-i-ti*,
1. s. of *Šú-lí*, *CCT* I, 10a:26.
2. *CCT* III, 5a:1; *LTC* IV, 108:16; *KTS*, 43a:4; *Babyl.* II, 40, 15.

A-šír-kal-la-ma, *Babyl.* II, p. 44, lines 10, 21.

A-šír-ka-mu-šú, *TTC*, 25:19.

A-šur-kî-na-ra-am, gf. *Ma-nu-kî-A-šur*, *Babyl.* II, 40, line 17.

A-šír-lá. . . ,
1. s. of *A-lá-ḫi-im*, *BIN* IV, 71:7.
2. *KTS*, 37a:5.

A-šír-la-ma-zi, *A-šír-lá-ma-zi*, *A-šur-la-ma-zi*, *A-šur-lá-ma-zi*,
1. s. of *A-šur-ma-lik*, *LTC* IV, 69:2.
2. s. of *ŠÚ-Ku-bi-im*, *CCT* IV, 16c:6.
3. *BIN* IV, 47:7, 32, 35, 38; 68:5; 111:4, 12; 205:4; *NBC*, 3775:1, 3; *CCT* IV,

5a:7, 11; 19b:1; *TTC*, 19:1.

A-šír-lá-na-zi, s. of *ŠÚ-Ku-be-im*, *TTC*, 21:14.

A-šír-li-du-ul, *NBC*, 4000:33.

A-šír-ma-lik, *A-šur-ma-lik*,

1. s. of *Lu-zi-na*, f. of *A-šír-i-din*, *NBC*, 3905:27.
2. s. of *E-na-Sin*, gs. of *Zu-ga-li-a*, *Gol.*, 3:4.
3. *ḫamuštum*, s. of *Lu-zi-na*, *CCT* I, 6c:5.
4. *ḫamuštum*, s. of *Zu-ga-li-a*, *Gol.*, 10:6.
5. s. of *ᵈAdad-ta-ak-lá-ku*, *CCT* I, 20b:9.
6. s. of *A-ḫu-qar*, *LTC* IV, 81:22; 88:3.
7. s. of *A-lá-ḫi-im*, *BIN* IV, 216:LE 2; *CCT* I, 14a:13.
8. s. of *A-mur-ᵈZu*, *BIN* IV, 199:14.
9. s. of *A-šír-ba*..., *SCTP*, 28:7.
10. s. of *A-šír-mu-ta-bi-el*, *LC*, 239:4, 14.
11. s. of *A-šur-ta-ak-lá-ku*, *LTC* IV, 82:4; *KTS*, 49b:21.
12. s. of *A-ta-ta*, *BIN* IV, 165:12.
13. s. of *A-zu-za*, *CCT* II, 3:20.
14. s. of *E-na-nim*, *LTC* IV, 82:1; *CCT* I, 49a:17.
15. s. of *Ga-ra-wa*, *CCT* IV, 9b:18.
16. s. of *Ga-tí-im*, *BIN* IV, 5:20.
17. s. of *Ili-ba-ni*, *CCT* IV, 49b:6.
18. s. of *Ì-lí-iš-tí-gal*, *BIN* IV, 164:21.
19. s. of *I-na-a*, *CCT* I, 18a:12.
20. s. of *Ir-ra-a*, *CCT* II, 42:4; *CCT* III, 22a:29; *LTC* IV, 81:4, 9; *TTC*, 2:20.
21. s. of *La-*... *ᵈAdad*, *NBC*, 3929:7.
22. s. of *Lu-zi-na*, *BIN* IV, 152:18; *LTC* IV, 51:8; *TTC*, 3:5.
23. s. of *ŠÚ-Ištar*, *LTC* IV, 96:14.
24. s. of *ŠÚ-Ku-bi-im*, *Chantre*, 1:3.
25. s. of *Ú-za-ri-a*, *CCT* I, 28a:12.
26. s. of *Zu-ki-bi-im*, *KTS*, 51c:3.
27. s. of *Zu-tí-a*, *BIN* IV, 161:seal A.
28. f. of *ᵈAdad-rabi*, *CCT* III, 50a:11.
29. f. of *A-lá-be-im*, *NBC*, 3911:6.
30. f. of *A-mur-ᵈŠamaš*, *LTC* IV, 95:6, 8.
31. f. of *A-šur-la-ma-zi*, *LTC* IV, 69:3.
32. f. of *Buzur-Ištar*, *BIN* IV, 18:7.
33. f. of *Da-tí-a*, *LTC* IV, 65:13.
34. f. of *ᵈEn-lil-ba-ni*, *BIN* IV, 145:27.
35. f. of *Ib-ni-Sin*, *KTS*, 48c:22.
36. f. of *I-din-a-bi-im*, *LTC* IV, 79:5, 27.
37. f. of *I-din-Ištar*, *BIN* IV, 81:12; 172:11; *KTS*, 55a:37.
38. f. of *ᵈIlabrat-ba-ni*, *NBC*, 3745:9; *CCT* III, 46a:19.
39. f. of *Mâr-A-šur-ma-lik*, *CCT* IV, 25b:14.

40. f. of *ŠÚ-Ḫu-bur*, *BIN* IV, 161:22; 161case:2.
41. f. of *Ú-zur-šá-A-šír*, *CCT* II, 8:6; 10:70.
42. b. of *A-šur-i-din*, *CCT* IV, 45c:2.
43. *dub-šar*, *CCT* I, 20b:8.
44. *ḫamuštum*, *BIN* IV, 195:9; *LTC* IV, 91a:9; 91b:3; *KTS*, 44c:7; *Gol.*, 6:5.
45. *lîmu*, *CCT* I, 4:20.
46. *BIN* IV, 9:27; 10:4; 25:1, 36; 41:4, 32; 46:5; 50:2; 75:2; 76:6; 82:4; 93:3; 103:40; 107:2, 4, 11; 155:16; 170:17; 196:3; 218:8; 222:1; *NBC*, 1642:22; 1897:11; 3744:5; 3753R:1; 3772:8; 3857:14; 3874:6; 3875:6; 3916:3; 3936R:7; 4004:21, 26; *CCT* I, 1a:5, 12; 4:17, 41; 26a:4; 27c:5; 28b:2; 31a:12; 36c:3; 36d:15; 39b:3; 50:21; *CCT* II, 29:7, 15; 40b:4; *CCT* III, 2b:10; 27a:32; 28b:27; 35b:3; 41a:6; 50a:1; *CCT* IV, 5b:11; 6a:3; 7a:4; 8b:31; 15b:3; 21b:2, 4; 45b:2; 48a:7; 49b:12; *LTC* IV, 3:2, 5, 9; 34:6; 44:4, 19; 85:10; 88:5; 89:4; 95:7; 96:5; 147:9; *KTS*, 4a:1; 22b:2; 23:35, 38; 28:3, 5, 9; 37a:3, 8, 25; *SCTP*, 15:14; 27:20; *Gol.*, 8:16; 14:2; 21:4; *Liv.*, 15:4.

A-šur-me-tî, *CCT* I, 15b:7.

A-šír-mu-ta-be-el, *A-šír-mu-ta-bi-el*, *A-šír-mu-ta-el*, *A-šír-mu-ta-bi*, *A-šír-mu-ta-bíl*, *A-šur-mu-ta-be-el*, *A-šur-mu-ta-bi-el*, *A-šír-me-ta-be-el*,

1. s. of *Bu-šú-ki-in*, *LTC* IV, 22:19.
2. s. of *I-din-na-bi-im*, *LC*, 239:2.
3. s. of *ŠÚ-A-nim*, *LTC* IV, 63:seal A.
4. s. of *ŠÚ-be-lim*, *BIN* IV, 105:27.
5. f. of *A-šír-ma-lik*, *LC*, 239:5, 14.
6. *BIN* IV, 26:46; 55:10; 59:1; 97:4; 106:1; 167:3; 231:3, 13; *NBC*, 3753:6; 3878:2; 4044:1; *CCT* III, 26a:2; 41b:1; *LTC* IV, 63:3, 5; 79:12, 17, 23; *KTS*, 49c:8; 52b:7; 60d:6.

A-šír-na-da, *A-šur-na-da*,

1. s. of *Dam-ga-a*, f. of *Bi-lá-aḫ-Ištar*, *CCT* IV, 25a:30.
2. s. of *A-mur-Ištar*, *LTC* IV, 71:7.
3. s. of *A-šur-i-din*, *BIN* IV, 119:6; 154:23.
4. s. of *A-zu. . .*, *LTC* IV, 124:14.
5. s. of *E-na-ma-a*, *BIN* IV, 196:17.
6. s. of *Na-be-li-šú*, *LTC* IV, 88:2.
7. s. of *Šarrum-Sin*, *BIN* IV, 206case:4.
8. s. of *Zu-tî-a*, *BIN* IV, 173:6.
9. f. of *Be-lá-aḫ-A-šur*, *CCT* I, 1a:24.
10. f. of *Ku-ta-a-a*, *LTC* IV, 81:35.

11. f. of *Ṭâb-zi-lá-A-šur*, *KTS*, 44a:20.
12. *ḫamuštum*, *KTS*, 43c:11.
13. *lîmu*, *BIN* IV, 196:16; *NBC*, 3787:8; *Gol.*, 6:14.
14. *BIN* IV, 19:14; 49:3; 51:1; 52:3; 54:2; 60:2; 64:1; 71:1; 88:1; 92:3; 147:4; 148:25, 30; 154:8; 170:5; 195:6; 206:22; 225:2; 229:1; *NBC*, 3909:2; 3913:10; 3937:3; 3937R:7; *CCT* I, 12b:11; 22a:11; 24b:4, 10; 34b:20; 41a:5; *CCT* II, 23:4, 22, 35; 26b:2; *CCT* III, 2b:2; 3b:2, 18, 26; 4:2; 5a:2; 5b:2; 6b:2; 7a:1; 7b:5; 8b:2; 9:3; 10:2; 16b:1; 48a:2; *CCT* IV, 1a:2; 2a:2; 2b:2; 3a:1; 3b:1; 5a:1, 9, 13, 17, 20; 6f:1; 10a:2; 12a:1; 13a:2, 34; 13c:1; 14a:15; 17b:2; 19c:1; 21c:1; 34b:1; *LTC* IV, 2:2; 4:2; 8:2; 11:2; 13:4; 15:2; 18:2; 27:1; 29:2; 71:13; 80:6, 13, 27, 34, 41; *KTS*, 8b:1; 9a:1; 9b:2; 10:2; 11:13; 12:3; 13a:1; 13b:1; 14a:2; 14b:2; 32a:15; 33a:3; 43c:11; *SCTP*, 15:1; 45:9; *TTC*, 14:1; 15:18; 17:2; 22:3; 23:1; 27:2, 14; *RT*, 31, 55, 2.

A-šír-ni-me-tî, *A-šur-ni-me-tî*, *BIN* IV, 58:1; *CCT* I, 23:28; *KTS*, 8b:3.

A-šír-ni-im-ri, *A-šur-ni-im-ri*,
1. s. of *I-din-Sin*, *CCT* I, 4:27.
2. *BIN* IV, 65:1; 164:4.

A-šur-ni-si-im, *CCT* III, 43b:2.

A-šír-ni-šú, *A-šur-ni-šú*, *A-šur-ni-šá-am*,
1. f. of *En-na-Sin*, *LTC* IV, 66:7.
2. f. of *Šú-me-a-bi-a*, *CCT* I, 4:2.
3. *BIN* IV, 103:3, 33; *CCT* I, 12b:3, 9; 13a:17; *CCT* III, 37b:29; *LTC* IV, 76:1, 4; *KTS*, 59a:7; *Liv.*, 15:11; *Chantre*, 6:2.

A-šur-ni-wa-ri, f. of *I-din-Sin*, *BIN* IV, 127:17.

A-šír-rabi, *A-šur-rabi̊*,
1. s. of *A-da-da*, *LTC* IV, 82:24.
2. s. of *Ì-lí-ba-ni*, *LTC* IV, 81:47.
3. s. of *I-na-a*, *BIN* IV, 167:2.
4. s. of *Lá-ki-ib*, *PSBA* 1881, p. 34, line 21.
5. s. of *Ma-nu-um-šú-um-šú*, *CCT* I, 36c:5.
6. s. of *Ni-tì-ba-ni*, *BIN* IV, 101:15.
7. f. of *I-din-a-be-im*, *BIN* IV, 152:21.
8. f. of *Lá-ki-be-im*, *BIN* IV, 197:18.
9. *ḫamuštum*, *Babyl.* II, p. 38, line 6.
10. *BIN* IV, 104:33; 108:1, 3; 111:1, 7, 9; 164:16; 167:5; *NBC*, 3775:2, 4, 18; 3858:1; *CCT* II, 18:37; 49b:1; *CCT* III, 14:2; 28b:29; 29:23, 34; 42b:2; *LTC* IV, 20:34, 35; 37:2; 91a:7; 91b:2; *KTS*, 2a:1;

Gol., 6:3, 19; 8:3, 12; *Chantre*, 14:9.

A-šír-rê'ûm, A-šur-rê'ûm,
1. s. of *Za-ba...-a, NBC*, 3748:1.
2. f. of *A-šur-iš-tí-gal, CCT* I, 15a:16.
3. f. of *Bi-lá-aḫ-Ištar, BIN* IV, 211:19; 211case:2.
4. *ḫamuštum, BIN* IV, 146:5.
5. *BIN* IV, 29:36; 210:16; 210case:1; *NBC*, 3748:4; 3783:4, 7; 3883:4; 3916:1; *CCT* I, 24a:3, 8; 27b:5, 9; 40a:10; *CCT* II, 36b:4; 37a:19; *CCT* III, 10:5, 7, 23; *LTC* IV, 36:3; *KTS*, 21a:11; 21b:25; 36b:2; 36c:1; *Babyl.* IV, 80, 3:31.

A-šír-ri-zi, A-šur-ri-zi,
1. s. of *Bûr-si-lim, BIN* IV, 200:3.
2. f. of *A-šír-damiq, CCT* II, 10:52.
3. *NBC*, 1643:3; 3734:4; 3774:1, 3; 3774R:4; *CCT* II, 47b:2; 48:2; *CCT* III, 13:22; *CCT* IV, 10b:1, 6, 13; 38b:1; *KTS*, 32c:2.

A-šír-sa-tu-e, BIN IV, 145:24.

A-šur-šá-du-ni, CCT IV, 40b:4.

A-šír-šá-am-si, A-šír-šamši(-ši), A-šír-^{d}šamši(-ši), A-šur-šamši(-ši), A-šur-^{d}šamši(-ši),
1. s. of *Am-..., BIN* IV, 91:7.
2. s. of *A-ma-a, BIN* IV, 154:24; *NBC*, 3905:21.
3. s. of *Ga-a-tim, LTC* IV, 24:53.
4. s. of *Ib-ni-Ì-lí, LTC* IV, 14:24; *KTS*, 28:22.
5. s. of *Ì-lí-ba-ni, LTC* IV, 91a:1, seal A.
6. s. of *La-ki-ib, BIN* IV, 173:45; *CCT* III, 19b:12.
7. s. of *ŠÚ-..., NBC*, 3905:32.
8. f. of *Ib-ni-lí, LTC* IV, 107:7.
9. *BIN* IV, 25:9; 26:12; 79:1; 82:2; 86:2; 92:7, 20; 130:7; 154:9; *NBC*, 1891R:9; 3795:4; 3852:9; 3854:7; *CCT* I, 36a:5, 13; *CCT* II, 16a:10; 48:30; *CCT* III, 21b:6, 9; *CCT* IV, 1a:23; 34a:7; *LTC* IV, 22:27; 24:55; 74:14; 91a:6; 91b:2; *KTS*, 6:25; 28:26; 31b:10; 35b:1; 35c:1; 36a:3; *Liv.*, 9:7; *Babyl.* II, p. 42, line 2; *RT*, 31, 55, 7.

A-šur-ta-..., s. of *A-am-ri-a, NBC*, 3730:4.

A-šír-ta-ak-la-ku, A-šír-ta-ak-lá-ku, A-šír-ta-ak-lá-ak-ku, A-šír-ták-lá-ku, ^{d}A-šír-ta-ak-lá-ku, A-šur-ta-ak-lá-ku, A-šur-ták-lá-ku,
1. *ḫamuštum*, s. of *A-lá-ḫi-im, CCT* I, 3:55; *KTS*, 45a:8.
2. s. of *A-lá-ḫi-im, BIN* IV, 127:14; *CCT* I, 2:3, 13; 3:55; 4:25, 37; *CCT* II, 47a:25; *KTS*, 45a:8; 49a:12.
3. s. of *Bu-ur-ki-a, CCT* I, 3:49.
4. s. of *E-na-ni-a, CCT* I, 1a: 25.
5. s. of *I-ga-lí, LTC* IV, 20:8.

6. s. of *ŠÚ-ᵈEn-lil*, *BIN* IV, 42:18.
7. f. of *A-šur-ma-lik*, *LTC* IV, 82:5; *KTS*, 49b:22.
8. *ḫamuštum*, *BIN* IV, 196:7; *CCT* I, 8c:4.
9. *BIN* IV, 19:13; 20:9; 34:25; 42:21; 49:2; 51:2; 52:2; 53:3, 19; 67:1; 69:3; 71:2; 151:15, 19, 29; 160:17; 164:7; 172:5; 188:11; 216:*LE;* 218:28; 220:2; *NBC*, 3725:1; 3730:11; 3732:3; 3909:30; *CCT* I, 25:20; 31a:15; 40a:8; *CCT* II, 2:15; 12b:3; 13:21; *CCT* III, 3b:3, 23; 4:3, 14, 34, 36, 40; 5a:15, 26; 5b:4; 7b:3; 8b:36; 25:33, 37; 30:39; 43b:3; *CCT* IV, 1b:3, 16, 17; 2b:3, 20; 19a:6; 19c:3; 21c:3; 24b:3, 11; 25a:32; 31a:6; 38b:2; *LTC* IV, 2:8; 12:2; 15:37; 17:3; 20:9, 20; 27:2; 47:2; 51:7, 20, 24; 80:7, 16, 32; *KTS*, 2b:2; 12:35; 43c:9, 18; 48b:2, 7, 13, 16; 50d:4; 55a:5; *SCTP*, 9:2; 23:5, 7; *TTC*, 27:5.

A-šír-ta-a-a-ar, s. of *ŠÚ-Ištar*, *Gol.*, 1:3.

A-šír-ṭâbu, *A-šur-ṭâbu*,

1. s. of *Ki-ki-i*, f. of *Mâr-A-šur-ṭâbu*, *BIN* IV, 233:5.
2. s. of *A-lá-ḫi-im*, *CCT* II, 9:28.
3. s. of *E-na-ma-nim*, *CCT* I, 4:39.
4. s. of *Ḫu-ra-za-nim*, *BIN* IV, 199:15.
5. s. of *I-ku-be-a*, *LTC* IV, 52:2.
6. s. of *Ì-lí-dan*, *Babyl.* IV, 78, 2:2, 4.
7. s. of *I-na-Sin*, *Chantre*, 1:6.
8. s. of *Ki-ki*, *LTC* IV, 105:12.
9. s. of *Lá-ki-ib*, *CCT* I, 22a:18.
10. s. of *Lu-lu-a*, *CCT* I, 18a:20.
11. s. of *Si-nu-nu-tim*, *BIN* IV, 120:16.
12. s. of *Ú-za-ri-a*, *BIN* IV, 28:5.
13. f. of *Bu-zu-a*, *BIN* IV, 173:17.
14. f. of *E-ni-ba-aš*, *CCT* I, 11b:13; *KTS*, 47c:2.
15. f. of *Gár-wa-a*, *LTC* IV, 82:3.
16. f. of *Ì-lí-aš-ra-ni*, *CCT* I, 9a:1.
17. f. of *Mâr-A-šur-ṭâbu*, *CCT* IV, 33b:29.
18. *ḫamuštum*, *BIN* IV, 197:8.
19. *lîmu*, *CCT* I, 22a:14.
20. *BIN* IV, 23:28; 28:4; 71:9, 17; 103:20, 26; 233:16; *NBC*, 3775:7; 3796:6; 3917:8; 3931:8; *CCT* I, 4:41; 19b:18; 25:18; 34b:17; 37a:7, 23; *CCT* II, 6:2, 3; 9:31; 11a:5, 10, 16, 22, 24; 46b:2, 18, 33, 35, 36; *CCT* III, 2a:3; 42b:3; *CCT* IV, 16c:1; 22b:6; 33b:21; 42a:8; 46a:2; *LTC* IV, 19:34; 24:2, 13, 35; 30:26; 106:8; *KTS*, 19b:11; 29a:7; 35b:7, 10; 38b:7; *SCTP*,

40:7, 10; *TTC*, 9:15; *Gol.*, 12:3, 4; *Babyl.* IV, 78, 2:15.

A-šír-ur-ḫi, s. of *Bu-da-tim*, *BIN* IV, 122:19.

A-šír-ú-si-ri-ba-ni, *Babyl.* II, p. 44, lines 5, 15.

A-šír-uš-ta-na-ad-ga, *LTC* IV, 5:7.

A-šír-zu-lu-li, *A-šur-zu-lu-li*,
1. *ḫamuštum*, *BIN* IV, 153:5.
2. *BIN* IV, 91:10, 14; *CCT* II, 35:4; 42:3; *CCT* IV, 20b:1; *TTC*, 30:2.

Aš-ku-tim, *Aš-ku-tum*, *Aš-ku-tì-a*,
1. s. of *A-dī-na*, *CCT* IV, 32a:2.
2. f. of *Ba-zi-a*, *BIN* IV, 145:18; *KTS*, 55b:8.
3. *BIN* IV, 74:12, 15; 79:4; 92:2; 147:3, 9, 14, 17, 20; *NBC*, 3905:5; *KTS*, 25b:2; 30:4, 8, 16, 40; 55b:3.

A-šú-ri-tim, *LTC* IV, 74:3.

A-šú-wa-an, *Gol.*, 5:2.

A-ta-a, *At-ta-a-a*,
1. s. of *Ku-uš-ku-zi-im*, *BIN* IV, 199:7.
2. f. of *A-bu-šá-lim*, *KTS*, 40:44.
3. f. of *I-ku-bi-a*, *LTC* IV, 79:10, 20.
4. *BIN* IV, 205:5; *CCT* III, 20:27; *CCT* IV, 13b:23; *LTC* IV, 24:16.

A-ta-i-lá-li-iḫ-šú(?), *BIN* IV, 146: 24.

A-ta-ni, *BIN* IV, 208:6; 208case:11.

A-ta-...-rabi, *BIN* IV, 168:10.

A-ta-ta,
1. s. of *A-mur-Ištar*, *CCT* I, 4:38.
2. s. of *A-šír-dan*, *BIN* IV, 138:9.
3. f. of *A-šír-ma-lik*, *BIN* IV, 165:13.
4. f. of *En-nam-A-šír*, *NBC*, 3755:3; *LTC* IV, 69:1.
5. *BIN* IV, 93:2; 144:3; 145:22; 166:10; 218:18; *NBC*, 3857:4; 4044:7; *CCT* I, 29:21; 38c:9; *CCT* II, 34:10; 49a:3; *CCT* III, 28b:13, 15, 18, 25; *CCT* IV, 6a:3; *LTC* IV, 20:43; *KTS*, 37a:4; 44b:19; *SCTP*, 30:17.

A-wi-el-Ì-lí, *CCT* I, 37a:14.

Az, f. of *A-šír-dan*, *BIN* IV, 225:9.

A-za-a, *CCT* III, 31:3.

A-za-nim, *BIN* IV, 96:4; 116:9; 169:5; *NBC*, 3905:5; *CCT* II, 32a:3, 12, 24; *CCT* III, 44b:1; *LTC* IV, 84:12; *KTS*, 47b:9.

A-zu,
1. f. of *Zu-na-wi-ir*, *SCTP*, 17:5.
2. *CCT* III, 9:42, 45; *KTS*, 60c:2; *SCTP*, 22:4; *TTC* 13:7.

A-zu-..., f. of *A-šír-na-da*, *LTC* IV, 124:15.

A-zu-e-el-ga, *TTC*, 26:1, 3.

A-zu-ma-nim, *CCT* III, 35b:2.

A-zu-na-a, *CCT* I, 9b:2.

A-zu-ta-a, *A-zu-da*,
1. s. of *E-me-me*, *CCT* I, 32a:2; *Chantre*, 10:19.
2. f. of *E-me-me*, *BIN* IV, 28:15.
3. *CCT* IV, 3b:5, 11; 5a:7, 11, 14; *LTC* IV, 34:1.

A-zu-za, *A-zu-za-a*,
1. f. of *A-šír-ma-lik*, *CCT* II, 3:21.
2. f. of *Mâr-A-zu-za-a*, *BIN* IV, 213:3.
3. *BIN* IV, 63:2.

Ba-ba-lá, *Ba-ba-lá-a*,
1. s. of *Bi-ru-a*, h. of *Ba-al-ḫa-zi-a*, *LTC* IV, 68:4, 7.
2. *KTS*, 52a:19; *Chantre*, 2:6; 13:4.

Ba-ba-lá-nim, *Ba-ba-lá-ni*, *Ba-be-lá-nim*,
1. s. of *A-na-aḫ-Ì-lí*, *Babyl.* IV, 77, 1:4.
2. *CCT* I, 23:33; *SCTP*, 3:24.

Ba-ba-li, *Ba-ba-lim*,
1. f. of *Dan-A-šur*, *BIN* IV, 176:7.
2. f. of *Mâr-Ba-ba-li*, *BIN* IV, 145:5; *CCT* IV, 50b:31.
3. f. of *ŠÚ-Sin*, *CCT* I, 48:24.

Ba-ba-zu-a, s. of *ŠÚ-A-nim*, *LTC* IV, 81:28.

Ba-be-lim, f. of *I-din-A-šír*, *CCT* II, 8:7.

Ba-bi-ru-um, *Ba-be-ra-am*, *Ba-bi-ra-am*, *Ba-bi-ri*, *NBC*, 3858:5; *CCT* III, 20:36, 37; 25:15; *Gol.*, 18:11.

Ba-bi-lá, *CCT* III, 25:4, 9.

Ba-bi-li, *KTS*, 39b:8.

Ba-bi-tî, f. of *Me-na-nim*, *CCT* I, 36c:8.

Ba-di-a, *CCT* I, 21d:10.

Ba-ga-ku-un, *CCT* I, 7a:20.

Ba-ḫi-im, *KTS*, 57c:10.

Ba-ḫu-lu, *Babyl.* VI, 189, 1:2, 12.

Ba-lá-a, *NBC*, 3863:15; *LTC* IV, 92:1.

Ba-al-du-bu, s. of *A-lá-ḫi-im*, *CCT* I, 18a:21.

Ba-al-du-šar, *BIN* IV, 40:2; 173:6.

ᶠ*Ba-al-ḫa-zi-a*, ᶠ*Ba-al-ḫu-si-a*,
1. w. of *Ba-ba-lá*, *LTC* IV, 68:5, 8.
2. *BIN* IV, 209:1; 209case:5.

Ba-na-ga, *CCT* I, 8a:14; 36d:6; *CCT* IV, 34a:6; *Gol.*, 4:16.

Ba-ni-a, f. of *Šá-ra-Sin*, *CCT* IV, 25a:26.

Ba-ni-A-šír, *CCT* III, 20:39.

Ba-ni-ni, *Babyl.* IV, 80, 3:31.

Ba-ra-nim, *LTC* IV, 81:27.

Ba-ar-si-ak, s. of *Ḫa-na-na-ri-im*, *CCT* III, 31:34.

Ba-ar-si-ba-lá, *Gol.*, 18:2.

Ba-ru-ga, *CCT* I, 41b:10.

Bar-wa-wa-šá, *CCT* I, 8b:16.

Ba-šú-ri-e, *Chantre*, 2:8.

Ba-at-a-na-aš-wa, *BIN* IV, 190:3.

Ba-za-za, f. of *Bu-zi-a*, *BIN* IV, 105:26.

Ba-zi-a,
1. s. of *Aš-ku-tim*, *BIN* IV, 145:17; *KTS*, 55b:7.
2. *CCT* III, 38:1, 17; *LTC* IV, 10:3.

Be-lá-ḫa-a, *Be-lá-aḫ-a-a*, *Bi-lá-ḫa-a*,
1. s. of *Ni-ra-aḫ-zu-lu-li*, *Liv.*, 7:2.
2. *CCT* III, 27a:1; *KTS*, 38a:1.

Be-lá-ḫa-nim, s. of *Da-nim-Ili*, *BIN* IV, 160:29.

Be-lá-aḫ-A-šír, *Be-lá-aḫ-A-šur*, *Bi-lá-aḫ-A-šír*, *Bi-lá-aḫ-A-šur*,
1. *ḫamuštum*, s. of *Ga-di*, *Gol.*, 4:5.
2. s. of *A-al-ṭâbu*, *CCT* II, 9:40; *KTS*, 16:12.
3. s. of *A-šur-na-da*, *CCT* I, 1a:24.
4. f. of *A-al-ṭâbu*, *Gol.*, 9:12.

5. *NBC*, 3770:3, 4; 3912:4, 6; 3935:6; *CCT* I, 23:25, 27; *CCT* III, 47b:1; *KTS*, 16: 15, 18, 24; 51a:24; 60c:9.

Be-lá-aḫ-Ištar, *Bi-lá-aḫ-Ištar*,
1. s. of *A-šír-na-da*, gs. of *Dam-ga-a*, *CCT* IV, 25a: 29.
2. s. of *A-šír-ba-ni*, *LTC* IV, 79:3.
3. s. of *A-šír-rē'ûm*, *BIN* IV, 211:18; 211case:2.
4. s. of *Ú-zu-a*, *CCT* II, 7:38.
5. f. of *ᵈAdad-damiq*, *LTC* IV, 67:4.
6. f. of *A-šír-du-kúl-tí*, *NBC*, 1708:8.
7. *BIN* IV, 58:2; 151:15, 19; 196:19; *NBC*, 4003:10; *CCT* I, 39a:21; *CCT* IV, 17b:10, 14; *LTC* IV, 65:14; 87:29, 59; *KTS*, 54b:9; *SCTP*, 8:17; *Gol.*, 20:5, 13, 16, 21.

Be-lá-aḫ-Sin, *LC*, 241:9.

Be-lá-nim, *Be-lá-nu-um*, *Bi-lá-nim*, *Bi-lá-nu-um*,
1. s. of *ŠÚ-Ku-bi-im*, *LTC* IV, 81:51; *CCT* I, 11b:12.
2. f. of *A-aḫ-ᵈŠamaš*, *NBC*, 3755:13.
3. *rabizum*, *LTC* IV, 79:13.
4. *BIN* IV, 5:17; 202:3; *NBC*, 3730:1, 7; *CCT* I, 17b:14; *CCT* II, 24:1; *CCT* III, 12b:19; 48b:22; *CCT* IV, 4a:3; 31a:2, 4, 26; *KTS*, 26b:3; 49c:6, 13.

Bi-la-ti-A-šír, *Babyl.* II, p. 43, lines 2, 5, 7.

Be-lá-tum, *Bi-lá-tum*, *CCT* IV, 15c:4; *LTC* IV, 46:2; *KTS*, 23:4; 24:3, 5; 25a:3.

Be-lí-a, *Be-lí-a-a*, *CCT* III, 11:3, 24; 12a:3.

Be-li-li, *Be-lí-lí*, *BIN* IV, 103:35; *KTS*, 23:21.

Be-lim-ba-ni, *Be-lu-ba-ni*, *Bi-lim-ba-ni*,
1. s. of *A-šír-be-el-a-wa-tim*, *BIN* IV, 108:21; *CCT* I, 7b:1.
2. s. of *Na-ra-am-Zu*, *CCT* I, 49b:28.
3. f. of *A-ri-lí*, *LTC* IV, 81:45.
4. *BIN* IV, 160:23; 164:8; *NBC*, 3856:4, 13; 3931:3; *CCT* I, 12a:23; *CCT* II, 40b:3; *CCT* III, 1:26.

Be-lim-na-da, f. of *A-šír-. . .*, *NBC*, 3796:3.

Bi-ra-tí, *Gol.*, 6:2.

Be-ru-a, *Bi-ru-a*,
1. s. of *Wa-lá-aḫ-si-na*, *KTS*, 46a:3, 7; 46b:2.
2. f. of *Ba-ba-lá*, *LTC* IV, 68: 4, 8.
3. *BIN* IV, 146:25; *CCT* I, 8b:4; *CCT* II, 45b:16; *CCT* IV, 20a:19; *LTC* IV, 62:1, 11; 122:20; *KTS*, 46a:12; 46b:6.

Bi-ri-a, *BIN* IV, 42:4.

Be-ru-wa, *Bi-ru-wa*,
1. s. of *Da-da*, *CCT* I, 33b:15.
2. *CCT* I, 41b:5; *LTC* IV, 78:4; *SCTP*, 43:5, 6, 24, 26.

Be-ir-wa-aḫ-šú, s. of *Ma-lá-aš*, *BIN* IV, 190:14.

Be-za, f. of *Šál-me-Ištar*, *BIN* IV, 145:21.

Bu-. . ., f. of *Ú-zu-ur-šá-A-šur*, *NBC*, 1889:8.
Bu-ba-li-a, *Gol.*, 9:21.
Bu-bu-ra-nim, *CCT* II, 7:3; 35:2; *CCT* III, 46b:3, 24.
Bu-da-tim,
1. f. of *ᵈAdad-ba-ni*, *CCT* I, 35:32.
2. f. of *A-šír-ur-ḫi*, *BIN* IV, 122:20.
Bu-du-du, f. of *Na-na-a*, *KTS*, 50a:12.
Bu-uḫ-a-ta-a, *BIN* IV, 225:16.
Bu-uk-da-šú, s. of *A-ni-nim*, *NBC*, 3716:6.
Bu-ku-la-am, *Gol.*, 18:12.
Bu-lá-el-. . ., *Babyl.* VI, 190, 5:5.
Bu-li-. . ., *LTC* IV, 87:54.
Bu-li-a, *Chantre*, 5:12.
Bu-li-na, f. of *Ni-wa-šú*, *LTC* IV, 68:3.
Bu-ra-ma, *LTC* IV, 44:1.
Bu-ra-ma-ma, *LTC* IV, 64:6.
Bûr-A-šír, *Bûr-A-šur*, *Bu-ur-A-šír*, *Bu-ur-A-šur*, *BIN* IV, 4:8, 14; 98:2; 233:6; *NBC*, 3731:2; 3882:3; *CCT* I, 20b:4; *CCT* II, 12b:2; *CCT* III, 35a:27; 49a:2; 50b:2; *CCT* IV, 29b:9; 47b:2; *LTC* IV, 9:2; *KTS*, 44b:17.
Bu-ur-Ištar, *KTS*, 43c:2.
Bu-ur-ki-a, f. of *A-šur-ta-ak-lá-ku*, *CCT* I, 3:49.
Bûr-Nu-nu,
1. s. of *A-di-a*, *BIN* IV, 207:13; 207case:1.
2. s. of *Na-ú-šá*, *BIN* IV, 187:24.
Bûr-si-lim, f. of *A-šur-ri-zi*, *BIN* IV, 200:4.
Bu-ur-Sin, *(Bu)Bûr-Sin*,
1. s. of *ŠÚ-Ma-ma*, *CCT* I, 28a:19.
2. *CCT* IV, 11a:6, 11.
Bu-ur-Šamaš, *KTS*, 31c:4.
Bu-šá-li, *BIN* IV, 157:31, 32, 33; *LTC* IV, 78:7, 11.
Bu-šá-lim, *BIN* IV, 171:5; *CCT* III, 38:32.
Bu-šú-ba-ni(?), *CCT* II, 45b:30.
Bu-šú-ki-in, *Bu-šú-ki-en*,
1. s. of *Šá-ra-wa*, *CCT* IV, 16a:6, 8, 12.
2. s. of *Zu-e-a*, *BIN* IV, 113:19; *KTS*, 43c:19.
3. f. of *A-ḫa-ḫa*, *LTC* IV, 79:9.
4. f. of *A-šur-mu-ta-be-el*, *LTC* IV, 22:20.
5. f. of *Bu-za-zu*, *LTC* IV, 79:7.
6. f. of *I-ku-ba-šá*, *LTC* IV, 79:8.
7. f. of *Zu-e-a*, *LTC* IV, 79:6; *CCT* I, 9a:16.
8. *BIN* IV, 1:1; 6:1; 7:1; 8:1, 19; 9:1; 10:1; 11:1; 12:1; 13:1; 14:1; 15:1; 16:1; 17:2; 18:2; 19:2; 20:2, 5; 21:3, 16; 22:2; 23:1; 24:3; 25:2; 26:2, 7; 27:2; 28:2, 33; 29:2; 30:3; 31:1, 28; 32:3; 33:2; 80:1; 81:1; 82:1; 85:1; 87:3; 90:1, 23, 31; 107:1, 3, 18; 139:6; 149:14; 168:2, 12; 184:8; 221:1; 226:4; 227:1; 232:4; *NBC*, 1895:2; 3704:2, 8; 3704R:5; 3713:5; 3722:1; 3733:1; 3735:2; 3741:1; 3750:3; 3751:8; 3766:4; 3780:1; 3783:2; 3794:2; 3795:1; 3861:3; 3865:12; 3876:1,

5; 3884:2; 3916:1; 3918:4; 3922:2; 4071:2; *CCT* I, 5b:5; 8c:2; 13a:3, 6; 13b:18; 15c:3; 16b:13; 17a:3, 17; 20a:22, 28; 35:5; 49b:20; *CCT* II, 1:2; 2:2; 3:2; 4a:2; 4b:3; 5b:2; 7:35; 28:2; 34:1, 27, 34; 35:3; 36a:1; 36b:2; 38:1; 41a:2; 44a:2; 44b:2; 45b:2, 4; 47:10; *CCT* III, 9:30; 19b:1; 20:1; 21a:2, 28; 21b:3; 22a:3; 22b:4; 36a:2; 49b:21; *CCT* IV, 4a:1; 5b:2; 6e:1; 9a:2; 11a:1; 12a:3; 15c:1; 16a:1, 3, 21, 26; 20a:1, 14, 22; 21b:1, 8; 23a:1; 25b:2; 27a:21; 29a:1, 13; 32b:1; 34c:1; 35a:1; 40b:1; 42c:1; 49a:2, 32, 33; 50b:2; *LTC* IV, 3:1; 6:1; 7:1; 14:3; 16:36, 38; 17:3; 26:2, 36; 28:2; 30:3; 31:1; 46:1; 49:2; 55:1, 9; 73:3, 8, 13; 79:11, 15, 16, 21, 22, 25, 26; *KTS*, 21a:3, 21; 21b:4; 22a:2; 22b:1; 23:1; 24:1; 25a:1, 28; 25b:1; 26a:1; 26b:1; 27a:2, 9; 27b:2; 28:2; 29a:2; 29b:3; 30:2; 57e:3, 8; *SCTP*, 35:2; *TTC*, 4:4, 5; 5:1; 6:3; 24:2, 4; *Liv.*, 10:5.

Bu-ta, *BIN* IV, 103:40.

Bu-ut-ki-im, *ḫamuštum*, *Chantre*, 4:6.

Bu-za, *BIN* IV, 2:2; *CCT* IV, 33a:24.

Bu-za-zu,
1. s. of *Bu-šú-ki-in*, *LTC* IV, 79:7.
2. f. of *A-šír-i-din*, *LC*, 239:8.
3. f. of *Ḫa-nu-nu*, *LTC* IV, 99:7.
4. f. of *Mâr-Bu-za-zu*, *KTS*, 50d:6.
5. f. of *ŠÚ-Sin*, *CCT* II, 4a:9.
6. *ḫamuštum*, *BIN* IV, 160:31.
7. *BIN* IV, 35:2; 38:2; 48:4; 59:9, 10, 18; 72:11; 86:1; 96:1; 103:21; 109:1, 3, 10; 110:1, 3, 9; 112:1, 2; 114:4, 17, 18; 166:2; 203:18; *NBC*, 1655:4; 3795:1; *CCT* I, 7b:8; 12a:23; 17b:12; *CCT* II, 16a:2; 29:34; 30:2; 31a:2; 31b:2; 32a:4; 47b:18; *CCT* III, 12b:15; 26b:2; 32:8, 21, 28, 29; 39a:1; 41a:2; *CCT* IV, 31a:1, 35; 31b:6, 10; 33a:22; 35b:1; 36a:2; 36b:1; 39b:8, 21, 28, 29; 48a:2; *LTC* IV, 21:2; 34:5; 50:2; *KTS*, 3a:1; 7a:3, 27; 44a:7; 49b:11.

Bu-zi, *Gol.*, 20:2.

Bu-zi-a, *Bu-zu-a*,
1. s. of *A-šur-ṭâbu*, *BIN* IV, 173:17.
2. s. of *Ba-za-za*, *BIN* IV, 105:26.
3. s. of *En-nam-A-šír*, *Liv.*, 7:12.
4. *BIN* IV, 62:2, 17, 22; 70:4; *NBC*, 3783:5; 3863:13; *CCT* I, 31b:7; *CCT* III, 16a:3; 29:14, 41; *CCT* IV, 10b:3.

Bu-zu, *CCT* III, 30:33.

Bu-zu-li-a, *KTS*, 60c:1.

Buzur-. . .,

1. f. of *A-ku-a*, *BIN* IV, 112:43.
2. *NBC*, 3790:3; 3803:9; 3861:2; *CCT* II, 12a:2; *CCT* III, 33b:2; *CCT* IV, 38c:1.

Buzur-^{d}Adad,
1. s. of *ŠÚ-Ḫu-bur*, *CCT* II, 10:53; *KTS*, 51c:8.
2. *NBC*, 3911:3.

Buzur-^{d}Amurru(MAR.TU), *Buzur-Amurru(MAR.TU)*,
1. s. of *Ili-be-lá-aḫ*, *LTC* IV, 63:1.
2. *LTC* IV, 76:21.

Buzur-A-na,
1. s. of *E-la-ni*, *BIN* IV, 61:29.
2. s. of *I-din-^{d}Adad*, *CCT* IV, 16c:25, 28.
3. s. of *Ì-lí-a-lim*, *BIN* IV, 185:8; *CCT* II, 47b:3.
4. f. of *Mâr-Buzur-A-na*, *BIN* IV, 225:12.
5. b. of *Ga-ri-a*, *Gol.*, 2:12.
6. *BIN* IV, 148:36; 151:28; 155:12; *CCT* II, 47b:19; *CCT* III, 10:6; *CCT* IV, 30b:33; *LTC* IV, 29:45; 110:8, 20; *KTS*, 10:3; *Liv.*, 14a:3, 10; 14b:6, 11.

Buzur-A-šír, *Buzur-A-šur*,
1. s. of *A-bi-a*, *CCT* I, 10a:27.
2. s. of *A-lá-ḫi-im*, *CCT* III, 38:6.
3. s. of *A-šír-...*, *LTC* IV, 65:3.
4. s. of *A-šír-dan*, *NBC*, 3755:5; 3755R:7.
5. s. of *Da-mu-tî*, *CCT* I, 16b:31.
6. s. of *En-um-^{d}Adad*, *BIN* IV, 192:7.
7. s. of *I-dūr-Ili*, *LTC* IV, 19:26; *TTC*, 25:20.
8. s. of *Ì-lí-a*, *BIN* IV, 135:2.
9. s. of *Ili-kúr-ub*, *CCT* I, 28a:17.
10. s. of *I-li-šú-da-a*, *CCT* I, 15c:5.
11. s. of *I-šar-ki-id-A-šur*, *CCT* I, 48:37.
12. f. of *A-...*, *NBC*, 3755:6.
13. f. of *A-gu-a*, *KTS*, 23:25.
14. f. of *Dan-A-šír*, *KTS*, 45a:1; *TTC*, 21:13.
15. f. of *I-din-Ku-bu-um*, *CCT* I, 46a:3.
16. f. of *ŠÚ-Ištar*, *LC*, 239:7, 13.
17. f. of *Šú-li*, *CCT* IV, 2b:15.
18. *BIN* IV, 2:1; 3:1; 4:1; 18:4; 21:2, 7, 17; 27:4; 31:2, 3; 34:1; 35:1, 12, 15, 31, 35; 36:1; 37:1; 38:1; 39:1; 43:1; 44:1; 47:4; 48:1; 68:4, 13; 84:2; 89:3, 4; 99:2; 103:28; 104:2, 5, 20; 112:6, 10, 11; 131:3; 151:12; 164:12; 174:5; 221:2; *NBC*, 1646:3; 1714:1; 1887:1; 1889:1; 3704:5, 7; 3746:2; 3752:1; 3773:2; 3780R:2; 3782:4; 3786:1; *CCT* I, 21c:5; 26c:10; 32c:4; 43:6; *CCT* II, 1:14; 7:13, 29, 35; 12b:4; 13:1; 14:1; 15:1; 16b:1; 24:15; 29:2, 35; 30:1; 31a:1; 31b:1; 35:5; 37b:1; 38:2; 39:1; 40a:3; 47b:18; 48:5, 16, 20; *CCT* III, 12b:3; 18a:2; 25:7, 17, 40; 30:1, 26, 28; 32:1, 15, 19; 41a:1; 45b:5;

46a:14, 27; 49a:3; 49b:1; *CCT* IV, 4a:2; 6a:1; 6c:1; 7b:1; 12b:1; 18a:2; 29b:1; 31b:5; 33a:3; 36a:1; 37b:1, 11; 38a:1; 38b:4; 39b:1, 15, 19; 40a:1, 29; 40b:2; 42b:2; 43a:31, 45; 45a:21; 47b:3; 48b:1; *LTC* IV, 6:2; 20:45; 21:3; 25:1; 51:1; 53:5, 13; 54:19; 103:1, 4; *KTS*, 5a:1; 5b:1; 6:1; 7a:1, 18; 7b:2; 18:5; 23:5, 15; 29a:2, 13, 22; 29b:24; 35a:6; 38b:11; 52b:6; 60c:5; *TTC*, 5:14; 24:6, 9, 21; 30:3; *Gol.*, 6:20; 12:10; *Chantre*, 16:13.

Buzur-EL.ŠÚ.GAL, *KTS*, 8a:8.

Buzur-E-na,
1. s. of *E-li-a*, *KTS*, 46a:1.
2. *KTS*, 46b:11.

Buzur-Ili, *Buzur-Î-lí*,
1. s. of *El-ba-ni*, *CCT* III, 22b:10.
2. f. of *Kúr-ub-Ištar*, *BIN* IV, 129:17; *KTS*, 40:43.
3. *BIN* IV, 77:2; *NBC*, 3787:13; 3864:8; 3912:1; *CCT* II, 50:2; *CCT* III, 17b:12; 23a:14; *CCT* IV, 15a:4; 44a:21.

Buzur-Ištar,
1. s. of *A-šír-ma-lik*, *BIN* IV, 18:6.
2. s. of *Da-lá-aš*, *BIN* IV, 137:6; *CCT* I, 32a:12.
3. s. of *I-ga-a*, *BIN* IV, 198:10.
4. s. of *Im-tí-lim*, *CCT* IV, 16b:14.
5. s. of *ŠÚ-Ilabrat*, *BIN* IV, 119:8; 206case:3.
6. f. of *A-šur-du-ri*, *NBC*, 1889:6; *LTC* IV, 81:7.
7. f. of ...-*A-šur*, *NBC*, 3748:3.
8. f. of *En-nam-A-šur*, *CCT* I, 41a:19.
9. f. of *I-din-Ku-bu-um*, *CCT* I, 47a:24.
10. f. of *I-ku-bi-A-šír*, *BIN* IV, 138:8.
11. f. of *Na-ab-Sin*, *BIN* IV, 173:41.
12. f. of *ᵈŠamaš-ba-ni*, *CCT* IV, 1a:19.
13. f. of *Ṭâb-A-šur*, *NBC*, 1889:29.
14. f. of *Zu-ba*, *LTC* IV, 30:17.
15. *BIN* IV, 5:3; 23:14; 42:28; 47:8; 57:4; 65:2, 34, 44, 50; 70:2; 82:3; 88:25; 104:1, 4; 151:34; 192:5; 206:20; 219:3; 232:1, 7; *NBC*, 3892:1; 3905:2; *CCT* I, 5a:3; 17a:10, 20; 32c:18; 36d:7; *CCT* II, 11a:3, 25, 26, 31; 40b:5; 45b:1; 46a:5; 46b:4; *CCT* III, 40b:3; *CCT* IV, 5b:3; 16b:2, 3, 5, 8, 10; 34a:18; *LTC* IV, 24:1, 3; 83:22; *KTS*, 1b:2; 19b:2; 25a:4; 29b:6; 54c:11; 56e:4; *TTC*, 12:2; *Chantre*, 4:4.

Buzur-Ni-ra-aḫ, *lîmu*, *BIN* IV, 161:24.

Buzur-sa-du-e, *Buzur-sa-tu*,
1. f. of *Lá-ki-ib*, *CCT* I, 1a:15; *LTC* IV, 34:24.
2. *ḫamuštum*, *CCT* I, 4:43.
3. *BIN* IV, 5:12, 18; 80:11; *KTS*, 8a:14, 18; 9b:13, 15; 60c:7.

Buzur-Sin,
1. s. of *I-ga-lá*, *LTC* IV, 11:20.
2. s. of *I-šá-a*, *CCT* II, 22:34.
3. f. of *Ni-mar-Ištar*, *BIN* IV, 160:28; 164:22; *CCT* I, 7b:5.
4. *CCT* I, 12a:4, 7, 10, 15, 18, 22; 31c:6; *CCT* II, 12b:1; *CCT* III, 10:5; 49a:1; 49b:26; *CCT* IV, 8a:18; 37b:9; 47b:1; *LTC* IV, 11:23; 72:25; *KTS*, 3c:1; *SCTP*, 36:14.

Buzur-ᵈŠamaš, *BIN* IV, 82:8; 104:9, 22; *NBC*, 3790:15; *KTS*, 5a:2.

Buzur-šá-a-du-e, *Buzur-šá-tu-e*,
1. s. of *Du-i-me-im*, *CCT* II, 44b:3.
2. *LTC* IV, 49:2.

Buzur-We-ir, *BIN* IV, 172:26.

Bu-zu-ta-a,
1. f. of *Aḫ-šá-lim*, *CCT* I, 2:2, 13.
2. f. of *Lá-ki-be-im*, *LTC* IV, 34:22; 81:37.
3. f. of *Mâr-Bu-zu-ta-a*, *BIN* IV, 173:24.
4. *ḫamuštum*, *KTS*, 45b:6.
5. *lîmu*, *LTC* IV, 21:15.
6. *BIN* IV, 20:1; 87:1; 150:2; 152:7, 15, 22; 184:3; 192:10; *CCT* I, 20a:4, 19; *CCT* III, 22b:3; *LTC* IV, 17:1; 58:1; *KTS*, 21b:4; 29a:1; *SCTP*, 22:4; *Liv.*, 4:LE.

Bu-zu-zu, *Bu-zu-zi-im*,
1. *lîmu*, *BIN* IV, 27:38; 210:15; 210case:12.
2. *CCT* I, 12b:12.

Da-a-a,
1. s. of *Ma-nu-a*, *CCT* II, 9:41.
2. f. of *I-ku-be-a*, *CCT* IV, 6f:6.
3. *CCT* I, 17a:24; *CCT* IV, 19c:5.

Da-da, *Da-da-a*, *Da-da-a-a*,
1. s. of *A-šír-i-me-tí*, *CCT* I, 2:22; *KTS*, 45a:2.
2. s. of *Dī-li-a*, *CCT* I, 48:11; *CCT* IV, 12b:22.
3. s. of *I-be-zu-a*, *CCT* III, 45b:7.
4. s. of *Ili-mu-ta-bi-el*, *CCT* I, 6a:14.
5. s. of *Ku-du-. . .*, *LTC* IV, 9:24.
6. s. of *Ku-um-ri-im*, *CCT* IV, 19a:12.
7. f. of *A-mur-Ištar*, *CCT* II, 8:23.
8. f. of *Bi-ru-wa*, *CCT* I, 33b:16.
9. *BIN* IV, 3:6; 194:5, 11, 21; 199:16; 205:1; *CCT* III, 45b:12; *CCT* IV, 6b:6, 11; *LTC* IV, 9:21, 23; 115:4; 119:9; *KTS*, 16:4, 7; 53a:17, 25; *TTC*, 21:19; *Chantre*, 10:16; *LC*, 241:13; *Babyl. II*, p. 44, lines 2, 11.

Da-da-nim, f. of *ŠÚ-Ištar*, *BIN* IV, 13:6; *LTC* IV, 70:24.

Da-ga-ni-a, *BIN* IV, 146:4, 19.

Da-gan-ma-al-ki-im, f. of *Li-ib-tí-Ištar*, (*Li-bi-it-Ištar*) *CCT* I, 9a:3; *CCT* III, 11:6.

Da-ak-lí-iš, *LTC* IV, 90a:3; 90b:3; *KTS*, 33a:4.

Da-ku-na, *LC*, 242:1.
Da-lá-aš, *Da-lá-šú*,
1. s. of *Ḫa-ma-ra-a*, *KTS*, 46a:4.
2. f. of *Buzur-Ištar*, *BIN* IV, 137:7; *CCT* I, 32a:12.
3. f. of *I-din-*^{d}*Šamaš*, *BIN* IV, 111:22.
4. *NBC*, 3764:3; *CCT* I, 6c:3; *KTS*, 29a:7; 46b:12; 57c:8; 57d:5.
Da-me-si-e-it, *KTS*, 57c:13.
Dam-ga-a,
1. f. of *A-šír-na-da*, gf. of *Bi-lá-aḫ-Ištar*, *CCT* IV, 25a:30.
2. *CCT* IV, 25a:37.
Damqu-be-i-A-šír, *CCT* IV, 14b:3.
Da-mu-tî, f. of *Buzur-A-šur*, *CCT* I, 16b:31.
Da-na-a, *LTC* IV, 37:2.
Dan-A-šír, *Dan-A-šur*, *Dan-*^{d}*A-šur*, *Dan-na-A-šír*,
1. s. of *A-šur-iš-ta-gal*, *PSBA*, 1881, p. 34, line 23.
2. s. of *Ba-ba-li*, *BIN* IV, 176:6.
3. s. of *Bu-. . .*, *LTC* IV, 105:14.
4. s. of *Buzur-A-šír*, *KTS*, 45a:1; *TTC*, 21:12.
5. s. of *Šál-me-ḫi-im*, *BIN* IV, 173:46; *LTC* IV, 70:27.
6. f. of *I-din-A-šír*, *CCT* II, 30:21.
7. b. of *En-um-A-šír*, *CCT* II, 8:19.
8. *BIN* IV, 8:5, 16, 28; 14:4; 15:3; 19:40; 26:27; 31:40; 47:2, 25; 85:6; 104:34; 144:16; 148:33; 168:3; 173:26, 31; *NBC*, 3767R:1; 3888:7; *CCT* I, 15b:22; 16b:30; 40c:10; *CCT* II, 1:21, 28; 24:4; 36a:5, 22, 26; *CCT* III, 9:21; 18b:3; 20:5; *CCT* IV, 9a:33; 25c:6; 29a:30; 35a:3; *LTC* IV, 14:11; 73:3, 14, 17; *KTS*, 41a:6, 10, 26; 42d:4; 57e:1; *SCTP*, 7:5, 7; *TTC*, 5:15; 9:13; 17:2.
Da-na-dam, *LTC* IV, 38R:13, 15.
Dan-na-i-el, f. of *Mâr-Dan-na-i-el*, *BIN* IV, 19:37.
Da-nim, s. of *A-ba-zi-a-šú*, *LTC* IV, 99:4.
Da-nim-Ili, *Da-nu-Ì-lí*, *Da-nu-me-el*,
1. f. of *Be-lá-ḫa-nim*, *BIN* IV, 160:30.
2. f. of *Mâr-Da-nu-Ì-lí*, *CCT* II, 28:27.
3. f. of *Ì-lí-aš-ra-ni*, *CCT* I, 9a:4.
Da-ra-ak-šú, *LTC* IV, 100:25.
Da-ar-ḫa-si-at, *LC*, 242:3.
Da-tî-a,
1. s. of *A-šír-ma-lik*, *LTC* IV, 65:13.
2. s. of *Na-ni-be-im*, *Gol.*, 3:3.
3. f. of *I-ti-A-šír*, *CCT* IV, 18a:6.
4. *BIN* IV, 192:9; *NBC*, 4044:2; *KTS*, 48a:2, 7, 14; *SCTP*, 17:7; *Babyl.* VI, p. 190, 4:3.
Da-tim, f. of *Šú-li*, *BIN* IV, 173:15.
Di-am-šú, *CCT* I, 41b:9.
Di-ba-zi-a, *BIN* IV, 104:2, 16.
Dī-bu-lá, *BIN* IV, 209:19; 209 case:2.

Dī-dī-a, *Dī-dī-e*,
1. s. of *E-nam-A-šur*, *CCT* I, 32a:13.
2. f. of *En-um-A-šur*, *CCT* III, 46a:20.
3. *BIN* IV, 96:12.

Dī-dī-na-ri, f. of *E-na-na-tim*, *LTC* IV, 67:2.
Dī-li-. . ., f. of *Ar-si-. . .*, *LTC* IV, 119:8.
Dī-li-a, f. of *Da-da-a*, *CCT* I, 48:12; *CCT* IV, 12b:23.
Di-ma-a,
1. f. of *I-ku-nim*, *BIN* IV, 173:46; *CCT* III, 22b:7.
2. *lîmu*, *CCT* I, 7b:13.

Di-mu-tum, *BIN* IV, 162:4, 35.
Dī-ri-ku-da, *LTC* IV, 100:22.
Di-zi-a, *CCT* I, 30a:24; *LTC* IV, 4:33.
Du-ud-ḫa-li-a, *CCT* I, 34a:17.
Du-ud-ḫi-tî-šú, *LTC* IV, 87:58.
Du-du, *Du-du-a*, *Du-du-ú*,
1. s. of *dAdad-ba-ni*, *LTC* IV, 81:16.
2. f. of *. . .-Ku-bu-um*, *KTS*, 47c:6.
3. *BIN* IV, 57:1; 95:8, 16; 208:17; 208case:2; *NBC*, 3921:12; *CCT* I, 22b:2, 20; 25:2; 34a:21; *CCT* IV, 49b:3, 11, 15; *LTC* IV, 19:41; 84:9; 87:11; *KTS*, 3a:2; 13b:31.

Du-du-li, *CCT* III, 9:43.
Du-uḫ-lí-iš, *BIN* IV, 113:1, 8, 12.
Du-ḫu-si-li, *LTC* IV, 100:23.
Du-ú-i-du-ú-i, *Liv.*, 13b:2.
Du-i-me-im, f. of *Buzur-šá-a-du-e*, *CCT* II, 44b:4.
Du-ul-du-ma, *Gol.*, 10:13.
Du-ma-ḫi-ir, *SCTP*, 15:2.
Du-ma-na, *Gol.*, 10:11.
Du-nu-um-na,
1. s. of *Ḫa-za-al-bu-na*, *LTC* IV, 87:3, 16.
2. *BIN* IV, 208:3; 208case:4, 8; *CCT* I, 8b:15; *Chantre*, 2:3.

Du-ra-am-Ili, *Du-ra-am-Î-lí*, *Du-ra-me-el*, *BIN* IV, 69:1, 4; *CCT* I, 6b:13; *CCT* III, 43b:1, 4, 8; 44a:13; *LTC* IV, 101:15.
Du-ru-uḫ-na, *CCT* III, 48b:9.
Du-šá-lá, *LTC* IV, 78:5.
Du-tî-ki, f. of *Mâr-Du-tî-ki*, *KTS*, 48c:8.
E-. . ., f. of *Šarrum-Sin*, *NBC*, 3756:7.
E-a-ba-aš-tî, *BIN* IV, 145:19.
Ê-a-dan, f. of *Iš-ma-A-šír*, *LTC* IV, 75:16.
E-a-nim, s. of *A-šír-i-me-tî*, *KTS*, 47c:23.
E-a-šar, *BIN* IV, 1:2; *TTC*, 5:2.
E-bi-bu-ni, *CCT* III, 23a:29.
E-dī-na-a, *BIN* IV, 147:10, 14, 17; *NBC*, 1903:14; *CCT* IV, 14a:19.
E-din-A-šír, *E-dī-in-A-šír*, *NBC*, 1701:12; *CCT* IV, 14a:2, 4; *LTC* IV, 4:3.
E-lá, *CCT* I, 37a:4, 21; *CCT* II, 2:3, 31, 41, 47; *LTC* IV, 70:23.
E-lá-ma, *E-lam-ma*,
1. s. of *I-din-Sin*, *TTC*, 25:13.
2. *BIN* IV, 19:13; *NBC*, 3903:9; *CCT* IV, 13a:14, 39; *TTC*, 14:38.

E-lá-ni, *E-lá-nim*, *E-lá-nu*, *E-lá-nu-um*,

1. s. of *ŠÚ-Ku-bi-im*, *BIN* IV, 91:11; *CCT* III, 25:34.
2. f. of *A-šur-i-me-tî*, *NBC*, 3746:8.
3. f. of *Buzur-A-na*, *BIN* IV, 61:30.
4. f. of *En-na-Sin*, *BIN* IV, 31:35; *Gol.*, 2:4.
5. f. of *I-ku-nim*, *LTC* IV, 81:53.
6. f. of *I-na-a*, *BIN* IV, 173:7; *CCT* I, 4:23; 20b:3.
7. f. of *Mâr-E-lá-ni*, *CCT* IV, 4a:4.
8. *ḫamuštum*, *LTC* IV, 63:8.
9. *CCT* III, 13:22; 18a:2; 37a:4; 43a:17; *CCT* IV, 24b:3; 30a:2; *LTC* IV, 20:4, 20, 23; 34:9; 54:12, 18; *KTS*, 26a:16, 22, 25; 31b:6; 31c:12; 34a:1; 36a:5; 51b:7; 54c:4; 58d:3.

El-ba-ni,
1. s. of *A-mur-A-šur*, *BIN* IV, 112:41.
2. s. of *I-a-. . .*, *BIN* IV, 79:3.
3. f. of *Buzur-Î-lí*, *CCT* III, 22b:10.
4. f. of *I-ku-nim*, *LTC* IV, 90a:2; *CCT* I, 14b:11.
5. *ḫamuštum*, *BIN* IV, 147:21.
6. *BIN* IV, 100:3; 170:18; *CCT* I, 13a:15; *CCT* II, 41a:23; *CCT* III, 42a:1, 11; *LTC* IV, 101:6; *KTS*, 23:16; 29a:4, 25; *TTC*, 10:2; *Chantre*, 7:3.

El-be-. . ., f. of *Î-lí-a-lim*, *BIN* IV, 173:21.

El-ga-si-id, *CCT* IV, 12a:5.

E-li-a, *El-li-a*,
1. f. of *Buzur-E-na*, *KTS*, 46a:1.
2. f. of *Id-na-a*, *BIN* IV, 206case:1.

El-ku-li, f. of *A-šur-i-me-tî*, *LTC* IV, 82:6.

El-me-da-ku, *LTC* IV, 50:1.

El-me-tî,
1. s. of *ŠÚ-Ištar*, *CCT* I, 7b:19.
2. f. of *ŠÚ-Sin*, *LTC* IV, 67:3.
3. *BIN* IV, 50:5; 164:18.

El-wa-da-ku, *El-wa-da-ak*, *BIN* IV, 34:2; 35:5; 37:2, 19; 38:5; 39:3; 43:2; 45:25; 104:8, 21; 109:1, 4, 7; 110:1, 4, 7; 112:1, 22; 130:10; 160:10; *NBC*, 1646:6, 7; *CCT* II, 12b:2; 13:2; 14:2; 15:2; 16a:1; 16b:2; 31a:3; 39:2; *CCT* IV, 7b:2; 12b:2; 31a:5, 11; 36a:14, 17; 38a:2; *LTC* IV, 22:2; *KTS*, 5b:2; 6:2, 5; 53c:3.

E-me-me, *E-me-ma*,
1. s. of *A-zu-ta-a*, *BIN* IV, 28:14.
2. f. of *A-zu-ta-a*, *CCT* I, 32a:3; *Chantre*, 10:19.
3. *ḫamuštum*, *BIN* IV, 196:8.
4. *BIN* IV, 49:1; *CCT* III, 7b:2; 9:1; *KTS*, 43c:12; 60b:10.

E-na-. . ., *CCT* III, 33b:1.

E-na-a, *CCT* III, 47a:1; *KTS*, 31c:2.

E-na-aḫ-Ili, *E-na-aḫ-Î-lí*,
1. f. of *A-lá-ḫu-um*, *LTC* IV, 82:2.
2. *LTC* IV, 50:5, 23.

E-na-na-tim,
1. s. of *Dī-dī-na-ri, LTC* IV, 67:1.
2. *BIN* IV, 233:28; *CCT* IV, 4b:25; *TTC*, 27:9.

E-en-A-šír, E-en-A-šur, E-in-A-šur, NBC, 3710:5; *LTC* IV, 5:15; *KTS*, 15:43.

E-na-aš-ru-ú, CCT I, 10b:10.

En-bi-A-šur, KTS, 40:44.

E-ni-ba-aš, E-ni-ba-šá-at,
1. s. of *A-šír-ṭâbu, CCT* I, 11b:13; *KTS*, 47c:1.
2. *LTC* IV, 25:13, 20; *Gol.*, 18:1.

E-ni-iš-ru, LTC IV, 68:9, 13.

E-ni-Sin, SCTP, 25:15.

ᵈEn-lil-ba-ni, ᵈEn-ba-ni, En-lil-ba-ni,
1. s. of *A-šír-ma-lik, BIN* IV, 145:26.
2. s. of *Ì-lí-ba-ni, CCT* II, 8:5.
3. s. of *Iš-ma-A-šur, LTC* IV, 81:10.
4. *BIN* IV, 68:1; 108:1, 4, 11; 154:10, 16, 22; 194:13, 15, 17, 20; *NBC*, 3779:1, 5; 3884:4; *CCT* I, 2:4, 14, 22; 3:32, 38, 44, 50, 55; 4:7, 29; 11b:4, 15; *CCT* III, 13:2, 14:1; 27a:3; 29:2, 7; *CCT* IV, 1a:21; 13b:1; 23b:3; 24b:2; *LTC* IV, 10:2; 20:2; 35:5; 57:3; 88:12, 18; *KTS*, 38a:3; 45a:6; 53a:16; *SCTP*, 35:13; *TTC*, 21:2, 9; *Liv.*, 1:1; *Babyl.* II, p. 38, lines 2, 15; *Babyl.* IV, p. 80, 3:32.

E-na-za, s. of *En-na-nim, BIN* IV, 113:21.

En-na-. . . , *Babyl.* VI, p. 189, 3:3.

En-nam-A-a, E-nam-A-a, E-na-ma-a,
1. f. of *A-šur-na-da, BIN* IV, 196:18.
2. f. of *ᵈŠamaš-ba-ni, LC*, 239:21.
3. *BIN* IV, 230:6, 16; *Gol.*, 8:2.

En-nam-ᵈAdad, En-um-ᵈAdad,
1. f. of *Buzur-A-šur, BIN* IV, 192:8.
2. *NBC*, 3770:10, 14.

En-na-ma-nim, En-nam-ma-nim, En-na-nim, En-na-ni, En-na-ni-a, En-na-nu, En-na-nu-um, E-na-ma-nim, E-na-ni-a, E-na-nim, E-na-nu-um,
1. s. of *A-be-a, CCT* I, 40c:11.
2. s. of *A-bu-di, CCT* II, 10:47.
3. s. of *Am-ri-a, BIN* IV, 122:17.
4. s. of *Ku-ku-a, KTS*, 44a:16.
5. s. of *Kúr-ub-Ištar, LTC* IV, 117:2.
6. s. of *ŠÚ-Ḫu-bur, CCT* IV, 49a:37.
7. s. of *Za-zi-a, TTC*, 19:6.
8. f. of *A-bi-a-a, KTS*, 50a:14.
9. f. of *. . .-A-šír, BIN* IV, 165:7.
10. f. of *A-šur-i-me-tì, BIN* IV, 29:1; 173:2, 11, 19, 33; *CCT* III, 19b:19.
11. f. of *A-šur-ma-lik, CCT* I, 49a:18; *LTC* IV, 82:1.
12. f. of *A-šur-ták-lá-ku, CCT* I, 1a:25.
13. f. of *A-šur-ṭâbu, CCT* I, 4:40.

14. f. of *E-na-za*, *BIN* IV, 113:22.
15. f. of *En-um-A-šur*, *BIN* IV, 127:19.
16. f. of *I-din-Sin*, *CCT* I, 49b:31.
17. f. of *Ma-nu-um-ba-lim-A-šur*, *BIN* IV, 108:15; *CCT* I, 14b:13.
18. f. of *Šú-da-a*, *BIN* IV, 61:42, 66.
19. f. of *ŠÚ-Ku-be-im*, *BIN* IV, 165:8.
20. *ḫamuštum*, *BIN* IV, 146:6; *CCT* I, 3:33, 39; 11b:6; *Chantre*, 16:7.
21. *BIN* IV, 206case:8; 219:17; *NBC*, 3745:7; 3782:1; *CCT* I, 12b:13; 20a:23; 34a:11; 41b:7; 44:8; *CCT* II, 7:2; 10:61; 22:4, 36, 39; 35:2; 36b:5; 37a:20; *CCT* III, 2b:6; 11:2, 28; 31:24; 45a:28; 46b:2, 26; *CCT* IV, 14a:1; 23b:2; 24a:43, 45; 45b:9; *LTC* IV, 74:16; 80:40; 85:9; 103:2, 14; *KTS*, 8a:3; 8b:2; 40:6; 43b:10; *SCTP*, 3:11; 32:2, 8; *TTC*, 6:4; 12:1; 27:11; 29:2; *Chantre*, 4:3; 5:5.

En-nam-A-šír, *En-nam-A-šur*, *En-na-A-šír*, *En-na-A-šur*, *En-nu-um-A-šír*, *En-nu-um-A-šur*, *En-um-A-šír*, *En-um-A-šur*, *En-um-^{d}A-šír*, *E-na-A-šír*, *E-na-A-šur*, *E-na-ma-A-šur*, *E-nam-A-šur*, *E-um-A-šír*,

1. *ḫamuštum*, s. of *Sin-na-da*, *KTS*, 44b:6.
2. s. of *A-ni-nim*, *BIN* IV, 103:37; 105:1; *CCT* I, 9a:5, 8, 14; 49b:2, 13; *TTC* 4:7.
3. s. of *A-ta-ta*, *NBC*, 3755:3; *LTC* IV, 69:1.
4. s. of ...*-ba-aḫ*, *BIN* IV, 210case:3.
5. s. of *Buzur-Ištar*, *CCT* I, 41a:18.
6. s. of *Dī-dī-a*, *CCT* III, 46a:20.
7. s. of *E-na-nim*, *BIN* IV, 127:18.
8. s. of *En-na-Sin*, *BIN* IV, 78:20; *CCT* I, 20b:6.
9. s. of *E-ra-tî*, *Gol.*, 3:16.
10. s. of *Ḫa-ba*, *BIN* IV, 209case:1.
11. s. of *Šál-ma-ḫi-im*, *BIN* IV, 184:11; *CCT* I, 4:24; *CCT* II, 8:18; *CCT* III, 50b:6; *CCT* IV, 33a:22.
12. s. of *ŠÚ-A-šur*, *LTC* IV, 30:21.
13. s. of *ŠÚ-^{d}En-lil*, *LTC* IV, 19:6.
14. s. of *Ú-za-ri-a*, *CCT* II, 9:29.
15. s. of *Zi-li-Ištar*, *LTC* IV, 95:5; 96:11.
16. f. of *A-šur-i-me-tî*, *LTC* IV, 66:1.
17. f. of *Bu-zi-a*, *Liv.*, 7:13.
18. f. of *Dī-dī-a*, *CCT* I, 32a:13.
19. f. of *En-na-Sin*, *LTC* IV, 75:24.
20. f. of *Ga-zu-a*, *TTC*, 10:19.
21. f. of *Ḫa-nu-nu*, *CCT* I, 49a:14.
22. f. of *Ili-šú-rabu*, *TTC*, 10:4.
23. f. of *Ištar-be-lá-aḫ*, *CCT* I, 46a:2; 47a:22.

24. f. of *Šá-lim-a-ḫi-im*, *LTC* IV, 69:5.
25. f. of *Šál-ma-A-šur*, *BIN* IV, 176:3.
26. b. of *Dan-A-šur*, *CCT* II, 8:18.
27. *BIN* IV, 12:2, 12; 23:9; 40:11; 73:4; 83:3, 6, 11, 46, 51, 53; 88:23; 105:13; 121:15; 164:6; 185:6; 209:18; 210:18; 225:3; 229:5, 7, 232:3; *NBC*, 3849:14; 3916:2; 4000:2; *CCT* I, 4:37; 12a:16, 19; 17a:4, 6, 14, 22, 23; 29:35; 34a:2; 43:1, 2; *CCT* II, 16b:7; 21a:2, 4; 23:5, 8, 14, 19, 24, 31, 38; 42:11; 50:12, 18, 19, 23; *CCT* III, 13:10; 35a:29; 47b:3; *CCT* IV, 4a:8, 21; 9a:21; 9b:2, 4; 20b:5; 21a:1; 23a:3; 25b:5; 26b:2; 30b:4; 33a:2; 35a:19; 44a:4, 11, 13; 45a:1; 49b:1; *LTC* IV, 41:1, 2; 48:24; 76:2, 5, 15; 77:5; 97:7; 105:11; *KTS*, 38b:10, 14; 44c:17; 48a:15; 52a:10; 58d:2; *TTC*, 1:20; 2:16; 30:1; *Gol.*, 7:21; 24:12; *Chantre*, 15:1, 2; *LC*, 241:6.

En-nam-be-lim, *En-na-be-lim*, *En-nim-be-lim*, *En-nu-be-lim*, *En-nu-um-be-lim*, *En-be-li*, *En-um-be-lim*, *E-na-be-lim*, *E-na-bi-lim*, *E-nu-be-lim*, *E-nu-*^{d}*be-lim*, *E-nu-bi-lim*,

1. s. of *ŠÚ-Lá-ba-an*, *BIN* IV, 173:42; *CCT* I, 16b:32; *TTC*, 25:17.
2. *BIN* IV, 5:15; 56:2; 66:3; 87:2; 101:10; 184:6; *NBC*, 3863:17; *CCT* II, 8:1, 4; 9:33; 10:52, 64; 21b:1; 35:1, 17, 46, 47; 42:2; *CCT* III, 5a:19; 11:1, 32; 15:2; 16a:4; 44b:23; *CCT* IV, 8b:7; 17a:6; 18b:2; 22b:2; 26b:20; 28a:36; 34b:13; 46b:1; *LTC* IV, 27:22, 27; *KTS*, 3c:7; 20:19; 29a:1.

En-na-Sin, *E-na-Sin*,

1. s. of *Zu-ga-lí-a*, f. of *A-šur-ma-lik*, *Gol.*, 3:4.
2. *lîmu*, s. of *Aḫ-me*, *CCT* I, 1a:31.
3. *lîmu*, s. of *ŠÚ-A-šur*, *CCT* I, 3:54; *LTC* IV, 66:13.
4. *lîmu*, s. of *ŠÚ-Ištar*, *CCT* I, 4:9.
5. s. of *A-šur-ni-šú*, *LTC* IV, 66:6.
6. s. of *E-lá-ni*, *BIN* IV, 31:35; *Gol.*, 2:3.
7. s. of *En-nam-A-šír*, *LTC* IV, 75:23.
8. s. of *I-din-a-be-im*, *CCT* IV, 33b:4.
9. s. of *Ì-lí-a-lim*, *NBC*, 1891:6; *CCT* I, 48:19.
10. s. of *Ku-ra-ra*, *CCT* IV, 24a:26.
11. s. of *ŠÚ-A-nim*, *CCT* IV, 16c:3.
12. f. of *En-nam-A-šur*, *BIN* IV, 78:21; *CCT* I, 20b:6.
13. *ḫamuštum*, *CCT* I, 3:45; *Gol.*, 6:6.

14. *BIN* IV, 15:13; 77:3; 142:3; *NBC*, 1891:8; 3701:13; 3865:15, 19; 3892:8; 3937:4; 3937R:5; *CCT* I, 21d:8; 27c:3; *CCT* II, 20:34; 24:21, 31; *CCT* III, 12b:2; 25:6; 45a:6; *CCT* IV, 24a:28; 43a:12, 37; 48a:27; *LTC* IV, 42:1; *KTS*, 26a:15; 56d:3; *SCTP*, 2:24; *Babyl.* VI, p. 190, 4:1.

En-nam-šá-. . ., s. of *ŠÚ-A-šír*, *KTS*, 50b:13.

En-nam-Šá-ra, *LTC* IV, 80:37.

En-na-Zu,
1. f. of *ŠÚ-A-nim*, *KTS*, 31a:2.
2. *CCT* I, 6b:12.

E-nu-a, f. of *A-mur-^{d}Šamaš*, *KTS*, 31a:6.

En-um-. . ., *CCT* IV, 27b:2; *NBC*, 3936R:3.

En-um-Ì-lí, *BIN* IV, 161:10.

E-ra-a, f. of *Mâr-E-ra-a*, *BIN* IV, 26:23.

E-ra-da-an, *Gol.*, 8:9, 15.

E-ra-tí, *E-ra-tim*,
1. f. of *E-na-A-šur*, *Gol.*, 3:17.
2. f. of *Ili-kúr-ub*, *NBC*, 1889:28.
3. f. of *Mâr-E-ra-tí*, *CCT* IV, 6c:14.
4. *Babyl.* II, p. 39, line 20.

E-ri-ri-a, *Gol.*, 18:10.

E-ri-iš-tí, *LTC* IV, 60:8.

E-ri-šum, *CCT* IV, 19b:16.

E-šú-ba-ni, f. of *Ṭâb-A-šur*, *CCT* III, 17a:24.

E-wa-ri-mu-šá, *LTC* IV, 109:6, 12.

Ga-ba-tim, f. of *Ḫa-nu*, *LC*, 239:1.

Ga-ba-zi, *CCT* I, 25:29.

Ga-áb-ri-a, *ḫamuštum*, *BIN* IV, 195:8.

*f**Ga-áb-zi-a*, w. of *Wa-ak-li-a*, *CCT* I, 10b:4, 8.

Ga-di, f. of *Bi-lá-aḫ-A-šur*, *Gol.*, 4:6.

Ga-du-du, *LTC* IV, 87:19.

Ga-ga-da-nim, *Ga-ga-ta-nim*,
1. f. of *A-šír-e-mu-qi*, gf. of *Za-ḫa-. . .*, *Gol.*, 9:5.
2. f. of *ŠÚ-be-lim*, *LTC* IV, 80:36.

Ga-gi-a, *Ga-ki*, *Ga-ki-i*, *CCT* III, 1:19; *TTC*, 5:11; 9:7.

Ga-li-. . ., *KTS*, 59a:5.

Ga-lu-lu-uš, *LTC* IV, 87:11.

Ga-lu-me, *CCT* I, 18b:4.

Ga-ni,
1. s. of *Na-ni-ib*, *LTC* IV, 33:10.
2. *LTC* IV, 33:12.

Ga-ni-si-im(?), *Ga-ni-si-ú*, *Ga-ni-si-e*, *CCT* II, 40a:6, 14; *SCTP*, 4:26.

Ga-ni-zi-a, *BIN* IV, 208:4; 208 case:5, 9.

Ga-nu-a, *CCT* I, 35:24.

Ga-ra-šú, *LTC* IV, 99:15.

Ga-ra-wa, f. of *A-šur-ma-lik*, *CCT* IV, 9b:19.

Ga-ri-a, *Gár-ri-a*,
1. s. of *ŠÚ-be-lim*, *BIN* IV, 101:17; *Gol.*, 3:18.
2. f. of *Mâr-Ga-ri-a*, *NBC*, 3856:7.
3. b. of *Buzur-A-na*, *Gol.*, 2:11.
4. *LTC* IV, 34:19; *KTS*, 43b:3; *Gol.*, 11:1, 16.

Ga-ar-na-lá-[*dī*], *CCT* I, 34a:8.

Gár-tum-^{d}Adad, *CCT* I, 45:11.

Ga-ru-bu-a, *TTC*, 23:3.

Gár-wa-a, Ga-ar-wa-a, Ga-ru-wa-a,
1. s. of *A-šur-ṭâbu*, *LTC* IV, 82:3.
2. f. of *Mâr-Ga-ar-wa-a*, *BIN* IV, 42:31.
3. *ḫamuštum*, *LTC* IV, 74:7.
4. *BIN* IV, 8:32; 16:10; 17:11; 19:14, 39; 41:36; 203:10; *NBC*, 3755R:5; 3927:5; *CCT* III, 22a:6; *LTC* IV, 73:16.

Ga-si-im,
1. s. of *Ma-zu*, *CCT* I, 26b:14.
2. b. of *A-šír-be-lí*, *CCT* II, 30:8.
3. *ḫamuštum*, *CCT* I, 3:33; 5b:7; 11b:5; *LTC* IV, 90a:7; 90b:6.
4. *BIN* IV, 124:7; 145:16; *LTC* IV, 145:4.

Ga-ta-tim,
1. s. of *I-din-Ištar*, *CCT* I, 18a:18.
2. *CCT* IV, 16b:1.

Ga-tì-im, Ga-a-tim,
1. f. of *A-šur-ma-lik*, *BIN* IV, 5:21.
2. f. of *A-šír-šamši(-ši)*, *LTC* IV, 24:53.
3. f. of *Mâr-Ga-a-tim*, *LTC* IV, 46:9.

Ga-wa-a, *CCT* I, 7a:4; 26a:2.

Ga-wa-lá, *KTS*, 43b:11.

Ga-za-bi-id, *BIN* IV, 72:1.

Ga-za-ri, Ga-za-ri-e, *NBC*, 3873:19; *LTC* IV, 16:7.

Ga-za-za, f. of *Mâr-Ga-za-za*, *CCT* III, 43a:8.

Ga-zi-a, Ga-zu-a,
1. s. of *En-nam-A-šur*, *TTC*, 10:18.
2. *ḫamuštum*, *CCT* I, 9b:7.
3. *BIN* IV, 150:11; *SCTP*, 35:11.

Ga-zu-ma(?), *BIN* IV, 23:6.

Gi-lu-lu, *Babyl.* IV, p. 80, 3:32.

Ḫa-ba, f. of *En-um-A-šur*, *BIN* IV, 209case:2.

Ḫa-ba-ta-lí, *LC*, 240:1, 6, 7, 12, 15, 19, 21.

Ḫa-bi-a, *CCT* I, 10b:3.

Ḫa-bu-a-lá, Ḫa-a-bu-ú-lá,
1. f. of *I-li-šá-ki*, *BIN* IV, 22:8.
2. *BIN* IV, 143:4; 157:1; 171:8; 231:1; *LTC* IV, 87:30; *KTS*, 51a:13, 16, 26; *Gol.*, 13:6.

Ḫa-bu-a-šú, Ḫa-bu-wa-šú, *BIN* IV, 143:4; *CCT* II, 30:9; *LTC* IV, 87:22; *TTC*, 16:22; *NBC*, 3723R:3.

Ḫa-da-a,
1. f. of *ŠÚ-A-nim*, *BIN* IV, 165:10; *LTC* IV, 88:1.
2. *CCT* IV, 9b:20, 28.

Ḫa-da-a-ni, *LTC* IV, 83:14.

Ḫa-du, *BIN* IV, 171:9; *KTS*, 51a:14.

Ḫa-du-wa, *BIN* IV, 163:2.

Ḫa-ḫa-lu-an, Ḫa-ḫa-lu-wa-an, *LTC* IV, 122:2, 6.

Ḫa-lá-be-im, f. of *A-šur-i-me-tì*, *BIN* IV, 200:2.

Ḫa-lá-da, *LTC* IV, 87:20.

Ḫa-li-ma, f. of *Mâr-Ḫa-li-ma*, *CCT* I, 50:9.

Ḫa-al-ki-a, *TTC*, 16:13.

Ḫa-lu-li, *BIN* IV, 189:14; 195:17; *CCT* I, 35:23; *CCT* III, 9:41.

Ḫa-ma-na-ni, *Liv.*, 8:15.

Ḫa-ma-ra-a, f. of *Da-lá-aš*, *KTS*, 46a:4.
Ḫa-mu-ri-a, f. of *Šú-be-ú-ma-an*, *KTS*, 46a:5.
Ḫa-na-..., *NBC*, 3716:1; 3753:1; 3759:1.
Ḫa-na-a, *CCT* IV, 14b:13, 21, 26, 29; 46a:8, 10; *TTC*, 9:12.
Ḫa-na-na-..., *BIN* IV, 107:28; 218:1.
Ḫa-na-na-bi-im, *Gol.*, 14:1.
Ḫa-na-na-ri-im, *Ḫa-na-na-ru-um*,
1. f. of *Ba-ar-si-ak*, *CCT* III, 31:35.
2. *BIN* IV, 36:21; 218:31; *NBC*, 3878:1, 35; 3888:7, 11; 4044:8, 10; *CCT* I, 28d:4; *KTS*, 5a:21; 40:31; 60d:5.

Ḫa-na-nu-um, *Ḫa-na-nim*,
1. s. of *I-ku-be-a*, gs. of *I-ku-a*, *BIN* IV, 52:26.
2. s. of *I-ku-be-a*, *LTC* IV, 2:6.
3. f. of *Na-na-a-a*, *NBC*, 3712:6; *LTC* IV, 81:13.
4. f. of *Rabû-A-šur*, *Gol.*, 23R:4.
5. f. of *Ta-ki-el-A-šír*, *LTC* IV, 65:2.
6. *ḫamuštum*, *BIN* IV, 146:18.
7. *CCT* I, 18b:13.

Ḫa-na-zu, *CCT* IV, 6d:3.
Ḫa-nu,
1. s. of *Ga-ba-tim*, *LC*, 239:1.
2. s. of *I-dūr-Ili*, *CCT* I, 49a: 2, 5.
3. *CCT* III, 38:1; *LTC* IV, 74:2; 81:17; *KTS*, 58b:5; *TTC*, 2:21; *Gol.*, 11:17.

Ḫa-nu-ú-a, *LTC* IV, 87:21.
Ḫa-nu-nu, *Ḫa-nu-nu-um*,
1. s. of *Bu-za-zu*, *LTC* IV, 99:6.
2. s. of *En-um-A-šur*, *CCT* I, 49a:14.
3. *dub-šar*, *LTC* IV, 81:33.
4. *BIN* IV, 42:14; 99:1; *CCT* I, 17b:25; *CCT* II, 48:4, 23; *CCT* III, 42b:20; *CCT* IV, 16c:31; *KTS*, 21b:25; 49c:4; *Liv.*, 13a:1; 13b:1.

Ḫa-ar-ḫa-ar-an, *CCT* I, 23:16.
Ḫa-ar-šú-um, *LTC* IV, 87:26.
Ḫa-ru-ḫu-ur, s. of *Ki-ki-da-ni-im*, *CCT* I, 10a:25.
ᶠḪa-šú-šá-ar-na, *Ḫa-šú-šar-na*, d. of *Ud-ga-ri-a*, w. of *Ta-li-a*, *LC*, 242:8, 12, 19.
ᶠḪa-ta-lá, *BIN* IV, 228:2; *CCT* III, 50a:2, 3.
Ḫa-ti, *KTS*, 36a:2.
Ḫa-tì-a-ar, *CCT* III, 48b:8.
Ḫa-tì-ni, *BIN* IV, 230:2.
Ḫa-tì-tim, *NBC*, 3720:1; *CCT* III, 31:2, 8; *TTC*, 21:17.
ᶠḪa-tì-tim, *BIN* IV, 55:1, 4; *KTS*, 53a:9, 11, 15.
Ḫa-za-al-bu-na, f. of *Du-nu-um-na*, *LTC* IV, 87:4, 16.
Ḫa-za-am-ri-im, *CCT* I, 41b:4.
Ḫi-ba-a-ni-a-im, *LTC* IV, 81:25.
Ḫi-ma-a, *CCT* II, 29:27.
Ḫi-na-a, *BIN* IV, 19:1; 21:1; 23:1; 25:10; 26:12, 15, 16, 38; 54:1; 119:2; *NBC*, 3791:2; 3852:9; 3937:2; *CCT* I, 30a:14; *CCT* II, 7:23; 23:23; 26b:1; 27:2; 28:1; *CCT* IV, 13a:15, 39; 49a:1; *LTC* IV, 14:27; *KTS*, 14b:1; 14c:2; 28:7, 10; *TTC*, 17:1.
Ḫi-na-ḫa, *LTC* IV, 83:8.

Ḫi-iš-ta-aḫ-šú, *Gol.*, 20:29.
Ḫi-iš-ta-aḫ-šú-šar, *CCT* I, 23:8; *LTC* IV, 87:8; *Liv.*, 8:17.
Ḫu-. . ., *LTC* IV, 119:6.
Ḫu-be-da-am, *CCT* I, 9b:21.
Ḫu-du-ur-lá, f. of *A-šur-ba-ni*, *BIN* IV, 197:6.
Ḫu-ma-da-šú,
1. f. of *Šá-ra-bu-nu-wa*, *LTC* IV, 99:13.
2. *LTC* IV, 122:1, 8.
Ḫu-ni-a, *BIN* IV, 103:2.
Ḫu-ra-za-nim, *Ḫu-ra-za-nu-um*, *Ḫu-ra-za-nam*, *AZAG-za-nim*,
1. f. of *A-šur-ṭâbu*, *BIN* IV, 199:15.
2. *ḫamuštum*, *BIN* IV, 207:6; 207case:6; *LTC* IV, 91a:8; 91b:3.
3. *BIN* IV, 27:8, 18; 56:20; 155:19; 223:4; *NBC*, 3865:25; *CCT* I, 26a:10; *CCT* II, 8:2; 47b:6; *CCT* IV, 32b:24, 30; *LTC* IV, 26:14; 30:24; 49:3; 52:14; *KTS*, 27b:18; *SCTP*, 20:5, 6, 10, 12; *TTC*, 6:29; *Babyl.* VI, p. 189, 1:1, 7.
Ḫu-ru-ta, *LTC* IV, 90a:4; 90b:4.
Ḫu-šá, *LTC* IV, 78:12.
Ḫu-ta-tim, *KTS*, 45b:20.
Ḫu-za-a, *BIN* IV, 183:14.
Ḫu-za-ru-a, *BIN* IV, 6:31.
Ḫu-za-ru-um, *Ḫu-za-ri-im*, *Ḫu-za-ra-am*, *BIN* IV, 12:3; 160:38; 165:5, 21; 220:3; *CCT* I, 15b:11; *CCT* IV, 16c:2; 29b:14; 42c:2; 43a:4, 9, 10, 13; *LTC* IV, 7:3; *KTS*, 33b:8; 50d:2.

I-a-. . ., f. of *El-ba-ni*, *BIN* IV, 79:3.
I-a-li-a, s. of *Šá-ra-bu-nu-a*, *LTC* IV, 87:6.
I-a-šar, *I-a-šá-ri-im*, *BIN* IV, 6:13; 9:5, 7, 11, 28; 31:5, 11, 13; 226:3, 6, 20; *CCT* II, 38:34; *CCT* III, 20:7; 22a:2; *KTS*, 29b:25; *SCTP*, 8:19.
I-a-tum(?), *LTC* IV, 16:6.
I-bi-Sin, ^{d}*I-bi-*^{d}*Sin*, *CCT* I, 14b:4; *LTC* IV, 90a:seal C.
I-bi-Zu-. . ., *SCTP*, 10:27.
I-bi-zu-a, *I-be-zu-a*,
1. f. of *A-lá-ḫa-am*, *SCTP*, 18:3.
2. f. of *A-mur-Ili*, *CCT* II, 8:20.
3. f. of *Da-da-a*, *CCT* III, 45b:7.
4. f. of *Mâr-I-bi-zu-a*, *CCT* III, 20:12.
Ib-ni-^{d}*Adad*,
1. s. of *Lá-ki-ib*, *CCT* I, 34a:28.
2. f. of ^{d}*Adad-ba-ni*, *KTS*, 49b:15.
3. f. of *I-din-A-šur*, *LTC* IV, 91a:4, seal B.
4. f. of *Mâr-Ib-ni-*^{d}*Adad*, *BIN* IV, 233:24.
5. *lîmu*, *LTC* IV, 30:34.
6. *CCT* I, 45:3, 20, 23; *CCT* IV, 4b:11; *KTS*, 48a:16.
Ib-ni-lí, *Ib-ni-Ì-lí*,
1. s. of *A-šur-*^{d}*šamši*(*-ši*), *LTC* IV, 107:6.
2. f. of *A-šír-*^{d}*šamši*(*-ši*), *LTC* IV, 14:24; *KTS*, 28:23.
3. f. of *Mâr-Ib-ni-lí*, *CCT* I, 33a:20.

Ib-ni-Sin,
1. s. of *A-šur-ma-lik*, *KTS*, 48c:21.
2. *BIN* IV, 62:9.

I-da-a,
1. f. of *Ú-zu-a*, *LTC* IV, 114:4.
2. *LTC* IV, 44:3, 16, 19.

I-di-a, *LTC* IV, 124:13.

I-din-. . . , f. of *I-din-Sin*, *KTS*, 46a:2.

I-dī-in-. . . , *BIN* IV, 168:8.

I-din-a-. . . , *CCT* IV, 33a:1.

I-din-A-a, s. of *Iš-ma-^dAdad*, *BIN* IV, 127:10.

I-din-a-bi-im, *I-din-A-be-im*, *I-din-a-bi*, *I-din-a-ba-am*, *I-din-a-bu*, *I-din-a-bu-um*, *I-din-na-bi-im*,
1. *lîmu*, s. of *Na-ar-be-tim*, *Babyl.* IV, p. 78, 2:9.
2. s. of *A-šír-dan*, *CCT* I, 28a:15; *LTC* IV, 86:15.
3. s. of *A-šír-ma-lik*, *LTC* IV, 79:5, 27.
4. s. of *A-šír-ra-bu*, *BIN* IV, 152:20.
5. s. of *I-dī-in-Ištar*, *BIN* IV, 61:39; *CCT* II, 10:69; *CCT* IV, 21c:9.
6. s. of *Mu-ni-ki-im*, *CCT* I, 6a:16.
7. s. of *ŠÚ-Ištar*, *BIN* IV, 197:15; *CCT* I, 22b:10.
8. f. of *A-šír-mu-ta-bi-el*, *LC*, 239:3.
9. f. of *En-na-Sin*, *CCT* IV, 33b:4.
10. *ḫamuštum*, *CCT* I, 1a:19, 29.
11. *lîmu*, *CCT* I, 9b:20; *Liv.*, 3:20.
12. *BIN* IV, 39:5; 47:1, 3; 50:11; 55:12; 80:4, 7, 9; 100:2, 5; 185:15; *NBC*, 3716:2; 3742:6; 3746:1; *CCT* I, 22b:16; 28a:2, 6; *CCT* II, 40a:1; *CCT* III, 30:1, 3; 43a:1; *LTC* IV, 21:31; 37:1, 21; 64:5; 86:1; *KTS*, 8c:5; 31b:2, 15; *TTC*, 14:24; *Gol.*, 15:1; *Liv.*, 17:1.

I-din-^dAdad,
1. s. of *A-šír-GIŠ*, *Liv.*, 14a:17; 14b:1.
2. f. of *Buzur-A-na*, *CCT* IV, 16c:25, 29.
3. *BIN* IV, 5:2; 135:6, 11; 192:11; *NBC*, 4000:25, 31; *CCT* II, 46a:1, 3; 50:4; *CCT* IV, 28b:2; 30b:2; 44a:4, 9; 50a:2, 45; *KTS*, 17:3, 9, 13; 18:34, 36; 19b:6; *TTC*, 30:12.

I-din-a-ḫi-im, *I-din-a-ḫu-um*,
1. *lîmu*, *CCT* I, 4:32.
2. *NBC*, 3782:2.

I-din-A-šír, *I-din-A-šur*,
1. *lîmu*, s. of *Ku-bi-din*, *BIN* IV, 207:12; *LTC* IV, 63:15.
2. s. of *A-aḫ-a-a*, *LTC* IV, 81:54.
3. s. of *A-ki-a-a*, *CCT* I, 32a:4.
4. s. of *A-šír-i-me-tî*, *CCT* II, 8:16; *CCT* IV, 26a:30.
5. s. of *Ba-be-lim*, *CCT* II, 8:7.
6. s. of *Dan-A-šír*, *CCT* II, 30:21.
7. s. of *Ib-ni-^dAdad*, *LTC* IV, 91a:4, seal B.

8. s. of . . .-*Sin*, *SCTP*, 21:3.
9. s. of *Ú-zu-a*, *BIN* IV, 211:2; 211case:1, 5.
10. f. of *ᵈAdad-ba-ni*, *KTS*, 45b:18.
11. f. of *Ì-lí-dan*, *BIN* IV, 161:3.
12. f. of *Mâr-I-din-A-šír*, *CCT* II, 41a:6.
13. f. of *Ú-zu-a*, *KTS*, 22b:6.
14. *ḫamuštum*, *CCT* I, 6a:6.
15. *BIN* IV, 31:30, 33; 34:28; 157:41; *NBC*, 1714:2, 12; 3792:7, 18; *CCT* I, 18b:8; 40c:2, 6; *CCT* II, 37b:2; *CCT* III, 46b:5, 12; *CCT* IV, 11a:5; 21c:23; 34a:2; 40a:2; *LTC* IV, 13:9; 22:31; 81:53; 91b:13; *KTS*, 22a:5, 7; 31b:9; *SCTP*, 10:27; 25:2, 5, 10.

I-din-be-el, *LTC* IV, 15:29.

I-din-Da-gan, *I-din-Da-ga-an*, *BIN* IV, 112:42; 161:13; *KTS*, 40:45; 44b:18; *Gol.*, 15:2.

I-din-Ištar, *I-dī-in-Ištar*,
1. s. of *A-šur-ma-lik*, *BIN* IV, 81:12; 172:10; *KTS*, 55a:37.
2. f. of *Ga-ta-tim*, *CCT* I, 18a:19.
3. f. of *I-din-a-bu-um*, *BIN* IV, 61:39; *CCT* II, 10:69; *CCT* IV, 21c:10.
4. f. of *I-din-Sin*, *CCT* IV, 13a:33.
5. f. of *Kúr-ub-Ištar*, *BIN* IV, 55:9.
6. f. of *Ma-ku-a*, *Chantre*, 10:18.
7. f. of *Mâr-I-din-Ištar*, *CCT* II, 5a:19.
8. *BIN* IV, 51:34; 54:17, 21, 25; 64:2; 95:3; 161:11; 172:9; *NBC*, 4070:13; *CCT* I, 6a:4; 6b:4; 10a:3; 19b:9, 12, 21; 22a:3; 35:17; *CCT* III, 16b:2; 17b:3; 27b:2; *CCT* IV, 2b:26, 30; 6f:2; 49b:2; *LTC* IV, 19:33, 38, 39; *KTS*, 4b:4, 9, 13; 19a:22; 55a:13.

I-din-Ku-be, *I-din-Ku-be-im*, *I-din-Ku-bi-im*, *I-din-Ku-bu-ma*, *I-din-Ku-bu-um*,
1. s. of *Buzur-A-šír*, *CCT* I, 46a:3.
2. s. of *Buzur-Ištar*, *CCT* I, 47a:23.
3. s. of *ŠÚ-A-nim*, *TTC*, 21:5.
4. f. of . . .-*Sin*, *KTS*, 2a:7.
5. *ḫamuštum*, *LTC* IV, 75:10.
6. *BIN* IV, 72:15, 16; *NBC*, 3733:2; 3734:2; *CCT* II, 37b:7; *CCT* IV, 4a:21; 4b:5; 11b:21; 30a:3; 42b:3; 46a:4; *LTC* IV, 75:6; *SCTP*, 2:2, 26.

I-din-Sin, *I-din-ᵈSin(EN.ZU)*,
1. s. of *A-lá-ḫi-im*, *CCT* II, 10:72.
2. s. of *A-šur-ni-wa-ri*, *BIN* IV, 127:16.
3. s. of *En-na-nim*, *CCT* I, 49b:30.
4. s. of *I-din-. . .*, *KTS*, 46a:2.
5. s. of *I-din-Ištar*, *CCT* IV, 13a:33.
6. s. of *I-na-Sin*, *CCT* I, 7b:23.
7. f. of *A-mur-Ištar*, *BIN* IV, 25:24.

8. f. of *A-šur-e-nam*, *CCT* II, 35:42.
9. f. of *A-šur-ni-im-ri*, *CCT* I, 4:27.
10. f. of *E-lá-ma*, *TTC*, 25:14.
11. f. of *Mâr-I-din-Sin*, *KTS*, 3c:13.
12. f. of ...*-um-Ili*, *NBC*, 3787:3.
13. *ḫamuštum*, *NBC*, 3788:21.
14. *BIN* IV, 41:17, 28; 52:11; 60:4; 75:15; 129:18; 189:14; 224:6; 225:1, 6; *NBC*, 3783:10, 12; 3788:5, 6, 9, 17; 3880:5; 3905:15; *CCT* I, 15b:20; 17a:5; *CCT* II, 1:29; 2:4, 7, 41; 27:1; *CCT* III, 10:3, 30; 20:4, 9; *CCT* IV, 6d:1; 13c:2; *LTC* IV, 37:4; *KTS*, 13b:2; 25a:25, 28; 33b:2; 46b:10; *SCTP*, 16:8, 14.

I-din-^{d}Šamaš,
1. s. of *Da-lá-aš*, *BIN* IV, 111:21.
2. *CCT* III, 14:4, 24; 48a:15; *CCT* IV, 23a:47, 49, 50; *LTC* IV, 80:25.

I-din-Za-bu-um, *TTC*, 9:10.

Id-na-a, *Id-na-a-a*,
1. s. of *El-li-a*, *BIN* IV, 206case:1, 7, 16.
2. s. of *Za-li-a*, *CCT* I, 15a:17.
3. *BIN* IV, 206:3, 18; 232:2, 14; *NBC*, 1645:2; *CCT* I, 34a:3; *CCT* IV, 47a:12; *KTS*, 60c:6.

Id-na-A-šur, *NBC*, 3782:2.

I-du-a, *lîmu*, *CCT* I, 10a:19.

Idu-A-na, *Chantre*, 12R:6.

I-dūr-..., *NBC*, 1891R:6; *CCT* IV, 22b:2.

I-dūr-Ili,
1. f. of *Buzur-A-šur*, *LTC* IV, 19:27; *TTC*, 25:21.
2. f. of *Ḫa-nu*, *CCT* I, 49a:2.
3. f. of *Mâr-I-dūr-Ili*, *CCT* I, 32c:6.
4. f. of *Šál-ma-^{d}A-šur*, *CCT* I, 37a:10.
5. *ḫamuštum*, *CCT* I, 4:43.
6. *BIN* IV, 5:13, 19; 28:6; 65:1, 10; 103:27, 34; 220:1; *NBC*, 3857:13, 17; *CCT* II, 11:5; *CCT* IV, 37b:26; 44b:2; *LTC* IV, 39:1; 82:17, 22; 95:39; 96:31; *KTS*, 43c:6, 8; *SCTP*, 8:1, 7; *TTC*, 24:1; *Gol.*, 4:3; 11:4; 14:2; 17:1; *Liv.*, 11:4.

I-dūr-šú-in, *CCT* I, 20a:9.

Idu-šá-A-šír, *Babyl.* II, p. 44, line 3.

Idu-šá-Ištar, f. of *A-šír-i-me-tî*, *Babyl.* II, p. 42, line 8.

I-ga-a, f. of *Buzur-Ištar*, *BIN* IV, 198:11.

I-ga-lá, f. of *Buzur-Sin*, *LTC* IV, 11:20.

I-ga-lí, f. of *A-šur-ták-lá-ku*, *LTC* IV, 20:8.

Ik-ra-a, f. of *A-šur-ga-si-id*, *LTC* IV, 81:29.

I-ku-..., s. of *A-bi-a*, *NBC*, 3795:2.

I-ku-a,
1. f. of *A-šur-i-me-tî*, *CCT* I, 32a:11; *KTS*, 21b:26.
2. f. of *I-ku-be-a*, gf. of *Ḫa-na-nu-um*, *BIN* IV, 52:27.

I-ku-ba-šá,
1. s. of *Bu-šú-ki-in*, *LTC* IV, 79:8.
2. *BIN* IV, 48:3; 59:3; 106:2; *NBC*, 3799:4; *CCT* IV, 31b:2; *KTS*, 3a:2, 12, 14.

I-ku-be-a, *I-ku-bi*, *I-ku-bi-a*,
1. s. of *I-ku-a*, f. of *Ḫa-na-nu-um*, *BIN* IV, 52:27.
2. s. of *A-da-. . .*, *NBC*, 3712:3.
3. s. of *A-da-làl*, *BIN* IV, 160:46.
4. s. of *A-ki-a-a*, *CCT* II, 30:22.
5. s. of *A-lá-bi-im*, *BIN* IV, 42:7.
6. s. of *A-šur-i-me-tî*, *KTS*, 44a:17.
7. s. of *A-ta-a*, *LTC* IV, 79:10, 20.
8. s. of *Da-a-a*, *CCT* IV, 6f:5.
9. s. of *ŠÚ-A-nim*, *KTS*, 20:10.
10. s. of *ŠÚ-I-li-el*, *BIN* IV, 119:10.
11. s. of *ŠÚ-Sin*, *BIN* IV, 145:20; 199:5; *NBC*, 3768:6.
12. f. of *A-šur-dan*, *BIN* IV, 161:6; *CCT* I, 16b:21.
13. f. of *A-šír-ṭâbu*, *LTC* IV, 52:2.
14. f. of *Ḫa-na-nu-um*, *LTC* IV, 2:6.
15. f. of *Mâr-I-ku-bi-a*, *CCT* II, 41a:22.
16. *dub-šar*, *CCT* III, 50b:12.
17. *BIN* IV, 5:22; 36:10; 44:5; 62:3; 75:19; 91:2, 3; 105:1, 3; 122:16; 164:13; *NBC*, 3722:3; 3743:2; 3873:20; *CCT* I, 4:6; 5b:22; 8c:16; 28d:11; 49b:14; *CCT* II, 11a:2; 23:13, 15, 23, 28; 24:18; 37b:17; *CCT* III, 20:11, 27; 26b:1; 49b:2; *CCT* IV, 24a:27, 46; 24b:2; 44b:2; 49a:7, 11, 12, 27; *LTC* IV, 20:3, 19; 21:38; 34:5; 48:5; 54:3; 114:1; *KTS*, 12:10; 21a:2; 49c:18; *SCTP*, 11:2; *Liv.*, 17:2.

I-ku-be-A-šír, *I-ku-be-A-šur*, *I-ku-bi-A-šír*, *I-ku-bi-A-šur*,
1. s. of *Buzur-Ištar*, *BIN* IV, 138:7.
2. *BIN* IV, 36:23; 41:1, 8, 13; 42:2, 13; 42 case; 76:1, 4; 151:32; 157:41; 169:16; *NBC*, 3876R:3; *CCT* II, 33:1; 38:26, 28; 45:3, 8, 12; *CCT* III, 28b:33; *LTC* IV, 6:13; 22:16, 37; *KTS*, 6:33, 34; 34a:2; 44c:3; 58c:6; *Liv.*, 9:4.

I-ku-be-Ištar, *I-ku-bi-Ištar*,
1. f. of *A-šur-i-me-tî*, *BIN* IV, 28:13; 173:36; *KTS*, 43c:21.
2. *BIN* IV, 63:18; *CCT* II, 14:16.

I-ku-uḫ-li-im, f. of *Na-na-a*, *KTS*, 10:9.

I-ku-nim, *I-ku-nu-um*,
1. s. of *A-ma-a*, *KTS*, 46a:6; 46b:1.
2. s. of *Di-ma-a*, *BIN* IV, 173:46; *CCT* III, 22b:6.
3. s. of *E-lá-ni*, *LTC* IV, 81:53.
4. s. of *El-ba-ni*, *CCT* I, 14b:10; *LTC* IV, 90a:2, seal A.

5. s. of *ᵈŠamaš-ba-ni*, *NBC*, 3727:11; *SCTP*, 24:1.
6. s. of *ŠÚ-be-lim*, *LTC* IV, 95:2; 96:9.
7. f. of *A-gi-a*, *LTC* IV, 81:24.
8. f. of *A-ma-a*, *LTC* IV, 81:42.
9. f. of *Šarrum-kênu*, *Babyl.* IV, p. 77, 1:seal.
10. *BIN* IV, 189:6; *NBC*, 3732:4; *CCT* I, 13a:2, 6; 15b:16; 20a:14; *CCT* II, 37a:22; *CCT* III, 23a:23; *CCT* IV, 9a:3; 29a:29; 32b:2; *LTC* IV, 30:2, 30; 42:3; 43:18; 90b:4, 16; 95:10, 23; *KTS*, 1a:2; 26a:2; 37a:9; 39a:27; 47a:19; *Gol.*, 23:6; *Chantre*, 16:14.

I-ku-uš-mu, s. of *I-ra-am*, *LTC* IV, 64:seal.

ᵈIlabrat-ba-ni, *I-lá-áb-ra-at-ba-ni*,
1. s. of *A-šír-ma-lik*, *NBC*, 3745:8; *CCT* III, 46a:19.
2. *BIN* IV, 8:14; 61:18; 94:1; 144:17; *NBC*, 3767:2, 5; 4070:3; *CCT* II, 3:3; *LTC* IV, 19:1; 26:3, 4; 55:7; *KTS*, 4b:1; 27b:5, 23; 41a:12; *TTC*, 1:15, 19; 2:11, 15.

I-lá-ni-šú, *BIN* IV, 165:16.

Ì-lí-. . ., *BIN* IV, 168:9; *LTC* IV, 70:9; *SCTP*, 20:11.

I-li-a, *Ì-lí-a*, *I-lu-a*, *I-lu-ú-a*,
1. f. of *A-šur-be-el-a-wa-tim*, *NBC*, 3765:5.
2. f. of *Buzur-A-šur*, *BIN* IV, 135:2.
3. f. of *Ì-lí-a-lim*, *LTC* IV, 75:26.
4. f. of *Ištar-du-li-zu*, *CCT* I, 46a:6; 46b:3.
5. f. of *Ku-lí-lim*, *LTC* IV, 107:1.
6. f. of *La-ki-ib*, *BIN* IV, 168:5.
7. f. of *Mâr-I-li-a*, *CCT* IV, 7b:5.
8. f. of *ŠÚ-Sin*, *CCT* I, 3:31.
9. f. of *Ú-zu-ur-šá-A-šur*, *CCT* III, 19b:16.
10. *BIN* IV, 1:16; 83:2; 95:1; *CCT* I, 20a:10; 39a:21; 47b:2, 3; *CCT* II, 34:32; *CCT* III, 17b:1; *CCT* IV, 10a:24; 11b:15, 27, 35; *LTC* IV, 101:2.

Ì-lí-a-lim,
1. s. of *A-gi-a*, *KTS*, 47c:7.
2. s. of *El-be-. . .*, *BIN* IV, 173:20.
3. s. of *Ì-lí-a*, *LTC* IV, 75:25.
4. s. of *Za-az*, *BIN* IV, 51:35.
5. f. of *Buzur-A-na*, *BIN* IV, 185:8; *CCT* II, 47b:3.
6. f. of *En-na-Sin*, *NBC*, 1891:6; *CCT* I, 48:20.
7. f. of *Ma-nim-ba-lim-A-šur*, *NBC*, 3859:2.
8. f. of *ᶠMârat-Ì-lí-a-lim*, *BIN* IV, 185:10.
9. *ḫamuštum*, *CCT* I, 26c:3.
10. *BIN* IV, 26:29, 48; 29:21; 51:1, 33, 39; 52:9; 53:3, 11, 29; 61:2; 64:16; 142:4; 148:26; 152:4, 5, 12; 173:38; *NBC*, 3704:4; 3859R:7; 3905:3; 3909:30; *CCT* I, 20a:20; *CCT* III, 3b:3, 13, 25; 5b:3, 10; 8b:6; *CCT* IV, 3b:2, 8;

13c:3; 21c:12; 34b:18; *LTC* IV, 12:3; 14:3; 18:20; 29:6, 44; 116:9; *KTS*, 10:27, 35, 37; 12:2; 55a:5, 12, 34; *SCTP*, 18:2; *TTC*, 14:2.

Ì-lí-a-na-Ì-lí, *BIN* IV, 97:2.

Ì-lí-aš-ra-ni, *I-li-aš-ra-ni*,
1. s. of *A-šur-ṭâbu*, *CCT* I, 9a:1.
2. s. of *Da-nu-me-el*, *CCT* I, 9a:4.
3. s. of *ŠÚ-be-lim*, *BIN* IV, 103:39.
4. s. of *Zu-ga-lí-a*, *CCT* II, 26a:20.
5. *BIN* IV, 25:2, 33, 39; 61:5, 24, 59, 71; *NBC*, 3745:4; *CCT* III, 12b:1; *LTC* IV, 23:1, 5; *TTC*, 27:25.

Ili-ba-ni, *Ì-lí-ba-ni*, *I-lu-ba-ni*,
1. s. of *Ma-ni-a*, *BIN* IV, 108:24; *NBC*, 3779:6; 3779R:4; *LTC* IV, 20:3; *TTC*, 3:13.
2. f. of *A-šír-ma-lik*, *CCT* IV, 49b:7.
3. f. of *A-šír-*[d]*šamši(-ši)*, *LTC* IV, 91a:2, seal A.
4. f. of *A-šur-rabi*, *LTC* IV, 81:48.
5. f. of [d]*En-lil-ba-ni*, *CCT* II, 8:5.
6. f. of *I-ku-nu-um*, *LTC* IV, 90a:seal A.
7. f. of *...-na-nim*, *BIN* IV, 114:45; 114case:1.
8. *BIN* IV, 10:33; 87:26; 98:2, 5; 135:12; 200:6, 8; *NBC*, 3730:2; 3859:1, 3; *CCT* I, 36d:5; 39a:20; *CCT* II, 20:28, 31; *CCT* III, 24:8; 33a:2; *CCT* IV, 19a:2; 24b:5, 14; 43b:1; *LTC* IV, 3:22; 20:6, 10, 13; 21:21; 56:5; 86:2, 5; *KTS*, 3b:3; *SCTP*, 16:17; 25:16; 35:6; *Gol.*, 7:20; 8:10, 13.

Ili-be-lá-aḫ,
1. f. of *Buzur-*[d]*Amurru*, *LTC* IV, 63:1.
2. *NBC*, 3873:8.

Ili-be-lá-lim, f. of *Zilli-Ištar*, *Babyl.* IV, p. 77, 1:14.

Ì-lí-dan, *Ili-dan-na*,
1. s. of *A-gi-a*, *LTC* IV, 81:31.
2. s. of *I-din-A-šur*, *BIN* IV, 161:2.
3. f. of *A-šur-ṭâbu*, *Babyl.* IV, p. 78, 2:2, 4.
4. f. of *Zu-zu-wa*, *LTC* IV, 71:16.
5. *lîmu*, *CCT* I, 8c:14.
6. *CCT* III, 2b:4.

Ì-lí-du-kúl-tí, *KTS*, 15:41.

Ì-lí-e-mu-qi, f. of *Zu-zu-a*, *BIN* IV, 114:46; 114case:2.

Ili-e-ri-iš, *Ili-e-ri-šú*, *BIN* IV, 32:5, 15.

Ili-ḫu-ni, *Liv.*, 1:5.

Ì-lí-eš-ta-ki-el, *Ì-lí-eš-tí-gal*, *Ili-eš-tí-gal*, *Ì-lí-iš-ta-gal*, *Ì-lí-iš-ta-ki-el*, *Ì-lí-iš-tí-gal*, *Ili-iš-tí-gal*,
1. f. of *A-šur-ma-lik*, *BIN* IV, 164:21.
2. f. of *ŠÚ-Ištar*, *BIN* IV, 103:19; 160:47; 163:7; *CCT* IV, 36a:19.
3. f. of *Za-ba-zi-a*, *BIN* IV, 15:6.

4. *ḫamuštum*, *BIN* IV, 170:7.
5. *BIN* IV, 224:4; *NBC*, 3741:3, 6; 3787:14; *CCT* II, 36b:5, 8; *CCT* III, 19:20; *KTS*, 5b:4; 47c:12, 15; *SCTP*, 32:10; *Babyl.* II, p. 38, lines 3, 16, 19; *Chantre*, 16:4.

Ili-kúr-ub,
1. s. of *E-ra-tî*, *NBC*, 1889:27.
2. f. of *Buzur-A-šír*, *CCT* I, 28a:18.

Î-lí-lim, f. of *Mâr-Î-lí-lim*, *CCT* II, 13:24, 26.

Ili-lu-ki, *LTC* IV, 31:6.

Ili-ma-lá-ak,
1. s. of *Sin-rê'ûm*, h. of *Wa-wa-lá*, *CCT* I, 11b:2, 11.
2. *CCT* III, 41a:11.

Ili-ma-lik, *BIN* IV, 154:4, 6, 29; 221:4, 11; *CCT* III, 19b:24; *CCT* IV, 15b:9.

Î-lí-me-tî, f. of *Ma-nu-šá-ni-šá*, *LTC* IV, 81:43.

I-li-me-a-ta, *BIN* IV, 62:1.

Ili-mu-ta-be-el, *Ili-mu-ta-bi-el*,
1. f. of *Da-da*, *CCT* I, 6a:14.
2. *CCT* I, 5b:4; *CCT* IV, 23a: 2, 4, 53; *LTC* IV, 3:24; 31:2.

Ili-na-da,
1. f. of *A-šír-i-din*, *KTS*, 44a:4.
2. *BIN* IV, 3:4; *CCT* IV, 6c:2; *LTC* IV, 85:11; 101:14; *KTS*, 1a:1; *Gol.*, 4:14.

Î-lí-nim, *CCT* I, 25:21.

Ili-rabi, *lîmu*, *Gol.*, 4:8.

Ili-rê'ûm, f. of *A-mur-A-šur*, *CCT* I, 12b:4.

Î-lí-sa-tu, *CCT* II, 32a:1.

Î-lí-šá-. . ., s. of *A-šír-. . .*, *KTS*, 45a:seal.

I-li-šá-ki, s. of *Ḫa-a-bu-ú-lá*, *BIN* IV, 22:7.

Î-lí-šú-. . ., *KTS*, 59a:6.

I-li-šú-da-a, f. of *Buzur-A-šír*, *CCT* I, 15c:6.

Î-lí-šú-du, *LTC* IV, 21:1.

Î-lí-ŠÚ.GAN,
1. s. of *Na-ni-. . .*, *CCT* IV, 1b:25.
2. *CCT* IV, 1b:2, 4.

Ili-šú-rabi, *Ili-šú-ra-be*, *Ili-šú-ra-bi*,
1. s. of *En-nam-A-šur*, *TTC*, 10:4.
2. *lîmu*, *BIN* IV, 174:13; *LTC* IV, 21:15.
3. *NBC*, 3912:7; *CCT* III, 4:12; *LTC* IV, 47:23.

Î-lí-uz-ra-ni, *I-lu-uz-ra-ni*, *NBC*, 1645:25; *SCTP*, 22:14.

Î-lí-wa-da, *BIN* IV, 4:2.

Î-lí-wa-da-ku, *CCT* III, 32:6, 10, 27, 30; 49b:10; *CCT* IV, 39b:6, 10, 27, 30.

Im-. . ., *NBC*, 1894:2.

I-ma-nim, *Babyl.* II, p. 43, line 13.

Im-ku-a, *Im-ku-ú-a*, *BIN* IV, 7:6; *CCT* II, 38:29.

Im-lá-ni, *LTC* IV, 19:22.

Im-li-ga-a, *CCT* I, 9b:3; *LTC* IV, 74:15.

Im-tî-du-Î-lí, *BIN* IV, 19:19.

Im-tî-li, *Im-tî-Ili*, *Im-tî-lim*,
1. f. of *Buzur-Ištar*, *CCT* IV, 16b:14.
2. *ḫamuštum*, *BIN* IV, 153:5; *Babyl.* IV, p. 78, 2:6.
3. *BIN* IV, 5:1; 27:4; 30:1; 33:30; 56:1; 66:6, 9, 13; 84:1; 87:4; 101:10; 103:14; 149:20; 155:18; 184:4; 215:4; *NBC*, 1645:1; 3777:4, 8;

3788:17; 4000:1; 4049:1; 4071:3; *CCT* I, 14a:3, 16; 15b:21; 25:15; *CCT* II, 5b:1; 6:1; 7:4; 8:1; 11a:1; 12a:1; 23:1; 35:3, 27, 32, 36, 37; 42:2; 44a:21; 46b:7; 49a:1; 50:1; *CCT* III, 1:2, 4; 2a:3; 11:1, 27; 15:1; 16a:1; 21a:2, 27; 22b:4; 34a:2; 40a:1; 45b:2; 46b:1, 18; *CCT* IV, 8b:1, 4; 10b:3; 18a:1; 18b:1; 22b:1; 26b:1; 27a:1; 27b:1, 3; 28a:1; 28b:29; 30b:1; 44a:1; 47a:2; 50a:1; *LTC* IV, 5:1; 16:1; 24:1; 53:1; 95:38; 96:30; *KTS*, 14c:1; 15:1; 16:1; 17:1, 14; 18:1; 19a:1, 24; 19b:1; 20:1; 21a:4, 22; *TTC*, 18:2; 27:1; 30:1, 30.

Im-ur-a-i, *KTS*, 21a:8, 15.

I-na-a,

1. *ḫamuštum*, s. of *A-mu-ra-a*, *CCT* I, 4:18.
2. s. of *A-mu-ra-a*, *BIN* IV, 87:9; *CCT* I, 4:18.
3. s. of *E-lá-ni*, *BIN* IV, 173:7; *CCT* I, 4:23, 37; 20b:3.
4. f. of *A-šur-ma-lik*, *CCT* I, 18a:13.
5. f. of *A-šír-rabi*, *BIN* IV, 167:2.
6. f. of *Mâr-I-na-a*, *BIN* IV, 45:3; *CCT* IV, 24a:37.
7. *ḫamuštum*, *KTS*, 44c:6.
8. *lîmu*, *LTC* IV, 21:6, 11; *CCT* I, 1a:7.
9. *BIN* IV, 55:11; 77:1; 89:1, 11; 91:1; 98:1; 217:1; 218:2, 16, 18, 26; 219:1; 220:1; 223:1; 233:1; *NBC*, 1708:5, 12; 3700:1; 3730:1; 3734:1; 3743:1; 3753:3; 3756:1, 3; 3759:2; 3768:1; 3779:1; 3779R:7; 3797:3; 3804:1; 3848:1; 3857:1, 2; 3859R:4; 3862:1, 8; 3931:1; 3937:2; 4003:1; 4044:3; *CCT* I, 30a:7; *CCT* II, 10:61; 19b:1; 20:1; 22:15; 25:1; 34:1, 16, 25; 43:1; 47b:1; 48:1; *CCT* III, 13:1; 18a:1; 18b:1; 23b:1; 24:1; 25:1; 33a:1; 34b:1; 35b:1, 14; 45a:1; 50b:1; *CCT* IV, 6b:1; 8a:1; 14b:1, 2; 16c:1, 20; *LTC* IV, 9:1; 20:1, 36; 33:4; 41:14; 45:1, 4; 54:1; 57:1; 124:4; *KTS*, 7b:1; 8a:1; 25a:25; 60c:8; *TTC*, 10:1; 11:1; *Liv.*, 10:9.

I-na-aḫ-Ili, *I-na-ḫi-Ili*,

1. f. of *ŠÚ-A-šur*, *CCT* I, 1a:26.
2. *BIN* IV, 79:9, LE 3; 89:2; *CCT* III, 45a:3; *CCT* IV, 7a:2; 42a:2.

I-na-ar, *BIN* IV, 22:33; *LTC* IV, 122:18; *KTS*, 10:27, 36.

I-na-ra-wa, *CCT* III, 40b:7.

I-na-Sin,

1. f. of *A-šur-ṭâbu*, *Chantre*, 1:7.
2. f. of *I-din-Sin*, *CCT* I, 7b:24.
3. f. of *^{d}Šamaš-ba-ni*, *BIN* IV, 109:20; 110:21; 110case:1.
4. f. of *ŠÚ-A-nim*, *BIN* IV, 212:4.

5. *lîmu*, *BIN* IV, 211:17; 211case:18; *Liv.*, 7:7.
6. *BIN* IV, 168:6; *CCT* I, 16b:14; *CCT* III, 40b:6; *CCT* IV, 29a:18.

In-ba-A-šur, *CCT* I, 9b:22.

In-bi-^{d}*Adad*, b. of *Šú-ma-a*, *LTC* IV, 30:15.

In-bi-Ištar, *In-be-Ištar*, *BIN* IV, 76:3; *NBC*, 3874:1; 3875:1; *CCT* II, 17a:1; 18:1; 19a:1; *CCT* III, 40c:1; *LTC* IV, 43:1; 48:1.

I-nu-ma-a, f. of *A-mur-Ili*, *Gol.*, 9:6.

I-nu-me-A-šur, *NBC*, 3804:3.

Ir, s. of *Lá-ki-ib*, *LTC* IV, 75:22.

I-ra-am, f. of *I-ku-uš-mu*, *LTC* IV, 64:seal.

Ȋr-A-šir, *BIN* IV, 124:14; *SCTP*, 38:3.

Ir-at-Ku-be, *LTC* IV, 43:19.

I-ri-si-im,
1. s. of *Ma-nu-ba-* . . . , *PSBA*, 1881, p. 34, line 2.
2. *CCT* IV, 19b:3; 35b:12.

I-ri-šum, *LTC* IV, 72:27; *PSBA*, 1881, p. 34, line 12.

Ir-ma, *CCT* II, 25:28.

Ir-ma-A-šír, *BIN* IV, 173:9, 27, 30.

Ir-nu-id,
1. f. of *Mâr-Ir-nu-id*, *CCT* I, 40a:17.
2. *CCT* IV, 6d:2.

Ir-ra-a, *I-ra-am*, *Ȋr-ra-a*,
1. f. of *A-šur-ma-lik*, *CCT* II, 42:4; *CCT* III, 22a:29; *LTC* IV, 81:4, 9; *TTC*, 2:20.
2. f. of *I-ku-uš-mu*, *LTC* IV, 64:seal.
3. f. of *Mâr-Ȋr-ra-a*, *BIN* IV, 144:9; *CCT* II, 10:66; 41a:8, 10.
4. *LTC* IV, 30:20.

Ir-tim,
1. f. of *Lá-ki-bi-im*, *LC*, 239:19.
2. *CCT* IV, 6d:3.

I-si-im-Sin, *SCTP*, 30:14.

Is-me-Ištar, *LTC* IV, 105:10.

I-šá-a, f. of *Buzur-Sin*, *CCT* II, 22:35.

Iš-a-ra, *BIN* IV, 112:1.

I-šar-be-li, *I-šar-bi-lí*, *CCT* I, 32a:10; *KTS*, 19b:12; 23:18; 24:24, 29; 30:39.

I-šar-ḫa-ri-im, f. of *Ma-nim-ki-i-E-lí-a*, *Chantre*, 1:9.

I-šar-ki-id-A-šur, f. of *Buzur-A-šur*, *CCT* I, 48:38.

Iš-ma-^{d}*Adad*, f. of *I-din-a-a*, *BIN* IV, 127:11.

Iš-ma-A-šír, *Iš-ma-A-šur*,
1. *lîmu*, s. of *Ê-a-dan*, *LTC* IV, 75:16.
2. f. of ^{d}*En-lil-ba-ni*, *LTC* IV, 81:11.
3. NBC, 1646:13; *LTC* IV, 39:3; 83:18; *KTS*, 3b:14; *SCTP*, 8:3; *TTC*, 18:1; *Gol.*, 17:3; *Babyl.* VI, p. 190, 4:10.

Iš-me-Sin, *CCT* I, 39b:2, 13; *CCT* III, 11:31; 46b:27.

Ištar- . . . , *NBC*, 3777:11.

Ištar-ba-li-el,
1. s. of *ŠÚ-Ku-be-im*, *CCT* I, 4:1; *Liv.*, 14b:2.
2. f. of *Zu-ba*, *BIN* IV, 174:4; *LTC* IV, 86:14.
3. *CCT* I, 6a:3; *Liv.*, 14a:19.

Ištar-ba-li-lu, *CCT* IV, 13b:21.

Ištar-ba-ni, *LTC* IV, 38:2.
Ištar-ba-aš-tí, *CCT* IV, 28a:2, 29; *KTS*, 1b:1.
Ištar-be-lá-aḫ, *Ištar-bi-lá-aḫ*, *Ištar-bi-lá-aḫ*,
1. s. of *A-ni-nim*, *CCT* II, 8:12.
2. s. of *A-dī-a*, *CCT* III, 26a:14.
3. s. of *En-nam-A-šír*, *CCT* I, 46a:1; 47a:21.
4. s. of *Ri-ḫa-am*, *LTC* IV, 83:3.
5. s. of *ŠÚ-A-...*, *Liv.*, 15:8.
6. f. of *ᶠMârat-Ištar-be-lá-aḫ*, *BIN* IV, 23:20.
7. *BIN* IV, 23:9; 172:33; *CCT* I, 30a:2, 20; 32b:7; *CCT* II, 26b:9; 28:8; *CCT* IV, 11a:3; 48b:7, 12.
Ištar-du-li-zu,
1. s. of *Ì-lí-a*, *CCT* I, 46a:5, 11, 14; 46b:2, 7, 9.
2. *KTS*, 60d:7.
Ištar-Ili-šú, *NBC*, 3937:4; *CCT* I, 18a:17; *CCT* IV, 24a:17.
Ištar-ki-iz-tim, *BIN* IV, 35:47.
Ištar-lá-ba,
1. f. of *A-al-ṭâbu*, *LTC* IV, 71:2, 6.
2. *Gol.*, 8:17.
Ištar-lá-ma-zi, *NBC*, 3892:3; *Gol.*, 20:3.
Ištar-na-da, *LTC* IV, 67:7.
I-šú-ḫi-im, s. of *Šú-li*, *BIN* IV, 137:3.
I-ti-A-šír, s. of *Da-tí-a*, *CCT* IV, 18a:5.
I-tí-lim,
1. s. of *Ṭâbu-Ì-lí*, *LTC* IV, 22:5.
2. f. of *A-mur-A-šur*, *SCTP*, 18:11.
3. *LTC* IV, 22:15.
I-za-li-a, f. of *Lá-ki-bu-um*, *BIN* IV, 161:seal B; 161case:3.
I-zi-..., *BIN* IV, 218:2.
I-zi-ḫi-im, f. of *Zu-tí-a*, *CCT* II, 15:16.
I-zi-za-am-Ili, *BIN* IV, 218:3.
I-zu-muš,
1. f. of *Mâr-I-zu-muš*, *NBC*, 3924:7, 12.
2. f. of *Šá-lim-A-šír*, *CCT* I, 14b:9.
I-zu-ur, *CCT* I, 33b:2.
I-zu-ri-ig,
1. f. of *Mâr-I-zu-ri-ig*, *BIN* IV, 19:29.
2. f. of *Šá-lim-A-šur*, *BIN* IV, 16:5.
Ki-ak-lá-nu, *BIN* IV, 70:1.
Ki-ib-si-im, *LTC* IV, 16:4.
Ki-da-ar, *LTC* IV, 87:12, 14, 41.
Ki-gár-šá-an, *Ki-ga-ar-šá-an*,
1. s. of *Šú-bu-na-aḫ-šú*, *LTC* IV, 68:1.
2. *CCT* I, 8b:5.
Ki-ki, *Ki-ki-i*,
1. f. of *A-šur-ṭâbu*, gf. of *Mâr-A-šur-ṭâbu*, *BIN* IV, 233:5.
2. f. of *A-šur-ṭâbu*, *LTC* IV, 105:13; *NBC*, 3915:15.
Ki-ki-da-ni-im, f. of *Ḫa-ru-ḫu-ur*, *CCT* I, 10a:25.
ᶠKi-lá-ri-tam, *CCT* III, 14:22.
Ki-li, *CCT* III, 27b:1.
Ki-li-a, f. of *Mâr-Ki-li-a*, *BIN* IV, 102:2.
Ki-na-aḫ-šú, *LTC* IV, 100:24.
Ki-ri-im, *CCT* I, 27c:12, 15; *TTC*, 9:3.
Ki-iz-..., *KTS*, 59a:3.
Ki-iz-ḫa-nu-el, *BIN* IV, 48:31.

Ku-bi-a, f. of *Mâr-Ku-bi-a*, *CCT* III, 19b:22.

Ku-be-din, *Ku-bi-din*,
1. f. of *I-din-A-šur*, *BIN* IV, 207:12; *LTC* IV, 63:15.
2. *BIN* IV, 207case:9.

Ku-bu-lim, f. of *Mâr-Ku-bu-lim*, *CCT* III, 17b:8.

Ku-da-ri-li, *BIN* IV, 25:34, 36.

Ku-da-tum, *Ku-da-tim*, *BIN* IV, 134:2; *CCT* IV, 6b:2; *SCTP*, 24:17.

Ku-du, *CCT* IV, 41a:16.

Ku-du-. . ., f. of *Da-da*, *LTC* IV, 9:24.

Ku-uk-ra-an, *BIN* IV, 209:3, 16; 209case:4, 9, 20.

Ku-ku-lá-nim, *Ku-ku-la-nu-um*,
1. s. of *Ku-ta-a*, *BIN* IV, 108:23.
2. f. of *A-šur-i-din*, *CCT* II, 20:34; *LTC* IV, 81:10.
3. *BIN* IV, 127:6, 12; 194:7; *CCT* I, 41a:16; *CCT* III, 27a:4, 6, 33; *CCT* IV, 5a:2; *KTS*, 9a:3; 38a:4, 7; *Babyl.* IV, p. 79, 3:12, 15.

Ku-ku-a, *Ku-ku-a-a*, *Ku-ku-i-im*, *Ku-ku-um*, *Ku-ku-wa*,
1. f. of *En-na-nim*, *KTS*, 44a:17.
2. *BIN* IV, 16:8; 17:9; *CCT* I, 37b:11; *KTS*, 34b:2; 49b:20; *Chantre*, 7:2.

Ku-ku-zi, *Ku-ku-zi-a*,
1. s. of *Zi-iḫ-ri-li*, *CCT* I, 1a:1; *KTS*, 44a:5.
2. f. of *Šál-ma-A-šur*, *KTS*, 49b:8.
3. *CCT* III, 48b:11.

Ku-lá, b. of *Šú-ki-tim*, *BIN* IV, 173:16.

Ku-lá-ku-lá-rabi, *Chantre*, 2:9.

Ku-li-a, *CCT* IV, 6d:13.

Ku-lí-lim,
1. s. of *Ì-lí-a*, *LTC* IV, 107:1.
2. *BIN* IV, 23:36; 119:4; *CCT* I, 19b:14; 22a:2; *CCT* II, 28:9, 11; *CCT* IV, 29a:3, 10.

Ku-ul-ku-lam, *LTC* IV, 16:11, 16.

Ku-lu-uk-lu, *BIN* IV, 210:3; 210 case:4, 5.

Ku-lu-ma-a,
1. s. of *A-šur-i-me-tì*, *CCT* I, 4:26.
2. f. of *Ú-zu-a*, *BIN* IV, 137:9.
3. *BIN* IV, 3:2; 7:5; 8:2, 3; 9:25; 13:2; 14:5; 23:5, 7; 103:2; 145:3; 163:3; 181:8; 190:6; *CCT* I, 16b:17; 17b:24; 38a:16; *CCT* II, 1:29; 2:39, 43, 45, 49; 28:21; 40a:2; *CCT* III, 20:3; 48b:21; *CCT* IV, 6a:2; 33a:4; *LTC* IV, 81:20; *KTS*, 29b:2; 49b:19; *TTC*, 17:3; *Chantre*, 12:13.

Ku-um-ri, *Ku-um-ri-im*,
1. f. of *Da-da-a-a*, *CCT* IV, 19a:13.
2. *Gol.*, 11:24.

Ku-na-ni-a, *CCT* IV, 21a:2, 4; *TTC*, 26:4.

Ku-ra,
1. s. of *Ú-lá-a*, *CCT* II, 11a:4; *KTS*, 19b:16.
2. s. of *Zu-tì-a*, *BIN* IV, 161:20; 161case:1.

3. f. of *A-šír-i-me-tí*, *CCT* III, 24:39.
4. *BIN* IV, 129:14; 210:17; 210case:2; *CCT* I, 45:44; *CCT* III, 12a:13; 16a:8; 25:2, 7, 16; 35a:18; *CCT* IV, 4b:2; 24a:2, 15; *LTC* IV, 131:2, 8; *KTS*, 54c:4; 56a:4; 56b:3, 5; 57b:7; *TTC*, 11:11; *Gol.*, 4:3.

Ku-ra-ra,
1. s. of *A-bu-šá-lim*, *BIN* IV, 94:5; *CCT* II, 8:24.
2. f. of *En-na-Sin*, *CCT* IV, 24a:26.
3. f. of *Ku-za-ri*, *BIN* IV, 207case:3.
4. f. of *ŠÚ-Iš-ḫa-ra*, *BIN* IV, 78:22; *CCT* I, 49a:16.
5. *BIN* IV, 31:22; 156:9; 225:5; *NBC*, 3746:3; *CCT* I, 42b:14; *CCT* II, 6:5; 37b:2, 26; *CCT* III, 8a:35; 12b:2; 40a:2; *LTC* IV, 4:11, 28; *KTS*, 22a:5; *SCTP*, 40:4.

Ku-ur-ku-. . . , *LTC* IV, 41:25.

Ku-ur-ku-ra, *Ku-ur-ku-ri-a*,
1. s. of *Za-aḫ-ri-li*, *KTS*, 44a:4.
2. *BIN* IV, 170:4; *NBC*, 3727:6; *KTS*, 56c:3.

Ku-ru-ub-. . . , *KTS*, 32a:6.

Kúr-ub-A-šír,
1. s. of *Zi-li-a*, *LTC* IV, 71:15.
2. *Gol.*, 12:12.

Kúr-ub-Ištar, *Ku-ru-ub-Ištar*,
1. *ḫamuštum*, s. of *A-lá-ḫi-im*, *NBC*, 3787:6; *CCT* I, 3:51.
2. s. of *A-na-ni*, *LTC* IV, 110:33.
3. s. of *Buzur-Ì-lí*, *BIN* IV, 129:16; *KTS*, 40:43.
4. s. of *I-din-Ištar*, *BIN* IV, 55:9.
5. s. of *ŠÚ-Ḫu-bur*, *BIN* IV, 23:13, 20.
6. f. of *A-šír-i-me-tí*, *KTS*, 47c:4; *Liv.*, 15:7.
7. f. of *En-na-nim*, *LTC* IV, 117:3.
8. f. of *Mâr-Kúr-ub-Ištar*, *CCT* IV, 38b:5.
9. f. of *ŠÚ-A-šur*, *KTS*, 2a:5.
10. *ḫamuštum*, *LTC* IV, 74:8.
11. *BIN* IV, 8:3, 11, 18, 20; 16:2; 17:3; 24:5; 26:30, 48; 29:26, 28; 63:1; 70:1; 88:15; 92:2; 154:4, 7, 15, 27; 173:35, 40; 198:4; 216:22; 220:6, 21; *NBC*, 3748:2; 3854:2, 4; 3854R:2; 3916:2; *CCT* I, 5a:18; 19a:8; 24b:2, 9, 12; 26a:8; *CCT* III, 4:31; 8:4; 16a:6; *CCT* IV, 5a:3; 7a:1; 17b:1; 32b:3; 42c:9; *LTC* IV, 11:1; 110:2, 28; 120:3; *KTS*, 1a:2; 14a:1; 21a:4, 5, 26; 36c:2; *SCTP*, 16:17; *TTC*, 12:9, 21; *Gol.*, 19:5, 8; 24:7; *Chantre*, 13:3.

Ku-uš-ku-zi-im, f. of *A-ta-a*, *BIN* IV, 199:7.

Ku-ta-a, *Ku-ta-a-a*,
1. s. of *A-šur-na-da*, *LTC* IV, 81:35.
2. f. of *A-šur-ba-ni*, *BIN* IV, 43:4; 108:22; 145:8.
3. f. of *Ku-ku-lá-nim*, *BIN* IV, 108:23.

4. *LTC* IV, 81:41; 114:2.

Ku-...-um, *NBC*, 3799:3.

Ku-za-am, *Ku-zi-im*, *CCT* I, 16a:4; *CCT* II, 16a:9.

Ku-za-ri,
1. s. of *Ku-ra-ra*, *BIN* IV, 207 case:3.
2. *BIN* IV, 207:2; 207case:4; *CCT* II, 1:4, 17.

Ku-za-tì-a, *CCT* IV, 6d:2, 11.

Ku-za-zu-um, *CCT* IV, 3b:3.

Ku-zi-a,
1. f. of *Ma-nu-um-ba-A-šír*, *LTC* IV, 75:4.
2. *NBC*, 1889:29; *CCT* I, 9a:7; 12a:14; *CCT* IV, 35a:7; *LTC* IV, 77:5, 11, 14.

Ku-zi-zi-a, *Ku-zi-zi-a-a*, *BIN* IV, 70:23; 218:27; *CCT* I, 34a:5; *CCT* II, 46b:1, 3; *LTC* IV, 17:9, 14; *KTS*, 13a:8; 13b:7; *TTC*, 12:15.

Ku-zu, f. of *Mâr-Ku-zu*, *KTS*, 51a:2.

Lá-...-^{d}Adad, f. of *A-šur-ma-lik*, *NBC*, 3929:8.

Lá-ba-na-da, *Gol.*, 12:2.

Lá-áb-du, *CCT* II, 50:21.

La-bi-a, *CCT* III, 34a:7.

Lá-bi-tim, *Lá-bi-tì-im*, *NBC*, 3720:8, 15.

Lá-aḫ-ra-aḫ-šú, *LTC* IV, 87:15.

Lá-ki-ib, *Lá-ki-ba-am*, *La-ki-bi-im*, *Lá-ki-be-im*, *Lá-ki-bu-um*,
1. s. of *^{d}Ab-ba-ni*, *BIN* IV, 113:20.
2. s. of *A-šur-rabi*, *BIN* IV, 197:17.
3. s. of *Buzur-sa-tu-e*, *LTC* IV, 34:23; *CCT* I, 1a:14.
4. s. of *Bu-zu-ta-a*, *LTC* IV, 34:21; 81:37.
5. s. of *I-li-a*, *BIN* IV, 168:4.
6. s. of *Ir-tim*, *LC*, 239:18.
7. s. of *I-za-li-a*, *BIN* IV, 161:seal B; 161case:3.
8. s. of *ŠÚ-A-šír*, *CCT* I, 3:54; *KTS*, 45a:3, 5.
9. f. of *A-šur-rabi*, *PSBA*, 1881, p. 34, line 22.
10. f. of *A-šír-^{d}šamši(-ši)*, *BIN* IV, 173:45; *CCT* III, 19b:13.
11. f. of *A-šur-ṭâbu*, *CCT* I, 22a:19.
12. f. of *Ib-ni-^{d}Adad*, *CCT* I, 34a:29.
13. f. of *Ir*, *LTC* IV, 75:22.
14. f. of *Mâr-Lá-ki-ib*, *CCT* II, 28:3.
15. f. of *ŠÚ-A-nim*, *NBC*, 3755:10.
16. f. of *ŠÚ-Ku-bu-um*, *BIN* IV, 217:3.
17. f. of *Ú-zu-a*, *CCT* I, 41a:4.
18. *ḫamuštum*, *CCT* I, 5b:8.
19. *BIN* IV, 26:2; 37:24, 28; 40:3; 61:2; 92:1; 95:2; 102:3; 107:25; 161:4, 7, 15, 18; 161case:6; 173:14; 182:6, 10; 228:1; *NBC*, 3874:2; *CCT* I, 38b:10; *CCT* II, 4a:2; 4b:2; 12b:9, 12; 15:21, 25; 28:5; *CCT* III, 12a:1; 17b:2; 21b:9; 38:12; 49a:3, 9, 15; 50a:4; *CCT* IV, 19b:3, 18, 19; 29b:2; 45a:20; 47b:3, 9, 15; *LTC* IV, 14:2, 17, 26; 26:36; 95:39; *KTS*, 2a:15; 57b:9; 60d:10; *SCTP*, 21:10; 30:16; 35:9; 38:6.

Lá-li-a, *NBC*, 3905:1; *CCT* I, 41a: 20; *LTC* IV, 24:2, 4, 35.

Lá-li-im,
1. f. of *Li-ib-ta-nim*, *CCT* I, 4:4.
2. f. of *Mâr-Lá-li-im*, *CCT* II, 39:14; *CCT* III, 38:23.
3. *CCT* III, 21a:6, 10, 15, 25; *Babyl.* II, p. 39, line 21.

Lá-ma-šá, *BIN* IV, 90:2; *NBC*, 3751:2; *CCT* III, 39a:4; 48b:2; *CCT* IV, 20a:3; 35b:2; 36b:2; *KTS*, 3a:3; 49c:3, 17.

La-ma-za-tum, *CCT* IV, 40b:5.

Lá-ma-zi, *BIN* IV, 135:9; 140:5; 155:6; *NBC*, 3741:2; 3903:7; *CCT* I, 37a:15; *CCT* III, 19b:2; 20:2; 23b:10; *CCT* IV, 21b:3; *LTC* IV, 70:19; *KTS*, 29b:27, 28; 60c:3; *Gol.*, 18:15; *Liv.*, 2:3.

ᶠLá-ma-zi, *BIN* IV, 9:2; 10:2; *CCT* II, 36a:2.

Lá-ta-ra-ak, f. of *A-lá-be-im*, *CCT* II, 19b:6.

Li-ba-a,
1. s. of *Ú-zu-a*, *BIN* IV, 173: 16.
2. *BIN* IV, 25:20; *LTC* IV, 17:7; *KTS*, 57b:6.

Li-bi-Ištar, *CCT* III, 28b:2.

Li-bi-it-Ištar, *Li-ib-tî-Ištar*,
1. s. of *Da-gan-ma-al-ki-im*, *CCT* I, 9a:2; *CCT* III, 11:6.
2. *KTS*, 60d:1.

Li-ib-ta-nim,
1. s. of *Lá-li-im*, *CCT* I, 4:3.
2. *lîmu*, *CCT* I, 4:14.
3. *BIN* IV, 125:2.

Li-lu-si-im, *ḫamuštum*, *Gol.*, 9:8.

Li-mur-šú-ma-an, *BIN* IV, 183:13.

Lu-ar-ra-aḫ-šú, *LTC* IV, 87:32.

Lu-ar-ra-ak-šú, *KTS*, 58a:5.

Lu-ar-ra-aḫ-šú-rabu, *Chantre*, 2:2.

LÛ-ba-ni, *BIN* IV, 1:7.

Lu-ḫa-du-ma-an, *BIN* IV, 189:2.

Lu-li-im, *CCT* III, 28a:30; 37a:14.

Lu-lu,
1. s. of *Am-ri-a*, *Liv.*, 17:4.
2. s. of *Zu-ku-ḫi-im*, *BIN* IV, 26:9.
3. *lîmu*, *CCT* I, 22a:13.
4. *BIN* IV, 14:2; 23:30; 29:23; 144:13; *NBC*, 3753:4; *CCT* I, 15c:2; 18a:5; *CCT* III, 45a:2; *CCT* IV, 23a: 39; 42b:9, 16; *SCTP*, 2:1; 38:2.

Lu-lu-a, f. of *A-šír-ṭâbu*, *CCT* I, 18a: 20.

Lu-zi-a, *CCT* II, 25:2.

Lu-zi-na,
1. f. of *A-šír-ma-lik*, gf. of *A-šír-i-din*, *NBC*, 3905: 27.
2. s. of *A-šír-ba-ni*, *BIN* IV, 142:8.
3. f. of *A-šír-ma-lik*, *BIN* IV, 152:19; *CCT* I, 6c:6; *LTC* IV, 51:8; *TTC*, 3:6.
4. f. of *Mâr-Lu-zi-na*, *BIN* IV, 37:3; 41:18; *CCT* IV, 36a:5, 18, 21.
5. f. of *ŠÚ-Ištar*, *BIN* IV, 173:8; *CCT* II, 31a:6; *CCT* IV, 6b:18; *LTC* IV, 19:8; *KTS*, 25b:11.
6. *ḫamuštum*, *CCT* I, 2:5, 15.
7. *CCT* I, 1b:5; *CCT* III, 29:4,

7, 10, 23, 34, 39; *CCT* IV, 4b:1; *LTC* IV, 65:16; *KTS*, 4a:2; *TTC*, 11:1.

ᶠMa-da-wa-da, *CCT* I, 9b:4.

ᶠMa-ga-ni-ga, *NBC*, 3858:2.

Ma-ḫa-i, *Ma-ḫa-i-a*, *TTC*, 19:4, 15.

Ma-ḫi-ra-aḫ-šú, *LTC* IV, 87:48.

Ma-ḫu-si, *LC*, 240:25.

Ma-ku-a, s. of *I-din-Ištar*, *Chantre*, 10:18.

Ma-lá-a-a, *CCT* I, 50:25.

Ma-lá-ba, *CCT* I, 6b:11.

Ma-lá-aš, f. of *Be-ir-wa-aḫ-šú*, *BIN* IV, 190:15.

Ma-lik-Ili-šú, f. of *ŠÚ-Ištar*, *LTC* IV, 95:4; 96:11.

Ma-lu-ku-lá-nim, *Babyl.* IV, p. 79, 3:6.

Ma-ma, *Ma-ma-a*, *BIN* IV, 88:20; *CCT* I, 29:26; *CCT* III, 18b:6; 19a:13.

Ma-ma-ḫi-ir, *BIN* IV, 104:35.

Ma-na-ki-li-a-ad, *CCT* I, 38c:11.

Ma-na-ma-na, *BIN* IV, 208:18; 208case:3.

Ma-na-na, f. of *Ú-ra-a*, *LTC* IV, 71:3.

Ma-ni-a, *Ma-ni-a-a*, *Ma-nu-a*,
1. f. of *A-lá-bu-um*, *BIN* IV, 74:2.
2. f. of *A-lá-ḫi-im*, *LTC* IV, 37:8.
3. f. of *Da-a-a*, *CCT* II, 9:41.
4. f. of *Ili-ba-ni*, *BIN* IV, 108:24; *NBC*, 3779:6; 3779R:5; *LTC* IV, 20:3; *TTC*, 3:14.
5. f. of *Mâr-Ma-ni-a*, *SCTP*, 8:16.
6. f. of *Šarrum-Sin*, *CCT* I, 1a:2, 16, 18; 7b:3.
7. *NBC*, 3756:1, 4, 19; *CCT* I, 33a:24; *LTC* IV, 145:13.

Ma-nim-. . . , *NBC*, 3882:2.

Ma-nu-ba-. . . , f. of *I-ri-si-im*, *PSBA*, 1881, p. 34, line 2.

Ma-nu-kî-šú, *CCT* III, 23a:28.

Ma-nu-ba-lu-um-A-na, *CCT* III, 31:12.

Ma-nu-ba-lim-A-šur, *Ma-nu-ba-lim-A-šír*, *Ma-nu-um-ba-lim-A-šír*, *Ma-nu-um-ba-lim-A-šur*, *Ma-nu-um-ba-A-šír*, *Ma-nim-ba-lim-A-šír*, *Ma-nim-ba-lim-A-šur*,
1. s. of *E-na-ma-nim*, *BIN* IV, 108:14; *CCT* I, 14b:12.
2. s. of *Î-lí-a-lim*, *NBC*, 3859:1, 4.
3. s. of *Ku-zi-a*, *LTC* IV, 75:4.
4. f. of *ᵈAmurru(MAR.TU)-ba-ni*, *CCT* I, 22b:22.
5. *ḫamuštum*, *CCT* I, 4:31.
6. *BIN* IV, 233:3; *NBC*, 3931:2; *CCT* I, 20a:16; 36d:14; *CCT* II, 19b:3; 20:2; 21a:3; *CCT* III, 27a:2; 29:9, 12, 22, 30; *CCT* IV, 4b:4; 33b:2; *LTC* IV, 28:3, 17; 30:18; 33:3; 81:38; *KTS*, 38a:2; *TTC*, 11:3; *Gol.*, 16:4.

Ma-nu-ki-a, *CCT* IV, 15a:7, 17.

Ma-nu-um-kî-a-bi-a, *KTS*, 45b:3.

Ma-nu-kî-A-šír, *Ma-nu-kî-A-šur*, *Ma-nu-um-kî-A-šír*, *Ma-nu-um-kî-A-šur*, *Ma-nu-um-kî-ᵈA-šír*, *Ma-nim-kî-A-šír*, *Ma-nim-kî-A-šur*,
1. s. of *A-da-ta*, *BIN* IV, 89:19.
2. s. of *A-ḫu-qar*, *CCT* I, 50:23.

3. s. of *ŠÚ-be-lim*, *CCT* I, 13a: 13.
4. gs. of *A-šur-kî-na-ra-am*, *Babyl.* II, 40:16, 19.
5. *CCT* II, 22:1; *CCT* III, 35b:5; 36b:2; *LTC* IV, 49:4, 21; *KTS*, 32a:2; 32b:2; *Liv.*, 5:2, 6, 9; *Gol.*, 23:9; *Babyl.* II, 40: 16, 19.

Ma-nim-ki-i-E-lí-a, s. of *I-šar-ḫa-ri-im*, *Chantre*, 1:8.
Ma-nu-kî-E-lí, *CCT* IV, 15a:2, 19.
Ma-nu-kî-Ištar, *Ma-nu-um-kî-Ištar*, *Ma-nim-kî-Ištar*, s. of *ŠÚ-be-lim*, *BIN* IV, 109: 17; 110:18; 110case:2; *CCT* IV, 16c:12.
Ma-nu-um-šú-um-šú, f. of *A-šír-rabi*, *CCT* I, 36c:6.
Ma-nu-šá-ni-šá, s. of *Î-lí-me-tî*, *LTC* IV, 81:42.
Mâr-A-gu-a, *CCT* IV, 10b:26.
Mâr-Aḫ-me, *BIN* IV, 177:2.
Mâr-Am-ri-a, *BIN* IV, 38:7; 49:4.
Mâr-A-mur-Ištar, *BIN* IV, 6:30; *KTS*, 5a:7.
Mâr-A-ni-nim, *BIN* IV, 79:19; *CCT* III, 7b:9; 12b:4; 17a:19.
Mâr-A-ra-wa, *NBC*, 4004:18.
Mâr-Ar-si-iḫ, *CCT* II, 41b:18.
Mâr-A-šur-ba-ni, *CCT* IV, 26a:28.
Mâr-A-šír-i-din, *CCT* II, 1:17.
Mâr-A-šur-ma-lik, *CCT* IV, 25b:14.
Mâr-A-šur-ṭâbu,
1. gs. of *Ki-ki-i*, *BIN* IV, 233:5.
2. *CCT* IV, 33b:29.

ᶠMârat-Î-lí-a-lim, *BIN* IV, 185:10.
ᶠMârat-Ištar-be-lá-aḫ, *BIN* IV, 23: 20.
ᶠMârat-Šá-lim-a-ḫi-im, *BIN* IV, 8 10.
Mâr-A-zu-za-a, *BIN* IV, 213:3.
Mâr-Ba-ba-li, *BIN* IV, 145:5; *CCT* IV, 50b:31.
Mâr-Bu-za-zu, *KTS*, 50d:6.
Mâr-Buzur-A-na, *BIN* IV, 225:12.
Mâr-Bu-zu-ta-a, *BIN* IV, 173:24.
Mâr-Dan-na-i-el, *Mâr-Da-nu-Î-lí*, *BIN* IV, 19:37; *CCT* II, 28:27.
Mâr-Du-tî-ki, *KTS*, 48c:8.
Mâr-E-lá-ni, *CCT* IV, 4a:4.
Mâr-E-ra-a, *BIN* IV, 26:23.
Mâr-E-ra-tî, *CCT* IV, 6c:14.
Mâr-Ga-a-tim, *LTC* IV, 46:9.
Mâr-Ga-ri-a, *Mâr-Ga-ar-wa-a*, *NBC*, 3856:7; *BIN* IV, 42:31.
Mâr-Ga-za-za, *CCT* III, 43a:8.
Mâr-Ḫa-li-ma, *CCT* I, 50:9.
Mâr-I-bi-zu-a, *CCT* III, 20:12.
Mâr-Ib-ni-ᵈAdad, *BIN* IV, 233:24.
Mâr-Ib-ni-lí, *CCT* I, 33a:20.
Mâr-I-din-A-šír, *CCT* II, 41a:6.
Mâr-I-din-Ištar, *CCT* II, 5a:19.
Mâr-I-din-Sin, *KTS*, 3c:13.
Mâr-I-dūr-Ili, *CCT* I, 32c:6.
Mâr-I-ku-bi-a, *CCT* II, 41a:22.
Mâr-I-li-a, *CCT* IV, 7b:5.
Mâr-Î-lí-lim, *CCT* II, 13:24, 26.
Mâr-I-na-a, *BIN* IV, 45:3; *CCT* IV, 24a:37.
Mâr-Ir-nu-id, *CCT* I, 40a:17.
Mâr-Ir-ra-a, *Mâr-Ìr-ra-a*, *BIN* IV, 144:9; *CCT* II, 10:66; 41a:8, 10.
Mâr-I-zu-muš, *NBC*, 3924:7, 12.
Mâr-I-zu-ri-ig, *BIN* IV, 19:29.
Mâr-Ki-li-a, *BIN* IV, 102:2.
Mâr-Ku-bi-a, *CCT* III, 19b:22.
Mâr-Ku-bu-lim, *CCT* III, 17b:8.

Mâr-Ku-lá-. . ., *SCTP*, 37:15, 21.
Mâr-Kúr-ub-Ištar, *CCT* IV, 38b:5.
Mâr-Ku-zu, *KTS*, 51a:2.
Mâr-Lá-ki-ib, *CCT* II, 28:3.
Mâr-Lá-li-im, *CCT* II, 39:14; *CCT* III, 38:23.
Mâr-Lu-zi-na, *BIN* IV, 37:3; 41:18; *CCT* IV, 36a:5, 18, 21.
Mâr-Ma-ni-a, *SCTP*, 8:16.
Mâr-Rabû-Šá-li-a, *CCT* IV, 6a:4.
Mâr-Ru-ba-im, *CCT* I, 26b:7.
Mâr-Šarrum-dAdad, *BIN* IV, 189:9.
Mâr-ŠÚ-A-šír, *BIN* IV, 26:20.
Mâr-ŠÚ-dEn-lil, *CCT* II, 41a:5.
Mâr-ŠÚ-Iš-ḫa-ra, *KTS*, 56a:10.
Mâr-ŠÚ-Ku-bi-im, *CCT* III, 25:28, 36.
Mâr-ŠÚ-Nu-nu, *CCT* II, 14:3.
Mâr-ŠÚ-Sin, *CCT* II, 41a:9.
Mâr-Um-me-a-na, *BIN* IV, 219:15; *CCT* II, 21a:18; 23:12.
Mâr-Ú-za-ri-a, *CCT* II, 45a:18.
Mâr-Ú-zu-a, *BIN* IV, 72:20; *CCT* II, 37b:20; *KTS*, 48c:6.
Mâr-Zi-ga-a, *CCT* IV, 18a:7.
Mâr-Zi-li-a, *BIN* IV, 146:3.
Mâr-Zilli(-li)-Ištar, *CCT* I, 32c:8.
Mâr-Zi-zi-im, *NBC*, 1903R:13.
Mâr-Zu-ga-lí-a, *CCT* II, 33:14.
Mâr-Zu-ku-ḫi-im, *CCT* I, 40a:20.
Maš-ba-ni, *Babyl.* II, p. 44, lines 9, 18, 21.
Mâ-ta-du-ú, *CCT* I, 41b:8.
Mâ-za-a, *BIN* IV, 50:1.
Mâ-zi-Ì-lí,
  1. *lîmu*, *CCT* I, 2:24; 3:56; *KTS*, 45a:10.
  2. *CCT* III, 34:8, 15.
Ma-zu, *Ma-zu-im*, *Ma-zu-e-im*,
  1. f. of *Ga-si-im*, *CCT* I, 26b:15.
  2. *CCT* I, 26b:1; 27a:6, 12.
Me-me-ib-ri, *Gol.*, 10:14.
Me-na-nim, s. of *Ba-bi-tî*, *CCT* I, 36c:7.
Me-ir, *CCT* I, 47:1, 3.
Me-šar-rabi, f. of *A-mur-dŠamaš*, *BIN* IV, 24:4.
Me-šú-rabi,
  1. f. of *A-mur-Ištar*, *KTS*, 58c:4.
  2. f. of *A-mur-dŠamaš*, *LTC* IV, 95:3, 23; 96:10.
  3. *LTC* IV, 97:6.
Mu-mu-lá-nim, f. of *A-šír-i-din*, *CCT* I, 35:22; *SCTP*, 18:10.
Mu-ni-ki-im, f. of *I-din-a-bi-im*, *CCT* I, 6a:17.
Mur-šá-lim, *CCT* II, 14:21; *LTC* IV, 58:3; 58R:3.
Mu-šú-ga-e(?), *TTC*, 16:17.
Mu-tî-Ili, *CCT* I, 36d:12.
Mu-za, *Mu-zi-e*, *BIN* IV, 171:4; *CCT* I, 38c:6.
f*Mu-za*, *BIN* IV, 90:1; *NBC*, 3751:1; *CCT* IV, 20a:1, 2.
Na-ba-ḫi-e, *Na-ba-ḫi-im*, *Na-ba-ḫi-ma*,
  1. f. of *. . .-ru-wa*, *Gol.*, 5:11.
  2. *CCT* I, 21a:6; 26b:9.
Na-be-li-šú, f. of *A-šur-na-da*, *LTC* IV, 88:2.
Na-ab-ra-ga, f. of *ŠÚ-Ištar*, *CCT* I, 13a:12.
Na-ab-si-im, *BIN* IV, 105:8; *NBC*, 3779R:11; *CCT* I, 49b:7.
Na-ab-Sin, *Na-áb-Sin*,
  1. s. of *Buzur-Ištar*, *BIN* IV, 173:41.
  2. s. of *ŠÚ-be-lim*, *CCT* I, 1a:3.
  3. *CCT* I, 1a:5; 3:38; 39a:7;

CCT II, 7:31; 10:59, 67; 40b:2; *CCT* IV, 16b:16; *LTC* IV, 35:9, 13; *KTS*, 60b:1; *SCTP*, 5:1, 8, 10, 13.

Na-ḫu-ma, *CCT* I, 23:16.

Na-ki-li-e-id, *Na-ki-li-id*,
1. s. of *Šú-be-a-aḫ-šú*, *BIN* IV, 190:16.
2. *LC*, 242:4.

Na-ki-iš-du-ar, *BIN* IV, 183:6.

Na-na, *Na-na-a*, *Na-ni-a*, *Na-an-ni*,
1. s. of *Bu-du-du*, *KTS*, 50a:12.
2. s. of *Ḫa-na-nim*, *NBC*, 3712:6, 10; *LTC* IV, 81:12.
3. s. of *I-ku-uḫ-li-im*, *KTS*, 10:8.
4. f. of *Ì-lí-ŠÚ.GAN*, *CCT* IV, 1b:25.
5. f. of *Rabû-A-šur*, *Gol.*, 2:10.
6. f. of *Zi-li-Ištar*, *LTC* IV, 63:2, seal B.
7. *BIN* IV, 90:29; 186:3; 186 case:3, 7; *CCT* I, 37a:4, 6; *LTC* IV, 89:6; 105:6; *KTS*, 36b:1; 50a:4; *SCTP*, 38:9.

Na-na-nim, *Babyl.* II, p. 39, line 22.

Na-ni-be-im, *Na-ni-ib*,
1. f. of *Da-tì-a*, *Gol.*, 3:3.
2. f. of *Ga-ni*, *LTC* IV, 33:10.

Na-ra-am-Zu,
1. f. of *Be-lu-ba-ni*, *CCT* I, 49b:29.
2. *ḫamuštum*, *BIN* IV, 146:17.
3. *LTC* IV, 108:8.

Na-ar-be-tim, f. of *I-din-a-bi-im*, *Babyl.* IV, p. 78, 2:9.

Na-aš, *BIN* IV, 209case:15.

Na-šú-a, *Gol.*, 18:20.

Na-ú-šá, f. of *Bûr-Nu-nu*, *BIN* IV, 187:25.

Na-zi,
1. s. of *A-mu-ru-ba-ni*, *CCT* I, 1a:13.
2. *NBC*, 3716:3; 3730:2; *CCT* III, 18b:2.

Ni-...-A-..., *LTC* IV, 81:52.

Ni-bi-si-im, *NBC*, 4045:7.

Ni-bu-um, *LTC* IV, 1:3.

Ni-ga-an, *BIN* IV, 163:1, 8.

Ni-ma-aḫ-šú, *CCT* I, 41b:6.

Ni-ma-A-šur, *CCT* III, 27a:1.

Ni-ma-Ištar, *Ni-mar-Ištar*,
1. s. of *Buzur-Sin*, *BIN* IV, 160:28; 164:22; *CCT* I, 7b:5, 7.
2. *BIN* IV, 160:33; *CCT* III, 43a:14; *LTC* IV, 34:2.

Ni-ra-aḫ-zu-lu-li, f. of *Be-lá-ḫa-a*, *Liv.*, 7:3.

Ni-tì, f. of *...-ma-A-šír*, *Babyl.* IV, p. 78, 2:18.

Ni-tì-ba-ni, f. of *A-šír-rabi*, *BIN* IV, 101:16.

Ni-wa-aḫ-šú-šar, *Ni-wa-aḫ-šú-šá-ar*, *LTC* IV, 33:2, 15; *LC*, 240:21.

Ni-wa-šú, s. of *Bu-li-na*, *LTC* IV, 68:2.

Nu-a-e, *Nu-a-im*, *CCT* III, 12a:11; *LTC* IV, 109:10; *TTC*, 13:4; 20:6; *Gol.*, 18:7.

Nu-nu, *Nu-ú-nu*,
1. f. of *...-ḫi-a*, *NBC*, 3911:5.
2. *BIN* IV, 186:3; 186case:3, 6; *CCT* III, 39b:6.

Nu-ur-Ištar, *BIN* IV, 26:46; 189:17; 198:15; *CCT* II, 4b:8.

Nu-ur-kì-li, *Nu-ur-kì-Ili*, *Nu-ur-kì-Ì-lí*, *BIN* IV, 160:14;

NBC, 3905:23; *CCT* I, 3:44; 31b:6; *CCT* III, 29:14, 40; *CCT* IV, 13b: 24; *KTS*, 56d:6; *Gol.*, 18: 21.
Nu-ur-Zu, f. of *A-lá-ḫi-im*, *LTC* IV, 81:8.
Nu-wa-nu-wa, *BIN* IV, 160:16.
Raba(-ba)-A-šur, *Rabû-A-šur*,
1. s. of *Ḫa-na-nim*, *Gol.*, 23R:4.
2. s. of *Na-na-a*, *Gol.*, 2:9.
3. *CCT* IV, 29a:2, 11; *LTC* IV, 60:21; *KTS*, 1a:29.
Rabû-Ku-be-im, *NBC*, 3889:2.
Rabû-Šá-li-a, f. of *Mâr-Rabû-Šá-li-a*, *CCT* IV, 6a:4.
Ri-a-a, s. of *A-ku-tim*, *KTS*, 47c:5.
Ri-en-šá, s. of *Ar-za-na-aḫ-šú*, *KTS*, 51a:11.
Ri-ḫa-am, f. of *Ištar-be-lá-aḫ*, *LTC* IV, 83:4.
Ri-ḫa-tí-e, *BIN* IV, 180:8.
Si-a-im, f. of *A-ni-na-a*, *CCT* I, 49a:1.
Si-a-at, *KTS*, 47b:1, 3.
Si-li-a-ra, *LC*, 240:2, 3, 16, 19, 22.
Si-ma-Sin, *BIN* IV, 67:2.
Si-ma-at-A-šír, *LTC* IV, 5:3.
Si-me-tí-Ili, *CCT* I, 24b:5, 7; *LTC* IV, 11:4, 8; *KTS*, 14a:5.
Si-im-nu-ma-an, s. of *Ta-ta-li-i*, *Liv.*, 8:4, 11.
Sin-. . ., *BIN* IV, 129:2.
dSin(EN.ZU)-ba-ni, *NBC*, 4003:2, 4.
Sin-bi-lá-aḫ, *CCT* II, 9:42.
Sin-damiq,
1. s. of *A-šír-i-me-tí*, *BIN* IV, 211:20; 211case:3.
2. *NBC*, 3905:9.
Sin-na-da,
1. f. of *En-um-A-šír*, *KTS*, 44b:7.
2. *BIN* IV, 207:3; *NBC*, 3797: 4; *CCT* IV, 23b:10.
Sin-na-wi-ir, *LTC* IV, 17:4, 6, 10; 58:2.
Sin-rê'ûm,
1. f. of *Ili-ma-lá-ak*, *CCT* I, 11b:3, 11.
2. *CCT* I, 13a:16.
Si-nu-nu-tim, f. of *A-šír-ṭâbu*, *BIN* IV, 120:17.
Si-šá-aḫ-šú-šar, *Si-šá-aḫ-šá-ar*, *KTS*, 13a:4; 13b:3.
fSi-šá-aḫ-šú-šar, *CCT* III, 7a:2.
Si-ta-ra-ma-an, *KTS*, 51a:18.
Si-wa-aš-me-i, *BIN* IV, 203:17; 209:2, 15; 209case:3, 8, 19; 231:2; *KTS*, 52a:11.
Šá-áb-ta, *LC*, 240:26.
Šá-bu-lí, *Babyl.* II, p. 43, line 6.
Šá-du-uḫ-bel-a, *Babyl.* II, p. 42, line 13.
Šá-aḫ-ga, *TTC*, 27:13.
Šá-ḫi-iš-ga-an, *LC*, 242:2.
Šá-ki-zu, *Babyl.* II, 40:9, 28.
Šá-ki-iš-ki-nim, *BIN* IV, 182:9.
Šá-ak-ri-aš-wa, *BIN* IV, 208:5; 208case:6, 10.
Šá-ak-ri-el-bi, *CCT* III, 14:3.
Šá-ak-ri-ú-ma-an, *CCT* III, 48b:17; *KTS*, 56b:8.
Šá-li-a-ta, *BIN* IV, 209:5, 12.
Šá-li-ba-a, *ḫamuštum*, *BIN* IV, 189:5.
Šá-lim-. . ., *NBC*, 3794:1.
Šá-lim-A-. . ., *Šál-ma-A-. . .*, *NBC*, 3735:1; *KTS*, 27a:1; *CCT* IV, 50b:1; *LTC* IV, 57:9.
Šá-lim-dAdad, *KTS*, 10:20, 25, 29.
Šá-lim-a-ḫi-im, *Šá-lim-a-ḫu-um*, *Šál-ma-ḫi-im*, *Šá-al-ma-ḫi-im*, *Šál-ma-a-ḫu-um*, *Šál-me-gim(?)*, *Šál-me-ḫi-im*,

1. s. of *En-um-A-šur*, *LTC* IV, 69:4.
2. f. of *Dan-A-šur*, *BIN* IV, 173:47; *LTC* IV, 70:27.
3. f. of *En-um-A-šur*, *BIN* IV, 184:12; *CCT* I, 4:24; *CCT* II, 8:18; *CCT* III, 50b:7; *CCT* IV, 33a:23.
4. f. of *ᶠMârat-Šá-lim-a-ḫi-im*, *BIN* IV, 8:10.
5. *BIN* IV, 11:24; 25:3; 26:1; 27:1; 61:1; 120:5, 21; 138:5; 144:2; 173:12; *NBC*, 3745:3, 5; 3767:1; 3922:1; *CCT* I, 15b:7; 28d:5; *CCT* II, 1:1; 2:1; 3:1; 4a:1; 4b:1; *CCT* IV, 5b:1; 11b:7; 25b:1; *LTC* IV, 14:1; 26:1; 70:17; *KTS*, 27b:1; 28:1; 60d:2; *TTC*, 1:7; 2:7; 6:2, 22, 25; *Gol.*, 18R:2; 19R:8, 9.

Šá-lim-A-šír, *Šá-lim-A-šur*, *Šál-ma-A-šír*, *Šál-ma-A-šur*, *Šál-ma-ᵈA-šur*,
1. *lîmu*, s. of *Ku-ku-zi-a*, *KTS*, 49b:7.
2. s. of *En-nam-A-šur*, *BIN* IV, 176:2.
3. s. of *I-dūr-Ili*, *CCT* I, 37a:9.
4. s. of *I-zu-muš*, *CCT* I, 14b:8.
5. s. of *I-zu-ri-ig*, *BIN* IV, 16:4.
6. f. of *ŠÚ-be-lim*, *CCT* II, 10:67.
7. f. of *Šú-ma-li-ba-A-šur*, *Liv.*, 7:15.
8. *BIN* IV, 8:22; 17:1, 4; 49:6; 226:2; *NBC*, 1647:1; 3766:3; 3865:11; 4071:4; *CCT* I, 5a:19; 20a:18; 26a:12; *CCT* III, 19:17; 21b:2; 45a:25; *LTC* IV, 28:1, 33; 30:1; 60:22; *KTS*, 22a:20; 29b:2; 37a:6; 50b:5; *TTC*, 6:12; 24:3, 23, 24, 29; *Gol.*, 17:14; 23R:7.

Šá-lim-be-in, *BIN* IV, 51:19.

Šá-lim-be-lí, *Šá-lim-bi-lí*, *BIN* IV, 54:6, 23; 148:19; 172:4; *CCT* IV, 3a:13; *KTS*, 47a:1, 3, 10, 15.

Šál-me-Ištar,
1. s. of *Be-za*, *BIN* IV, 145:21.
2. *CCT* III, 32:31; *CCT* IV, 39b:31.

Šá-lu-wa-an-ta, *BIN* IV, 209case:10, 16.

Šá-lu-wa-ta, *LTC* IV, 99:3.

ᵈŠamaš-a-bi, *NBC*, 3905:1.

ᵈŠamaš-ba-ni,
1. s. of *Buzur-Ištar*, *CCT* IV, 1a:19.
2. s. of *En-nam-A-a*, *LC*, 239:20.
3. s. of *I-na-Sin*, *BIN* IV, 109:19; 110:20; 110case:1.
4. f. of *I-ku-nim*, *NBC*, 3727:12; *SCTP*, 24:2.
5. f. of *ŠÚ-Ku-be-im*, *LTC* IV, 81:34.
6. *ḫamuštum*, *BIN* IV, 174:8; *CCT* I, 5b:8; *LTC* IV, 63:8; *Babyl.* IV, p. 78, 2:6.
7. *BIN* IV, 73:2; *NBC*, 4070:4; *CCT* III, 37a:26; *CCT* IV, 1a:34; 44b:5; *LTC* IV, 47:22; 81:50; *KTS*, 25b:4; 57b:4.

ᵈŠamaš-damiq, *KTS*, 37b:2.

^{d}Šamaš-rê'ûm, *NBC*, 1642:LE 2.
^{d}Šamaš-tab-ba-i, *BIN* IV, 154:3, 27, 28; *CCT* II, 40a:18; *CCT* III, 13:12, 20; 47a:15; *LTC* IV, 9:9; *Babyl.* II, p. 40, line 18; *Gol.*, 15:4, 14.
^{d}Šamaš-ta-ak-lá-ku, *BIN* IV, 133:5.
^{d}Šamaš-ṭâbu, *CCT* III, 11:29.
Šá-ra-bu-nu-a, *Šá-ra-bu-nu-wa*,
1. s. of *Ḫu-ma-da-šú*, *LTC* IV, 99:12.
2. f. of *I-a-li-a*, *LTC* IV, 87:6.
3. *CCT* I, 8b:3; *KTS*, 13b:32.
Šá-ra-ma, f. of *Šú-bu-na-aḫ-šú*, *Gol.*, 11:6.
Šá-ra-Sin,
1. s. of *Ba-ni-a*, *CCT* IV, 25a:26.
2. *CCT* IV, 25a:34.
Ša-ra-at-Ištar, *BIN* IV, 88:2.
Šá-ra-wa, f. of *Bu-šú-ki-in*, *CCT* IV, 16a:7, 9, 13.
Šá-ra-za-ma, *BIN* IV, 124:4.
Šá-ar-ni-ga, *Šá-ar-ni-ga-ar*, *KTS*, 1a:30; *TTC*, 16:15.
Šarrum-^{d}Adad, f. of *Mâr-Šarrum-^{d}Adad*, *BIN* IV, 189:9.
Šarrum-kênu, s. of *I-ku-nim*, *Babyl.* IV, p. 77, 1:seal.
Šarrum-Sin, *Šarrum-^{d}Sin*,
1. s. of *E-. . .*, *NBC*, 3756:7.
2. s. of *Ma-ni-a*, *CCT* I, 1a:2, 15, 17; 7b:3.
3. f. of *A-šír-na-da*, *BIN* IV, 206case:5.
4. *BIN* IV, 57:3; 164:17, 19; 224:3, 23; *NBC*, 1897:13; 3773:11; 3799:1; *CCT* III, 10:4; *LTC* IV, 20:11, 15; *KTS*, 3b:2; *SCTP*, 5:2; 12:5; *Liv.*, 4:1; *Chantre*, 10:14, 16.
^{f}Šá-šá-ma, *BIN* IV, 55:1, 22.
Šá-at-A-šír, *Šá-at-A-šur*, *BIN* IV, 8:9; 22:1; *CCT* I, 15b:15; *TTC*, 2:6; 26:4, 20.
^{f}Šá-at-A-šír, *^{f}Šá-at-A-šur*, *BIN* IV, 75:1; 212:3; *CCT* IV, 15b:1.
^{f}Šá-tí-a, *CCT* I, 8c:2.
Šá-at-Ì-lí, *CCT* I, 45:2, 4, 19, 22; *KTS*, 47a:16.
Šá-za-ga-ri-a, *LTC* IV, 87:2, 5.
Šá-zu-ḫa-ku, *BIN* IV, 35:3.
ŠÚ-. . ., f. of *A-šur-šamši(-ši)*, *NBC*, 3905:33.
ŠÚ-A-. . ., f. of *Ištar-bi-lá-aḫ*, *Liv.*, 15:8.
ŠÚ-^{d}Adad, *CCT* I, 5a:3; *CCT* IV, 10a:9.
ŠÚ-A-du, *KTS*, 60b:3.
ŠÚ-A-nim,
1. s. of *En-na-Zu*, *KTS*, 31a:2.
2. s. of *Ḫa-da-a*, *BIN* IV, 165:9; *LTC* IV, 88:1.
3. s. of *I-na-Sin*, *BIN* IV, 212:3.
4. s. of *Lá-ki-ib*, *NBC*, 3755:9.
5. s. of *Šú-da-a*, *KTS*, 47c:10.
6. s. of *ŠÚ-Ištar*, *SCTP*, 18:9.
7. f. of *^{d}Adad-zu-lu-li*, *KTS*, 48c:20.
8. f. of *A-gu-za*, *Babyl.* IV, p. 77, 1:8.
9. f. of *A-mur-A-šír*, *LTC* IV, 90a:seal B.
10. f. of *A-šur-mu-ta-bi*(?), *LTC* IV, 63:seal A.
11. f. of *Ba-ba-zu-a*, *LTC* IV, 81:28.

12. f. of *E-na-Sin*, *CCT* IV, 16c:4.
13. f. of *I-din-Ku-be-im*, *TTC*, 21:6.
14. f. of *I-ku-be-a*, *KTS*, 20:11.
15. f. of *ŠÚ-Ištar*, *LTC* IV, 9:16.
16. *ḫamuštum*, *BIN* IV, 170:7.
17. *BIN* IV, 1:11; 50:3, 6, 23, 28; 114:17; *NBC*, 1655:19; 3889:1; *CCT* III, 36b:1; 43a:2; 47b:2, 4; *CCT* IV, 7c:26; 10a:27; 34a:1; 41b:2, 22; 44b:1; *LTC* IV, 13:2; 41:5, 8; 45:5; 81:3; *KTS*, 31b:1; 31c:1, 13; 32a:1; 32b:1; 32c:1; 33a:2; 33b:2, 3; 34a:2; 34b:1; 35a:2; 35b:3; 37b:15; 39a:40; 47c:13; 56b:6; 57b:8; *Gol.*, 7:18; *Liv.*, 2:1; *Babyl.* IV, p. 79, 3:2, 14.

ŠÚ-A-šír, *ŠÚ-A-šur*, *ŠÚ-^{d}A-šír*,
1. s. of *A-lá-ḫi-im*, *CCT* II, 41a:15.
2. s. of *I-na-ḫi-Ili*, *CCT* I, 1a:26.
3. s. of *Kúr-ub-Ištar*, *KTS*, 2a:5.
4. s. of *ŠÚ-Sin*, *BIN* IV, 207:14; 207case:2.
5. f. of *En-um-A-šur*, *LTC* IV, 30:21.
6. f. of *En-na-Sin*, *CCT* I, 3:54; *LTC* IV, 66:13.
7. f. of *En-nam-šá-. . .*, *KTS*, 50b:14.
8. f. of *Lá-ki-be-im*, *CCT* I, 3:54; *KTS*, 45a:3, 6.
9. f. of *Mâr-ŠÚ-A-šír*, *BIN* IV, 26:20.
10. *NBC*, 1891R:2; *CCT* I, 1a:28; 39a:5, 9, 18; *CCT* III, 10:2; *LTC* IV, 8:6; 57:4; *KTS*, 12:1, 21; *TTC*, 23:2.

ŠÚ-be-. . ., *CCT* IV, 27b:1.

Šú-be-a-aḫ-šú, f. of *Na-ki-li-it*, *BIN* IV, 190:17.

Šú-be-a-aḫ-šú-šar, *CCT* III, 31:1, 5.

Šú-be-a-ni-ga, *Liv.*, 8:2, 6, 12.

ŠÚ-be-lam, *ŠÚ-be-lim*, *ŠÚ-bi-lim*,
1. s. of *A-mur-Ili*, *BIN* IV, 173:36; *TTC*, 25:15.
2. s. of *Ga-ga-ta-nim*, *LTC* IV, 80:35.
3. s. of *Šá-lim-A-šír*, *CCT* II, 10:67.
4. s. of *Zu-ur-zu-ur*, *CCT* II, 46a:11.
5. f. of *A-šur-mu-ta-be-el*, *BIN* IV, 105:28.
6. f. of *Gár-ri-a*, *BIN* IV, 101:18; *Gol.*, 3:19.
7. f. of *I-ku-nim*, *LTC* IV, 95:2; 96:9.
8. f. of *Î-lí-aš-ra-ni*, *BIN* IV, 103:39.
9. f. of *Ma-nu-um-kî-A-šur*, *CCT* I, 13a:14.
10. f. of *Ma-nu-um-kî-Ištar*, *BIN* IV, 109:18; 110:19; 110case:2; *CCT* IV, 16c:13.
11. f. of *Na-áb-Sin*, *CCT* I, 1a:3.
12. f. of *Ú-zu-a*, *TTC*, 3:12.
13. f. of *Wa-al-tî-lim*, *LTC* IV, 66:4, 5.
14. *BIN* IV, 31:23; 46:3; 69:2, 6; 98:21; 101:1, 4, 9, 13; 158:11; 191:8; *NBC*, 1647:2; 4071:3, 12, 13;

CCT I, 21d:6; 31a:17; 45:1, 4, 19, 21; *CCT* II, 21a:1, 15; 31b:4, 7; *CCT* III, 16a:15; 25:6; 43b:2; 44a:15; *CCT* IV, 22a:1; *LTC* IV, 45:3; 49:1; *KTS*, 33b:8, 10, 13; 36a:6; 60c:10; *SCTP*, 9:1; 22:13; 29:4; *TTC*, 11:4; *Gol.*, 12:13; *Liv.*, 16R:7.

Šú-be-ú-ma-an, *Šú-bi-ú-ma-an*,
1. s. of *Ḫa-mu-ri-a*, *KTS*, 46a:5.
2. *KTS*, 46b:13.

Šú-bu-ul-tum, *BIN* IV, 85:3; *SCTP*, 38:8.

Šú-bu-na-aḫ-šú,
1. s. of *Šá-ra-ma*, *Gol.*, 11:6, 17.
2. f. of *Ki-ga-ar-šá-an*, *LTC* IV, 68:2.
3. *LTC* IV, 87:35; *CCT* I, 10b:2; 23:10.

Šú-da-a,
1. *lîmu*, s. of *En-na-nim*, *BIN* IV, 61:42, 66.
2. f. of *ŠÚ-A-nim*, *KTS*, 47c: 10.
3. *lîmu*, *Babyl.* II, p. 38, line 12.
4. *LTC* IV, 81:38.

ŠÚ-Da-gan, *ŠÚ-Da-ga-an*,
1. f. of *A-bi-a*, *CCT* I, 5a:15; *LTC* IV, 86:13.
2. *NBC*, 3791:4.

ŠÚ-^{d}*En-lil*,
1. f. of *A-šur-ták-lá-ku*, *BIN* IV, 42:18; *KTS*, 43c:6.
2. f. of *En-um-A-šur*, *LTC* IV, 19:6.
3. f. of *Mâr-ŠÚ-*^{d}*En-lil*, *CCT* II, 41a:5.
4. *NBC*, 3759:5, 16; *CCT* I, 18b:11; 29:31; *CCT* III, 35b:13, 23; 38:2; *KTS*, 35a:1; 48a:1, 3, 9.

Šú-ga-tim, f. of *ŠÚ-Ištar*, *CCT* I, 4:39.

ŠÚ-Ḫa-bu-ra, *BIN* IV, 25:21.

Šú-ḫa-ir-^{d}*Adad*,
1. f. of *A-lá-bu-um*, *LTC* IV, 32:11.
2. *CCT* III, 4:13; 7b:11.

ŠÚ-Ḫu-bur, *ŠÚ-Ḫu-bu-ur*,
1. s. of *A-šur-ma-lik*, *BIN* IV, 161:21; 161case:2.
2. f. of *Buzur-*^{d}*Adad*, *CCT* II, 10:53; *KTS*, 51c:9.
3. f. of *En-na-nim*, *CCT* IV, 49a:37.
4. f. of *Kúr-ub-Ištar*, *BIN* IV, 23:13, 21.
5. *BIN* IV, 24:2; 32:1, 9; 33:1, 20; 173:29; 226:1; *NBC*, 1895:4; 1903:7; 3766:2; 3783:1; 3880:6; 3884:1; 3916:4; *CCT* I, 15b:8; 36c:2; *CCT* II, 7:2; *CCT* III, 21a:1; 21b:1; 22a:1; 22b:1; *CCT* IV, 9a:1; 43a:39, 40; *LTC* IV, 34:3, 7, 17; 70:18; *KTS*, 21a:2; 21b:1; 36a:1; 36c:4; *TTC*, 6:12; 18:5.

Šú-ḫu-ur, *LTC* IV, 122:19.

Šú-ḫu-ur-be-a, *Šú-ḫu-ur-bi-a*, *BIN* IV, 170:3; *CCT* I, 34a:24; *LC*, 242:6.

ŠÚ-^{d}*Ilabrat*, *ŠÚ-lá-áb-ra-at*, f. of *Buzur-Ištar*, *BIN* IV, 119:9; 206case:4.

ŠÚ-I-li-el, f. of *I-ku-bi-a*, *BIN* IV, 119:11.

ŠÚ-Iš-ḫa-ra,
1. s. of *Ku-ra-ra*, *BIN* IV, 78:22; *CCT* I, 49a:15.
2. f. of *A-mur-A-šír*, *KTS*, 43a.2.
3. f. of *Mâr-ŠÚ-Išḫara*, *KTS*, 56a:10.
4. *BIN* IV, 83:8, 15, 17, 25, 35, 36, 43; *NBC*, 3796:4; *TTC*, 29:15; *Chantre*, 12:1.

ŠÚ-Ištar,
1. s. of *A-ḫu-wa-qar*, *LTC* IV, 99:8, 17.
2. s. of *A-šur-e-mu-qi*, *BIN* IV, 197:3.
3. s. of *Buzur-A-šír*, *LC*, 239:7, 13.
4. s. of *Da-da-nim*, *BIN* IV, 13:5; *LTC* IV, 70:24.
5. s. of *Ili-iš-tí-gal*, *BIN* IV, 103:19; 160:47; 163:6; *CCT* IV, 36a:19.
6. s. of *Lu-zi-na*, *BIN* IV, 173:8; *CCT* II, 31a:6; *CCT* IV, 6b:18; *LTC* IV, 19:7; *KTS*, 25b:11.
7. s. of *Ma-lik-Ili-šú*, *LTC* IV, 95:4; 96:10.
8. s. of *Na-ab-ra-ga*, *CCT* I, 13a:12.
9. s. of *ŠÚ-A-nim*, *LTC* IV, 9:16.
10. s. of *Šú-ga-tim*, *CCT* I, 4:39.
11. f. of *A-ak-li-a*, *LTC* IV, 81:46.
12. f. of *A-ḫu-wa-qar*, *CCT* I, 4:3; *SCTP*, 24:19; *Babyl.* IV, p. 78, 2:1.
13. f. of *A-mur-A-šír*, *LTC* IV, 26:16.
14. f. of *A-šur-i-dī-in*, *CCT* I, 7b:22.
15. f. of *A-šur-i-me-tí*, *CCT* I, 15b:19; *CCT* IV, 6b:9.
16. f. of *A-šur-ma-lik*, *LTC* IV, 96:14.
17. f. of *A-šír-ta-a-a-ar*, *Gol.*, 1:4.
18. f. of *El-me-tí*, *CCT* I, 7b:20.
19. f. of *En-na-Sin*, *CCT* I, 4:9.
20. f. of *I-din-a-be-im*, *BIN* IV, 197:16; *CCT* I, 22b:11.
21. f. of *ŠÚ-A-nim*, *SCTP*, 18:9.
22. f. of *Ṭâbi(-bi)-A-šír*, and *Zu-za-a*, *CCT* II, 8:21.
23. *ḫamuštum*, *CCT* I, 4:8.
24. *límu*, *BIN* IV, 115:2.
25. *BIN* IV, 6:2; 7:2; 41:8; 81:2, 4, 8; 89:6, 15; 104:8, 20; 114:26; 117:2; 136:3; 151:16; *NBC*, 1655:26; 1759:11; 3716:4; 3746:4; 3756:5; *CCT* I, 22b:3, 12, 18; 28a:4; 28b:5; 32a:7; 40a:5; *CCT* II, 7:1; 9:44; 12b:9, 16; 13:3, 9, 14, 17; 29:23, 25; 31a:10; 32b:13; 37b:2, 29; 39:12; *CCT* III, 12b:18; 13:3, 5, 23, 24, 25, 30; 14:28; 18b:2; 28b:29; 32:4; 41a:3; 49a:2; 49b:23; *CCT* IV, 6b:14; 6d:3; 16b:4; 19a:1; 36a:11, 13; 39b:4; 43a:41; 47b:2; *LTC* IV, 10:1; 38:1; 89:6; 95:10, 24; 114:3; *KTS*, 3c:10; 5a:13, 17; 8c:3; 16:2; 25a:24, 26; 26a:4; 40:11; 44c:18; 60d:4; *SCTP*, 2:4, 5, 9; 8:4; *TTC*, 22:1; 29:2;

Gol., 12:11; 14:3; *Liv.*, 5:8, 12; 14a:3; 14b:4, 5; *Babyl.* VI, p. 190, 4:11.

Šú-ki-tim,
1. b. of *Ku-lá*, *BIN* IV, 173:17.
2. *BIN* IV, 165:15.

ŠÚ-Ku-ba-am, *ŠÚ-Ku-be-im*, *ŠÚ-Ku-bi-im*, *ŠÚ-Ku-bu-um*,
1. s. of *En-na-ma-nim*, *BIN* IV, 165:8.
2. s. of *Lá-ki-be-im*, *BIN* IV, 217:3.
3. s. of *ᵈŠamaš-ba-ni*, *LTC* IV, 81:33.
4. s. of *Šú-na-...*, *CCT* I, 50:2, 5, 10, 16.
5. f. of *A-šur-lá-ma-zi*, *CCT* IV, 16c:7; *TTC*, 21:15.
6. f. of *A-šur-ma-lik*, *Chantre*, 1:4.
7. f. of *Be-lá-nim*, *CCT* I, 11b:12; *LTC* IV, 81:52.
8. f. of *E-lá-ni*, *BIN* IV, 91:11; *CCT* III, 25:34.
9. f. of *Ištar-ba-li-el*, *CCT* I, 4:1; *Liv.*, 14b:3.
10. f. of *Mâr-ŠÚ-Ku-bi-im*, *CCT* III, 25:28, 36.
11. *ḫamuštum*, *CCT* I, 8a:6; 9b:6.
12. *BIN* IV, 1:16; 6:4; 12:7, 16; 153:2; 204:9; 230:23; *CCT* I, 1b:6; *CCT* II, 22:16, 23; 33:2; 34:2; *CCT* III, 31:22; 48a:4; *CCT* IV, 24a:12; 41b:3; 42c:4, 18, 21; *LTC* IV, 44:2, 5; 70:8; 124:16; *KTS*, 11:10, 16; *SCTP*, 21:9; 38:4; *Gol.*, 7:4; *Chantre*, 5:11; *LC*, 241:10.

Šú-ku-tum, *CCT* IV, 14a:15.

ŠÚ-Lá-ba-an,
1. s. of *A-al-ṭâbu*, *LTC* IV, 79:2.
2. s. of *A-mur-Ili*, *KTS*, 34a:24.
3. f. of *A-šír-iqbi*, *CCT* II, 8:8.
4. f. of *E-nu-be-lim*, *BIN* IV, 173:42; *CCT* I, 16b:32; *TTC*, 25:18.
5. f. of *Ú-zu-ra-nim*, *KTS*, 43c:5.
6. *CCT* I, 14a:3; *CCT* II, 10:50; 25:1; *CCT* III, 31:3; 34a:1; 35a:20; *LTC* IV, 23:2; *KTS*, 29b:26; 57b:5; *Gol.*, 17:19, 23.

Šú-li, *Šú-li-a*, *Šú-li-i-e*,
1. s. of *Buzur-A-šur*, *CCT* IV, 2b:15.
2. s. of *Da-tim*, *BIN* IV, 173:15.
3. f. of *A-šír-i-ti*, *CCT* I, 10a:26.
4. f. of *I-šú-ki-im*, *BIN* IV, 137:4.
5. *BIN* IV, 135:4; 156:12; *NBC*, 3875:4; *CCT* I, 6c:3; 29:4; *CCT* IV, 43a:4; *LTC* IV, 22:22; *KTS*, 60c:1; *Chantre*, 2:7.

ŠÚ-...-lim, *NBC*, 3863:11.

Šú-ul-mu-um, *NBC*, 3873:9.

Šú-ma, *Šú-ma-a*,
1. b. of *In-bi-ᵈAdad*, *LTC* IV, 30:15.
2. *CCT* II, 8:23.

Šú-ma-li-be-ᵈAdad, *BIN* IV, 205:7.

Šú-ma-li-ba-A-šír, *Šú-ma-li-ba-A-šur*,
1. s. of *Šál-ma-A-šur*, *Liv.*, 7:14.

2. *ḫamuštum*, *CCT* I, 7b:10.
3. *BIN* IV, 4:8, 23; 160:11; *CCT* I, 48:1, 4, 8, 13, 16, 21, 26; *CCT* IV, 29b:6; 43a:48; *LTC* IV, 72:27; *TTC*, 9:14.

Šú-ma-li-be-I-li-a, *CCT* II, 24:16.

ŠÚ-Ma-ma,
1. f. of *Bu-ur-Sin*, *CCT* I, 28a:20.
2. *TTC*, 29:11.

Šú-ma-a-be-a, *Šú-ma-a-bi-a*, *Šú-ma-bi-a*, *Šú-me-a-be-a*, *Šú-me-a-bi-a*,
1. s. of *A-šur-ni-šú*, *CCT* I, 4:2.
2. s. of *Zu-zu*, *CCT* III, 36b:9.
3. *BIN* IV, 50:1; 66:1; 121:2; 128:2; *CCT* I, 14b:3; *CCT* IV, 8a:5; 8b:2; *LTC* IV, 28:13; 30:19; 110:9; *KTS*, 3c:2; 44b:2; 48c:14; 60d:3; *SCTP*, 30:2; *PSBA*, 1881, p. 34, line 10.

Šú-me-bi-. . . , *LTC* IV, 37:20.

Šum-ma-ḫi-im, *Šum-ma-ḫu-um*, *CCT* IV, 13a:6, 20, 26, 31.

Šú-mu-um-li-ib-si, *NBC*, 3779:3.

Šú-na-. . . , f. of *ŠÚ-Ku-bi-im*, *CCT* I, 50:2.

Šú-na-bar, *CCT* IV, 14a:3.

ŠÚ-Nu-nu,
1. f. of *A-šír-i-me-tî*, *BIN* IV, 114:2.
2. f. of *Mâr-ŠÚ-Nu-nu*, *CCT* II, 14:3.
3. f. of *Ṭâb-zi-lá-A-šír*, *LTC* IV, 79:1.
4. *BIN* IV, 19:26; 82:7; *CCT* III, 4:25; *KTS*, 29b:17.

Šú-ra-ma, *lîmu*, *CCT* I, 46a:20; 46b:14.

ŠÚ-Sin,
1. *lîmu*, s. of *Ba-ba-lim*, *CCT* I, 48:23.
2. s. of *A-ku-a-a*, *BIN* IV, 187:22.
3. s. of *Bu-za-zu*, *CCT* II, 4a:9.
4. s. of *El-me-tî*, *LTC* IV, 67:3.
5. s. of *Ì-lí-a*, *CCT* I, 3:31.
6. f. of *A-šír-ba-ni*, *LTC* IV, 64:4.
7. f. of *I-ku-be-a*, *BIN* IV, 145:20; 199:6; *NBC*, 3768:7.
8. f. of *Mâr-ŠÚ-Sin*, *CCT* II, 41a:9.
9. f. of *ŠÚ-A-šír*, *BIN* IV, 207:15; 207case:2.
10. f. of *Zu-na-da*, *BIN* IV, 187:21.
11. *BIN* IV, 26:20; 55:3; 168:7; 222:2; *NBC*, 3730:3; 3774:4; 3791:5; 4004:10; *CCT* I, 21d:5; *CCT* II, 4a:27; 25:3; 26a:1; *CCT* III, 9:37; 29:6; *CCT* IV, 12a:2; 45a:16; *LTC* IV, 54:2; 57:2; *KTS*, 4a:5; 52cR:4; *SCTP*, 24:7; *Liv.*, 4R:5.

Šú-wa-ak-ru, *CCT* III, 19a:15.

Šú-zu-zu, *BIN* IV, 65:3.

Ta-be-ma(?), *BIN* IV, 38:29; *CCT* II, 50:22.

Ta-ki-e, *CCT* I, 36b:7.

Ta-ki-el-A-šír, *Ta-ki-el-A-šur*,
1. s. of *Ḫa-na-nim*, *LTC* IV, 65:1.
2. *Gol.*, 23:3.

Ta-li-a,
1. h. of *Ḫa-šú-šá-ar-na*, *LC*, 242:7, 11, 20.

2. *BIN* IV, 195:3; 220:9; *CCT* I, 32c:11; 34a:23; *TTC*, 20:3.

Ta-mu-ri-a, *BIN* IV, 190:4, 10.

Ta-ra-ku, *CCT* III, 25:1.

Ta-ra-am-Ku-be, *Ta-ra-am-Ku-bi*, *NBC*, 3700:3; *CCT* III, 23b:2; 24:2; *CCT* IV, 46a:26; *LTC* IV, 5:2.

Ta-ar-am-šá-Ili, *LTC* IV, 87:18.

Ta-ar-ḫu-nu, *BIN* IV, 195:4; *Gol.*, 10:3.

Ta-ri-eš-ma-tum, *Ta-ri-iš-ma-tum*, *CCT* IV, 15c:3; *LTC* IV, 46:2; *KTS*, 23:3; 24:2; 25a:2; 53a:10, 20; *SCTP*, 2:3; *Chantre*, 1:2.

ᶠTa-ri-iš-ma-tum, *Liv.*, 1:3.

Ta-ar-ma-na, *Tár-ma-na*, *CCT* I, 33b:12; *CCT* III, 48b:7; *KTS*, 3a:6; 29a:6.

Ta-ta-a, *BIN* IV, 186:5; 186case:8.

Ta-ta-li-i, f. of *Si-im-nu-ma-an*, *Liv.*, 8:5.

Tî-ta-a, *NBC*, 3734:4.

Ṭâb-a-ḫi, *Ṭâb-a-ḫi-e*, *CCT* IV, 7a:19, 21; *KTS*, 47a:18.

Ṭâb-ba, f. of *Zu-ki-ki*, *LTC* IV, 91a:3.

Ṭâb-ba-A-šur, *lîmu*, *LTC* IV, 91a:14; 91b:11.

Ṭâbu-A-šír, *Ṭâbu-A-šur*, *Ṭâbi(-bi)-A-šír*,
1. s. of *Buzur-Ištar*, *NBC*, 1889:28.
2. s. of *E-šú-ba-ni*, *CCT* III, 17a:24.
3. s. of *ŠÚ-Ištar*, *CCT* II, 8:21.
4. f. of *A-gu-a*, *KTS*, 27b:25.
5. *NBC*, 1708:5; *CCT* II, 9:46; 22:2; *CCT* IV, 10b:10; 16a:4.

Ṭâbu-Î-lí, f. of *I-tí-lim*, *LTC* IV, 22:6.

Ṭâbu-zi-lá-A-šír, *Ṭâbu-zi-lá-A-šur*, *Ṭâbu-zilli-A-šur*,
1. s. of *A-šír-i-din*, *BIN* IV, 103:38; *KTS*, 49a:10.
2. s. of *A-šur-na-da*, *KTS*, 44a:19.
3. s. of *ŠÚ-Nu-nu*, *LTC* IV, 79:1.
4. *BIN* IV, 48:2; 88:27; 180:5; 203:6; *CCT* I, 8c:15; *CCT* III, 17a:21; *CCT* IV, 19c:6; *LTC* IV, 11:6; 84:4; *KTS*, 14a:9, 23; 52a:4; 54b:12, 13.

Ṭâbu-zi-li, *LTC* IV, 39:6.

Ub-ḫa-ki-im, *Ub-ki-im*,
1. f. of *Ú-ur-si-si*, *BIN* IV, 206case:2.
2. *LTC* IV, 16:5; *KTS*, 57b:1.

Ud-ga-ri-a, f. of *Ḫa-šú-šá-ar-na*, *LC*, 242:9, 18.

Ú-di-nim, *CCT* II, 46b:1.

Ud-ni-iḫ-šú, *Liv.*, 8:16.

Ud-ru-wa-šú, *BIN* IV, 68:15.

Ú-ku-. . ., f. of *Zi-lu-lu*, *KTS*, 31a:5.

Ú-lá-a, *Ú-lá-a-a*, f. of *Ku-ra*, *CCT* II, 11a:4; *KTS*, 19b:16.

Ú-lá-me-el, *BIN* IV, 160:1.

Ú-ra-a,
1. s. of *Ma-na-na*, *LTC* IV, 71:3.
2. *NBC*, 3903R:7; *LTC* IV, 71:8, 10, 11.

Ú-ra-ni, *BIN* IV, 9:9, 12; *NBC*, 3735:3.

Ú-ra-ad-Ku-bi-im, *BIN* IV, 162:40.

Ur-da-A-šur, *LTC* IV, 82:17, 18.

Ur-ᵈLugal-marda, s. of *Ur-Nigin-gár*, *LTC* IV, 90a:seal C.

Ur-Nigin-gár, f. of *Ur-^{d}Lugal-marda*, *LTC* IV, 90a: seal C.

Ú-ur-si-si,
1. s. of *Ub-ḫa-ki-im*, *BIN* IV, 206case:2.
2. *BIN* IV, 206:21.

Ú-za-nim,
1. s. of *A-mur-A-šur*, *KTS*, 49a:8.
2. *CCT* I, 43:1, 16, 21; *CCT* IV, 44a:2, 20.

Ú-za-ri-a,
1. f. of *A-šír-ma-lik*, *CCT* I, 28a:13.
2. f. of *A-šur-ṭâbu*, *BIN* IV, 28:5.
3. f. of *En-um-A-šír*, *CCT* II, 9:29.
4. f. of *Mâr-Ú-za-ri-a*, *CCT* II, 45a:18.

Ú-zi-a, *Ú-zu-a*,
1. s. of *A-bi-a-a*, *CCT* II, 9:27.
2. s. of *I-da-a*, *LTC* IV, 114:4.
3. s. of *I-din-A-šír*, *KTS*, 22b:5.
4. s. of *Ku-lu-ma-a*, *BIN* IV, 137:8.
5. s. of *Lá-ki-be-im*, *CCT* I, 41a:4, 8, 12.
6. s. of *ŠÚ-be-lim*, *TTC*, 3:11.
7. f. of *Bi-lá-aḫ-Ištar*, *CCT* II, 7:39.
8. f. of *I-din-A-šír*, *BIN* IV, 211:2; 211case:1, 5.
9. f. of *Li-ba-a*, *BIN* IV, 173:16.
10. f. of *Mâr-Ú-zu-a*, *BIN* IV, 72:20; *CCT* II, 37:20; *KTS*, 48c:6.
11. *BIN* IV, 50:1; *NBC*, 1887:2, 6, 7; *CCT* II, 17a:20; *CCT* IV, 27a:2; *KTS*, 17:2; 18:3.

Ú-zu-be-iš-ki-im, *Ú-zu-be-iš-ku*, *Ú-zu-bi-iš-ki-im*, *CCT* I, 37a:8, 24; 40c:9; *CCT* III, 40b:1.

Ú-zur-. . ., *NBC*, 4071:4.

Ú-zu-ra-nim,
1. s. of *ŠÚ-Lá-ba-an*, *KTS*, 43c:4.
2. *BIN* IV, 102:1; 123:11; *CCT* II, 9:43; *LTC* IV, 110:10.

Ú-zur-šá-. . ., *NBC*, 3887:10; *CCT* II, 23:2.

Ú-zur-šá-A-šír, *Ú-zur-šá-A-šur*, *Ú-zu-ur-šá-A-šír*, *Ú-zu-ur-šá-A-šur*,
1. s. of *A-ku-a*, *BIN* IV, 105:25.
2. s. of *A-šur-be-el-a-wa-tim*, *BIN* IV, 24:13.
3. s. of *A-šír-ma-lik*, *CCT* II, 8:6; 10:70.
4. s. of *Bu-. . .*, *NBC*, 1889:8, 15.
5. s. of *Ì-lí-a*, *CCT* III, 19:16.
6. f. of *A-ni-na*, *LTC* IV, 79:4.
7. *ḫamuštum*, *CCT* I, 26c:4.
8. *BIN* IV, 19:25, 43; 24:15; 33:51; 38:10; 53:6; 160:44, 50; 173:25, 30; *NBC*, 3874:3, 15; 3878:3; *CCT* I, 35:7; 36d:13; 40c:3; 48:36; *CCT* II, 21b:2; 22:2; 36b:11, 15; 37b:3, 30; *CCT* III, 9:13; 30:9; 34a:6; *CCT* IV, 19c:2; 24a:36; 34b:3; 46b:2; *LTC* IV, 38:4; *KTS*, 4b:10, 16; 7a:6; 13a:3; 24:26; 25a:5; 48c:2.

Ú-zur-šá-Ištar, *Ú-zu-ur-šá-Ištar*, *Ú-zur-si-Ištar*,
1. s. of *A-šur-i-me-tî*, *CCT* II, 8:9.
2. *BIN* IV, 47:2, 25; 94:2; *NBC*, 3879:10, *CCT* I, 5b:21; 40c:8; *CCT* II, 8:10; 23:3; 35:4; *CCT* III, 40a:11; *CCT* IV, 17a:2; 28a:35; *KTS*, 19a:25, 26; *TTC*, 9:11.

Wa-da-ab-ra, *CCT* I, 6c:13.
Wa-ad-du-Ili(?), *CCT* I, 23:14.
Wa-ak-li, *Wa-ak-lim*,
1. h. of *Ga-áb-zi-a*, *CCT* I, 10b:3, 7.
2. *CCT* IV, 32a:1.

Wa-kúr-tim, *Wa-kúr-tum*, *BIN* IV, 21:19; 96:3; *CCT* I, 17b:20; *CCT* III, 41b:2.
Wa-lá-aḫ-si-na, f. of *Be-ru-a*, *KTS*, 46a:3, 8; 46b:3.
Wa-lá-wa-lá, *Liv.*, 13a:2.
Wa-li-si-id, *Chantre*, 2:4.
Wa-li-iš-ra, *SCTP*, 38:10.
Wa-li-wa-li, *KTS*, 3a:17, 19.
Wa-al-tî-lim, *Wa-al-tî-Ili*,
1. s. of *ŠÚ-be-lim*, *LTC* IV, 66:3, 5.
2. *BIN* IV, 80:1, 2.

Wa-ar-ḫi-lá, *CCT* I, 38c:2.
Wa-ri-zi, *dub-šar*, *CCT* I, 7b:4.
Wa-aš-ḫu-ru, *Gol.*, 20:2, 33.
Wa-aš-na-ni, *BIN* IV, 40:3.
Wa-tî-tum, *LTC* IV, 21:2.
ᶠ*Wa-wa-lá*, w. of *Ili-ma-lá-ak*, *CCT* I, 11b:3, 16.
Wa-wa-li, *KTS*, 7a:16, 23; *TTC*, 5:8.
Wa-wa-an-da, *KTS*, 51b:18.
Wa-za-wa, *LC*, 240:25.

Za-ba-zi-a, *Za-ba-zu*, *Za-ba-...-a*,
1. s. of *Î-lí-iš-ta-gal*, *BIN* IV, 15:5.
2. f. of *A-šur-rê'ûm*, *NBC*, 3748:1.
3. *BIN* IV, 15:9; 41:2; 42:3; 42 case; 160:7; *CCT* I, 12a:5; *CCT* III, 30:2; *CCT* IV, 37b:2; *LTC* IV, 51:2; *SCTP*, 16:1, 4.

Za-ḫa, *Za-ḫa-a*, *BIN* IV, 99:1; 165:18; *CCT* II, 43:5; 48:4, 22.
Za-ḫa-an, *CCT* I, 24b:12.
Za-ḫa-..., s. of *A-šír-e-mu-qi*, gs. of *Ga-ga-da-nim*, *Gol.*, 9:3.
Za-aḫ-ri-li, f. of *Ku-ur-ku-ri-a* and *Ku-ku-zi*, *KTS*, 44a:6.
Za-ki-...-Ili, *Gol.*, 5:2.
Za-ḫi-im, *BIN* IV, 56:9.
Za-ak-li-a, *BIN* IV, 57:2, 6; *KTS*, 5a:4, 28.
Za-li-a, f. of *Id-na-a*, *CCT* I, 15a:18.
Za-li-ti, f. of *A-mur-ᵈA-šur*, *CCT* I, 26c:7.
Za-am-ru, *BIN* IV, 188:9.
Za-az, f. of *Î-lí-a-lim*, *BIN* IV, 51:35.
Za-zi-a,
1. f. of *A-ba-be-a*, *TTC*, 19:18.
2. f. of *En-na-nim*, *TTC*, 19:7.

Za-zu-ni, *LTC* IV, 81:27.
Zi-ga-a, f. of *Mâr-Zi-ga-a*, *CCT* IV, 18a:7.
Zi-iḫ-ri-Î-lí, f. of *Ku-ku-zi*, *CCT* I, 1a:1.
Zi-ki-ki, *LTC* IV, 91b:12; *SCTP*, 27:18.
Zi-ku-ḫi-im, f. of *A-lá-ḫi-im*, *BIN* IV, 56:4.

Zi-kúr-Ì-lí, Zi-ku-ur-lí,
1. f. of *A-mur-A-šír, CCT* III, 39a:10.
2. *CCT* IV, 13a:3, 36.

Zi-li-a,
1. f. of *Kúr-ub-A-šír, LTC* IV, 71:15.
2. f. of *Mâr-Zi-li-a, BIN* IV, 146:3.

Zi-lá-dAdad, Zilli-dAdad,
1. f. of *dAdad-ba-ni, KTS,* 47b: 18.
2. *BIN* IV, 73:1; 78:23, 29; 192:12; 206:6; 206case:9; 230:1; *NBC,* 3860:2, 12; 3874:3, 4; *CCT* II, 17b:2; 18:2; 19a:2; 49b:3, 10; *CCT* III, 39b:1; *LTC* IV, 43:2; 48:2, 25.

Zi-li-Ištar, Zilli-Ištar,
1. s. of *Ili-be-lá-lim, Babyl.* IV, p. 77, 1:13.
2. s. of *Na-ni-a, LTC* IV, 63:2, seal B.
3. f. of *En-um-A-šír, LTC* IV, 95:5; 96:12.
4. f. of *Mâr-Zilli(-li)-Ištar, CCT* I, 32c:8.
5. *NBC,* 3911:4; *CCT* I, 20a:6; *SCTP,* 31:3; *Gol.,* 7:3.

Zi-lu-lu,
1. s. of *Ú-ku-. . . , KTS,* 31a:5.
2. *BIN* IV, 42:11; *LTC* IV, 90a:1; 90b:14.

Zi-lu-tî-ri-el-ga(?), NBC, 3720:3.

Zi-zi-i, Zi-zi-im,
1. f. of *Mâr-Zi-zi-im, NBC,* 1903:13.
2. *NBC,* 3874:2, 15.

Zu-a-ni-a, CCT I, 7a:19.

Zu-ba,
1. s. of *Buzur-Ištar, LTC* IV, 30:16.
2. s. of *I-din-a-be-im, BIN* IV, 189:15.
3. s. of *Ištar-ba-li-el, BIN* IV, 174:3; *LTC* IV, 86:13.
4. *BIN* IV, 42:37, 42; 88:3; *CCT* I, 25:4; 26c:5; 32c: 10; 47b:1, 4; *CCT* III, 21a:3, 5; *CCT* IV, 34b:2; 40b:2; 49a:2, 3; *LTC* IV, 86:1; *KTS,* 11:2; 12:2; 39a:2; *TTC,* 20:1.

Zu-e-a,
1. s. of *Bu-šú-ki-in, CCT* I, 9a: 16; *LTC* IV, 79:6.
2. f. of *Bu-šú-ki-in, BIN* IV, 113:20; *KTS,* 43c:19.
3. *BIN* IV, 31:2; 45:2; 105:9; 199:12; *CCT* I, 9a:7; 17b: 11; 49b:5, 6, 15; *CCT* III, 26a:1; 26b:2; *CCT* IV, 6e:3; 48a:9; 48b:3; *LTC* IV, 22:5, 11, 14; 77:6, 10, 13; 81:5; 105:4, 9; *KTS,* 5a:17, 19; 48c:3.

Zu-e-ta-ta, BIN IV, 100:1; *Gol.,* 9: 22.

Zu-ga-li-a, Zu-ga-li,
1. *ḫamuštum,* f. of *A-šír-ma-lik, Gol.,* 10:7.
2. f. of *E-na-Sin,* gf. of *A-šur-ma-lik, Gol.,* 3:5.
3. f. of *A-mu-ra, LTC* IV, 66:2.
4. f. of *A-mur-A-šur, BIN* IV, 8:33; 140:3; *CCT* I, 19a: 16; *CCT* III, 45a:22.
5. f. of *A-šur-iš-ta-ki-el, CCT* IV, 21b:6.

6. f. of *Ì-lí-aš-ra-. . .*, *CCT* II, 26a:21.
7. f. of *Mâr-Zu-ga-li-a*, *CCT* II, 33:14.
8. *CCT* I, 18b:6, 9; *CCT* II, 33:17; *CCT* III, 27b:7; *CCT* IV, 33b:23, 25; *KTS*, 33b:1, 17.

Zu-gu-ri-im, *BIN* IV, 219:8.

Zu-ḫu-za, *Zu-ḫu-za-a*, *BIN* IV, 186:4, 10; 186case:4, 7, 11.

Zu-ki-bi-im, f. of *A-šur-ma-lik*, *KTS*, 51c:4.

Zu-ki-ki, s. of *Ṭâb-ba*, *LTC* IV, 91a:3.

Zu-ku-a, *Zu-ku-ú-a*, *BIN* IV, 164:9; 197:7; *CCT* II, 46a:2; *CCT* IV, 4b:2; *TTC*, 11:2, 9.

Zu-ku-ḫi-im,
1. f. of *Lu-lu*, *BIN* IV, 26:9.
2. f. of *Mâr-Zu-ku-ḫi-im*, *CCT* I, 40a:20.

Zu-li-a-rabi, *BIN* IV, 160:5.

Zu-li-li, *BIN* IV, 206:13; 206case:13.

Zu-lu-la-a, *CCT* I, 15b:9.

Zu-na-da, s. of *ŠÚ-Sin*, *BIN* IV, 187:20.

Zu-na-nim, *CCT* II, 25:15, 25, 41, 43.

Zu-na-wi-ir,
1. s. of *A-zu*, *SCTP*, 17:4.
2. *LTC* IV, 58:4.

Zu-ur-zi, *CCT* I, 39b:7.

Zu-ur-zu-ni, f. of *A-ḫu-wa-qar*, *CCT* I, 36b:6.

Zu-ur-zu-ur,
1. f. of *A-ḫu-wa-qar*, *CCT* II, 5b:5.
2. f. of *ŠÚ-be-lim*, *CCT* II, 46a:11.

Zu-ta-A-šír, *BIN* IV, 83:36.

Zu-tî-a,
1. s. of *I-zi-ḫi-im*, *CCT* II, 15:16.
2. f. of *A-šír-ma-lik*, *BIN* IV, 161:seal A.
3. f. of *A-šur-na-da*, *BIN* IV, 173:6.
4. f. of *Ku-ra*, *BIN* IV, 161:20; 161case:1.

Zu-za-a,
1. s. of *ŠÚ-Ištar*, *CCT* II, 8:21.
2. *CCT* II, 9:46; 10:48.

Zu-zu, *Zu-ú-zu*,
1. f. of *Šú-ma-be-a*, *CCT* III, 36b:9.
2. *BIN* IV, 195:18; *CCT* I, 21d:19; 42a:15; *CCT* IV, 1a:17; *LC*, 242:3.

Zu-zu-a,
1. s. of *Ì-lí-e-mu-qi*, *BIN* IV, 114:46.
2. *NBC*, 1903:15; *CCT* I, 7a:17; *TTC*, 23:27, 32.

Zu-zu-li, *LTC* IV, 78:9.

Zu-zu-wa, s. of *Ì-lí-dan*, *LTC* IV, 71:16.

. . .-*^{d}Adad*, *BIN* IV, 78:2; *NBC*, 4000:3.

. . .-*a-dī-na-a*, *NBC*, 3889:4.

. . .-*aḫ-A-šur*, *NBC*, 3748:10.

. . .-*aḫ-Ištar*, *BIN* IV, 160:39.

. . .-*ak-lá-ku*, s. of *ŠÚ-^{d}En-lil*, *KTS*, 43c:5.

. . .-*A-šír*, . . .-*A-šur*,
1. s. of *En-na-nim*, *BIN* IV, 165:6.

2. s. of *Buzur-Ištar*, *NBC*, 3748:3.
3. *NBC*, 1889:2; 3787:20; 4000: 4; *LTC* IV, 22:1, 32; 42:8; *TTC*, 25:1; *Gol.*, 21:9.

...*-bi-Ištar*, *BIN* IV, 78:1.
...*-da-a*, s. of *Aḫ-me*, *NBC*, 3905:8.
...*-din-*^{d}*Adad*, *CCT* II, 6:3; 26a:10.
...*-e-a*, *NBC*, 1889:3.
...*-el-a-wa-tim*, *Babyl.* VI, p. 190, 5:2.
...*-ḫi-a*, s. of *Nu-nu*, *NBC*, 3911:5.
...*-i-A-šur*, s. of *A-šur-ba-ni*, *LTC* IV, 110:34.
...*-ir-ma-A-šír*, *BIN* IV, 13:9.
...*-Ištar*, *NBC*, 3772:3; 4045:11.
...*-ki-*^{d}*Adad*, *Liv.*, 6:3.
...*-Ku-be-im*, ...*-Ku-bu-um*,
1. s. of *Du-du-a*, *KTS*, 47c:6.
2. *CCT* IV, 4b:3.

...*-lá-*^{d}*Adad*, *BIN* IV, 76:2.
...*-lim-A-šur*, *Liv.*, 6:13
...*-ma-A-šur*,
1. s. of *Ni-tí*, *Babyl.* IV, p. 78, 2:18.
2. *Chantre*, 14:10.

...*-ma-lik*, *CCT* I, 6c:15.
...*-na-A-šír*, *LTC* IV, 41:3.
...*-na-ni*, f. of *A-šur-na-da*, *NBC*, 3787:9.
...*-na-nim*, s. of *Ili-ba-ni*, *BIN* IV, 114:45; 114case:1.
...*-ru-a*, *LTC* IV, 84:2.
...*-ru-wa*, s. of *Na-ba-ḫi-e*, b. of *Ar-za-na-aḫ-šú*, *Gol.*, 5:10.
...*-Sin*,
1. s. of *I-din-Ku-bi-im*, *KTS*, 2a:7.
2. f. of *I-din-A-šur*, *SCTP*, 21:3.
3. *NBC*, 3925:8.

...*-šá-lim*, f. of ...*-ta-ak-lá-ku*, *CCT* I, 43:25.
...*-*^{d}*Šamaš*, s. of *Da-lá-aš*, *BIN* IV, 111:21.
...*-šír-ṭâbu*, s. of *Ki-ki*, *NBC*, 3915: 15.
...*-ta-ak-lá-ku*, ...*-ták-lá-ku*,
1. s. of ...*-šá-lim*, *CCT* I, 43:25.
2. *NBC*, 3763:2.

...*-um-A-šír*, *BIN* IV, 165:24.
...*-um-Ili*, s. of *I-din-Sin*, *NBC*, 3787:3.
...*-zu-a*, s. of *Ì-lí-e-mu-qi*, *BIN* IV, 114case:2.

LIST OF ELEMENTS

a, *a-a*, hypocoristic ending, in *A-ba-a-a*, *A-ba-ba-a-a*, *A-bi-a-a*, *A-aḫ-a-a*, *A-ma-a*, *Am-ma-a*, *A-mu-ra*, *A-mu-ra-a*.

Aia, deity, in *Be-la-ḫa-a*, *E-na-ma-a*, *I-din-a-a*.

E-a, *Ê-a*, *I-a*, deity, in *E-a-ba-aš-tî*, *Ê-a-dan*, *E-a-šar*, *I-a-šar*, *I-a-šá-ri-im*, *Zu-E-a*(?).

E-a-nim, probably for *E-na-nim*.

i-a, hypocoristic ending, in *A-bi-a*, *Be-li-a*, *Zu-e-a*(?).

I-a-tum, cf. *Ia-a-tum*, *CPN*, p. 82.

אב, *abu*, father, in *A-ba*, *A-ba-a-a*, *A-ba-el*, *A-ba-ni-im*, *A-be-a-nim*, *A-be-Î-lí*, *A-be-ma-ni*, *A-be-na-zi-ir*, *A-bi-a*, *Áb-šá-lim*, *A-bu-um-Ili*, *A-bu-šá-lim*, *A-lá-be-im*, *A-lá-bu-um*, *Ḫa-lá-be-im*, *I-din-a-bu-um*, *Ma-nu-um-kî-a-bi-a*, *ᵈŠamaš-a-bi*, *Šú-ma-bi-a*, *Šú-me-a-bi-a*.

ᵈAb, deity, in *ᵈAb-ba-ni*.

áb, in *Áb-si-e-ni*.

a-be, in *A-be-zu-ra*.

A-ba-ba, (cf. *A-ba-ba*, *HPN*, p. 41, *UMBS*, XI(2), p. 148) in *A-ba-ba-a-a*.

A-ba-be-a, see above.

E-bi-bu-ni.

A-bu-di, from עבד(?), perhaps to be read *A-bu-šalim*.

A-ba-zi-a-šú, cf. *aba-aza*, *SPN*, p. 44.

Ub-ḫa-ki-im, *Ub-ki-im*.

A-be-lá, *A-be-i-lá*, Sem., *Ab-Ilu* or non-Sem., *Abbi-la*, cf. *ab-bi CPN*, p. 149.

A-bu-um-me-lim, perhaps אב, *abum;* אל, *e-lim* (cf. *I-lim*) but cf. *me-li*, *CPN*, p. 183.

ib-ri, friend, in *Me-me-ib-ri*.

A-ba-ta-na-nu, *A-ba-ta-na-nu-um*.

A-gi-a, *A-gu-a*, see also *Mâr-A-gu-a;* cf. *A-gu-ú-a*, *RPN*, p. 62; *A-gu-a*, *HPN*, p. 44, *UDT*, p. 80; *A-gi*, *CPN*, p. 150; אָגֵא, *Bi*.

I-ga-a, cf. *I-ka-ú-su*, *TAPN*, p. 95.

a-ga-áb, (cf. *a-gab*, *CPN*, p. 150) in *A-ga-áb-si*.

A-gu-za, cf. *A-ku-za;* *A-gu-zi*, *HPN*, p. 44.

I-ga-lá, cf. אגל, *TAPN*, p. 264; עֶגְלָה, יִגְאָל, *Bi*.

I-ga-li, cf. above.

A-ga-li-ú-ma-an, cf. *A-ga-li*, *CPN*, p. 150; *A-ga-la*, *TAPN*, p. 264; see also *ma-an*.

A-di-a, cf. *A-di-ia*, *CTK*, p. 109; עֲדָיָה, *Bi*.

A-du, *A-du-a*, *A-du-e*, *A-du-ú*, cf. *A-du*, *YBT* IV, p. 23.

a-du, *ad-du*, in *A-du-a-aḫ-si*, *Ad-du-aḫ-si*.

I-da-a, cf. *Id-du-u-a*, *TAPN*, p. 94; *Id-di-ia*, *RPN*, p. 95; *Id-da-a*, *NBPN*, p. 69; אדו, עדו, עדוא, *Bi.*

I-di-a, *I-du-a*, cf. above.

Adad, (written *ᵈIM*, *A-du*) deity; see names under *ᵈAdad-*, and the fol., *Buzur-ᵈAdad*, *E-um-ᵈAdad*, *Gár-tum-ᵈAdad*, *Ib-ni-ᵈAdad*, *I-din-ᵈAdad*, *In-bi-ᵈAdad*, *Iš-ma-ᵈAdad*, *Šá-lim-ᵈAdad*, *Šarrum-ᵈAdad*, *ŠÚ-ᵈAdad*, *ŠÚ-A-du*, *Šú-ḫa-ir-ᵈAdad*, *Šú-ma-li-be-ᵈAdad*, *Zi-lá-ᵈAdad*.

A-da-da, for *ᵈAdad*(?), cf. *A-ta-ta*; *A-da-da*, *HSS* III, p. 15, *YBT* IV, p. 23; *A-da-ta*, *HPN*, p. 44; *SPN*, p. 45.

A-di-da.

A-du-da, cf. above and *A-du-du*.

A-du-du, cf. *A-du-du*, *YBT* IV, p. 23.

Ud-ga-ri-a.

אדי, *a-dī*, unto(?), (perhaps scribal error for *I-din*) in *A-dī-A-šur*.

A-da-làl, see דלל.

A-dī-la-at, cf. *ada*, *SPN*, p. 45; *lada*, *SPN*, p. 131.

A-di-nim, *A-di-nu*, *A-dī-na*, cf. *E-dī-na-a*; עדינא, *Bi.*

E-din, *E-dī-na-a*, see נדן.

id-na, *id-na-a*, (cf. *E-dī-na-a*; *idnu*, *CPN*, p. 151; *Id-na-a-a*, *ADB*, p. 74; עדנה, *Bi.*) in *Id-na-a*, *Id-na-A-šur*.

I-du-a-na.

Ú-di-nim, cf. *Ú-di-ni*, eagle, *TAPN*, p. 264.

Ud-ni-iḫ-šú.

Ud-ru-wa-šú.

idu-šá, (cf. *Buzur*) in *Idu-šá-A-šur*, *Idu-šá-Ištar*.

A-da-ta, cf. *A-da-da*.

E-wa-ri-mu-šá.

az, *a-zu*, perhaps from אסי, physician (cf. *Az*, *DmlWTF*, p. 21; *Az-zu*, *Azuzu*, *TAPN*, p. 265, 252; *ᶠA-za-a-a*, *CTK*, p. 110) in *Az*, *A-za-nim*, *A-zu*, *A-zu-e-el-ga*, *A-zu-ma-nim*.

Ú-zi-a, *Ú-zu-a*, cf. *Ú-zu-a-a*, *YBT* V, p. 40; עזא, עזי, *Bi.*

Ú-zu-bi-iš-ki-im, perhaps אזב II_1, to spare, save; *išku*, child, *TAPN*, p. 272.

A-zu-da, cf. *A-zu-ta-a*; *Á-zid-da*, *YBT* IV, p. 24.

A-zu-za, cf. *Azuzu*, deity, *TAPN*, p. 252; צוזא, *Bi.*

I-zi-ḫi-im, cf. *I-šú-ḫi-im*.

I-za-li-a.

I-zu-muš. Probably to be read *I-zu-rig*; *muš* may have had the value *rig* in Cappadocian; see *I-zu-ri-ig* below.

Ú-za-nim, cf. *Ú-za-nu-ú-a*, *CPN*, p. 144.

A-zu-na-a, cf. *A-za-na-a*, *TAPN*, p. 265; אזניה, *Bi.*

I-zu-ur.

Ú-za-ri-a, cf. *A-za-ru*, *TAPN*, p. 265.

I-zu-ri-ig, see סרק.

A-zu-ta-a.

אח, *aḫ, a-ḫi-e, a-ḫu-um, a-ḫa-tum*, brother, sister, in *A-aḫ-a-a, A-aḫ-A-šír, A-ḫa-tum, A-aḫ-Ili, A-aḫ-Ištar, Aḫ-šá-lim, A-aḫ-ᵈŠamaš, A-aḫ-šú, A-a-aḫ-šú-nu* (cf. *YBT* V, p. 22), *A-ḫu-wa-qar, A-ḫu-qar, A-lá-ḫu-um, I-din-a-ḫu-um, Šá-al-ma-ḫi-im, Šá-lim-a-ḫi-im, Šál-me-ḫi-im, Šál-me-gim, Šum-ma-ḫu-um, Ṭâb-a-ḫi, Ṭâb-a-ḫi-e.*

A-ḫa-ḫa, cf. *aka-ka, SPN*, p. 46; *Aḫa(?)-a-a-ḫa-a, TAPN*, p. 14.

Aḫ-me, cf. *A-ḫi-me-e, TAPN*, p. 17; *A-ḫi-ma-a-a, YBT* V, p. 22.

A-ḫa-na-ar-si.

aḫ-si, in *A-du-aḫ-si.*

aḫ-šú, element or ending of non-Sem. names, in *Ar-za-na-aḫ-šú, Be-ir-wa-aḫ-šú, Ḫi-iš-ta-aḫ-šú, Ḫi-iš-ta-aḫ-šú-šar, Ki-na-aḫ-šú, La-aḫ-ra-aḫ-šú, Lu-ar-ra-aḫ-šú, Ma-ḫi-ra-aḫ-šú, Ni-ma-aḫ-šú, Ni-wa-aḫ-šú-šar, Si-šá-aḫ-šú-šar, Šú-be-a-aḫ-šú, Šú-be-a-aḫ-šú-šar, Šú-bu-nu-aḫ-šú.*

A-ki-a-a, A-ku-a, cf. *A-gi-a; Ak-ku-u-ia, CPN*, p. 152; *aki, TAPN*, p. 266; *A-ki-ia, CTK*, p. 109.

I-ku-a, perhaps scribal error for *I-ku-be-a.*

I-ku-ba-šá, I-ku-bi-a, see כון.

A-ku-za, cf. *A-gu-za.*

I-ku-uk-li-im.

A-ak-li-a, cf. *Wa-ak-li-a; aklu, RPN*, p. 221.

Ik-ra-a, cf. אכר, *TAPN*, p. 266.

ak-šú (cf. *aḫ-šú*), in *Da-ra-ak-šú.*

I-ku-uš-mu.

ak-ta (cf. *aktta, SPN*, p. 47), in *Ak-ta-ma-tim.*

A-ku-tum, cf. *A-gu-du, YBT* IV, p. 23.

אל, *Ilu*, god, (written *AN, al, a-lim, el, e-li, i-el, I-li, Ī-lí, i-lim*), in *A-lá-bu-um* (cf. אֱלִיאָב, *Bi.*), *A-lá-ḫu-um, Al-be-li, A-al-ṭâbu, A-al-ta-bu-a, E-li-a, El-li-a, E-la-nu-um, El-ba-ni, El-ga-si-id, El-ku-li, El-me-da-ku, El-me-tî, El-wa-da-ak, El-wa-da-ku, I-lá-ni-šú, I-li-a, Ī-lí-a, Ī-lí-a-lim* (cf. אֱלִיאֵל, *Bi.*), *Ī-lí-a-na-Ī-lí, Ili-, Ī-lí-, I-lu-a, I-lu-ú-a, A-ba-el, A-be-Ī-lí, A-bu-um-Ili, A-aḫ-Ili, A-mur-Ili, A-na-aḫ-Ī-lí, A-na-ku-Ili, A-wi-el-Ī-lí, A-zu-e-el-ga, Be-li-li, Buzur-Ī-lí, Dan-na-i-el, Da-nim-Ili, Da-nu-me-el, Du-ra-am-Ī-lí, Du-ra-me-el, E-na-aḫ-Ī-lí, En-um-Ī-lí, Ḫa-bu-a-la, Ib-ni-li, I-dūr-Ili, Im-tî-du-Ī-lí, Im-tî-lim, Im-tî-Ili, Im-tî-li, I-na-ḫi-Ili, Ištar-Ili-šú, I-zi-za-am-Ili, Ma-lik-Ili-šú, Ma-nim-ki-i-e-li-a,*

Ma-nu-kî-E-lí, Mâr-E-la-ni, Mâr-I-li-a, Ma-zi-Ì-lí, Mu-tî-Ili, Na-be-li-šú, Nu-ur-kî-li, Nu-ur-kî-Ì-lí, Si-me-tî-Ili, Šá-at-Ì-lí, Šú-ma-li-be-I-li-a, Ta-ra-am-šá-Ili, Ṭâb-Ì-lí, Wa-al-tî-lim, Wa-al-tî-Ilim, Wa-ar-ḫi-lá(?), Za-aḫ-ri-li, Za-ki-im-Ili, Zi-iḫ-ri-Ì-lí, Zi-kur-Ì-lí, Zi-ku-ur-Ì-[lí].

E-lá, cf. *E-la, CPN,* p. 71; *E-la-a, YBT* V, p. 25; אֵלָה, *Bi.*

Ú-lá-a, cf. *u-la, CPN,* p. 154.

Ili-be-lá-lim, perhaps scribal error for *Ili-be-lá-aḫ.*

ᵈIlabrat (written *ᵈNIN. ŠUBUR, I-lá-áb-ra-at*), deity, see names under *ᵈIlabrat-, I-lá-áb-ra-at-,* and *ŠÚ-ᵈIlabrat.*

A-lu-ud-ḫu-ḫa-ar-šá.

A-lá-ḫi-nim, cf. *Rab-A-lá-ḫi-nim, Gol.,* 11:7, an official(?).

A-lu-wa-zi, cf. *a-lu, SPN,* p. 47; *wa-zi, SPN,* p. 240.

A-lu-uk-ri-im.

Al-lu-uḫ-ru-um, cf. above.

אלל, *illatu,* strength, power, in *ᵈAdad-illat(-at).*

A-li-li, A-lu-lu, strong.

I-li-el (cf. W. Sem. ending of personal names, e.g. Jacob-el, Joseph-el, etc., or *Ellil*), in *ŠÚ-I-li-el.*

A-lu-la-a.

E-lá-ma, E-lam-ma, cf. *E-lá.*

Ú-lá-me-el.

EL.ŠÚ.GAL (see Intro., p. 2), in *Buzur-El.ŠÚ. GAL.*

אמד, *imdu,* support, in *Im-tî-lim.*

nimedu, dwelling, in *A-šur-ni-me-tî* (but perhaps to be read *A-šur-ì-me-ti).*

אמה, *amâtu,* word, in *A-šur-be-el-a-wa-tim, A-šur-bi-el-a-wa-tim.*

Im-ku-a, cf. *Im-gu-u-a, BE* VI (2), p. 132, *YBT* V, p. 29.

amêlu, man, servant, in *A-wi-el-Ì-lí.*

Im-li-ga-a.

Im-lá-ni.

אמם, *Am,* uncle, or deity, in *A-ma-a, Am-ma-a, Am-lá-ḫa-a* (cf. *ᶠAm-me-e-a, CTK,* p. 109; *Am-ma-a, YBT* VI, p. 16).

E-me-me.

I-ma-nim, perhaps for *I-ku-nim.*

אמק, *emûqu,* might, strength, in *A-šír-e-mu-qi, Ì-lí-e-mu-qi.*

אמר, *a-mur,* worshipper, *BDB,* p. 771b, or fullness, abundance, Bezold, p. 43, (probably not from *amâru,* to see, cf. *A-mur-šá-ᵈDagan, LC,* p. 15) see names under *A-mur-.*

Am-ri-a, cf. *Am-ra-ai, CPN,* p. 157; *amri, TAPN,* p. 269.

a-ma-ru-um (cf. *amar, TAPN,* p. 269), in *A-šur-a-ma-ru-um.*

Im-ur-a-a, cf. *Im-mu-u-ri-ia,* Eg., *CPN,* p. 157.

^{d}*Amurru* (written *MAR.TU*, ^{d}*MAR.TU*, *A-mu-ru*), deity, see names under *Amurru-*, and *Buzur-*^{d}*Amurru*.

imittu, right hand, support, in *A-šír-i-me-tì*, *Ì-lí-me-tì*.

im-tì-du (cf. *Im-ti-dam*, *YBT* IV, p. 28; *Im-ti-da*, *HPN*, p. 54), perhaps for *imdu*, in *Im-tì-du-Ì-lí*.

a-na, unto, in *Ì-lí-a-na-Ì-lí*.

a-ni, pron. suff. 1 sg., in *A-šír-ú-si-ri-ba-ni*.

a-ni, *a-nim*, *a-nu-um*, hypocoristic ending, in *A-ba-ni-im*, *A-be-a-nim*, *A-be-ma-ni*, *A-za-nim*, *A-zu-ma-nim*, *Ba-ba-la-nim*, *Be-lá-nim*, *Bi-lá-nim*, *E-lá-ni*, *E-lá-nu-um*, *E-lá-nim*, *Ḫa-da-a-ni*, *Na-na-nim*.

^{d}*Anu* (written *A-na*, ^{d}*A-na*, *A-nim*, *A-nu*, *E-na*(?)), deity, in *Be-lá-ḫa-nim*, *Buzur-*^{d}*A-na*, *Buzur-A-na*, *Buzur-E-na*, *Da-da-nim*, *En-na-nu*, *En-na-nim*, *Li-ib-ta-nim*, *Ma-nu-ba-lu-um-A-na*, *ŠÚ-A-nim*, *Ú-zu-ra-nim*, *Zu-na-nim*.

A-nu-a, *E-nu-a*, cf. *annu*.

אנב, *inbu*, fruit, in *En-bi-A-šur*, *In-bi-*^{d}*Adad*, *In-ba-A-šur*, *In-bi-Ištar*.

E-ni-ba-aš, *E-ni-ba-šá-at*, cf. ^{d}*Anu*; *ba-aš-tì*, power.

^{d}*A-na-da*, for ^{d}*A-šír-na-da*.

E-na-za.

A-ni-za-lá, perhaps for *A-ni-Šá-lá*, grace of *Šala*, but cf. *zala*, *SPN*, p. 244.

אנח, *anâḫu*, to sigh, in *A-na-aḫ-A-šur*, *A-na-aḫ-Ì-lí*, *E-na-aḫ-Ì-lí*, *I-na-ḫi-Ili*.

anâku, pron. 1 sg. (cf. *anâḫu*; *A-na-ku-Ilu-ma*, *CPN*, p. 55), in *A-na-ku-Ili*.

^{d}*En-lil* (also written *En-lil*), deity, see names under ^{d}*En-lil*, and *ŠÚ-*^{d}*En-lil*.

i-nu-me, when (cf. next element), in *I-nu-me-A-šur*.

אנן$_3$, *anânu*, to be gracious, in *E-na-ma-a*, *En-nam-a-a*, *E-nam-a-a*, *En-um-*^{d}*Adad*, *En-nam-*^{d}*Adad*, *En-na-ni-a*, *E-na-ni-a*, *En-na-nim*, *E-na-nim*, *E-na-ma-nim*, *En-na-ma-nim*, *En-nam-ma-nim*, *En-um-A-šír*, *En-nam-A-šur*, *E-nam-A-šur*, *En-nu-um-A-šur*, *E-na-A-šur*, *En-na-A-šír*, *E-na-ma-A-šur*, *E-nu-be-lim*, *En-nam-be-lim*, *En-um-be-lim*, *E-na-be-lim*, *En-nim-be-lim*, *En-nu-be-lim*, *En-na-be-lim*, *En-nu-um-be-lim*, *En-um-Ì-lí*, *En-na-Sin*, *E-na-Sin*, *E-ni-Sin*, *En-nam-Šá-ra*, *En-na-Zu*, *E-na-a*, *I-na-a*, *I-na-Ra-wa*, *I-na-Sin*, *I-nu-ma-a*, *A-šur-e-nam*.

annu, grace, in *A-ni-a*, *A-nu-a*, *E-nu-a*, *E-en-A-šur*, *E-in-A-šur*, *En-be-li*.

anînu, grace, in *A-ni-na-a*.

אנן$_4$, *anânu*, to overshadow, in *A-*

na-ni, A-na-na, A-na-nim, cf. עֻנִּי, *Bi.*

E-na-na-tim, cf. Enannatum, early ruler of Lagash.

A-nu-nu-uš, cf. *A-na-aš.*

I-na-ar.

A-na-aš, cf. אֱנוֹשׁ, *Bi.*

E-na-aš-ru-ú, E-ni-iš-ru.

Ir, cf. *eru;* עֵר, עִיר, *Bi.*

UR, servant, see names under *UR-.*

A-ri-a, cf. *A-ra-wa.*

eru, son, man (cf. *Ú-ra-a; Ìr-ra,* diety, *YBT* V, p. 43), in *Ir-ra-a, E-ra-a.*

Ú-ra-a, cf. *Ir-ra-a;* אוּרִיָּה, *Bi.*

erêbu III_1, to increase, in *A-šír-ú-si-ri-ba-ni.*

A-ra-wa, cf. *A-ri-a; a-ra, a-ri, CPN,* p. 160; see also *A-ra-wa-ur-ḫi.*

ar-za-na, in *Ar-za-na-aḫ-šú.*

ארח, *ur-ḫi, wa-ar-ḫi,* road, way, in *A-šír-ur-ḫi*(?), *Wa-ar-ḫi-lá*(?).

ur-ḫi (cf. *ur-ḫi, CPN,* p. 161), in *A-ra-wa-ur-ḫi.*

A-ri-li, lion of *Ilu*(?), cf. *A-ri-li, CPN,* p. 161; אֲרִיאֵל, *Bi.*

Ir-ma, cf. erma, *SPN,* p. 73, but see רמה.

ar-nu (cf. *ar-nu, CPN,* p. 161), in *Ar-nu-ma-an.*

Ú-ra-ni, cf. *Úr-ra-ni, HPN,* p. 83, *YBT* IV, p. 38; *Ur-an-ni, BIN* II, p. 74; *Ir-a-ni, TAPN,* p. 102.

Ir-nu-id, cf. *ernettu,* cry of triumph, *Bezold,* p. 257.

A-ru-ru, cf. *A-ri-ri, TAPN,* p. 29.

E-ri-ri-a, cf. *i-ri-ir, CPN,* p. 161.

A-ra-ar-ri-ḫi, cf. *A-ra-wa-ur-ḫi.*

Ar-si-iḫ, cf. *Ar-ši-iḫ, TrD,* p. 13, *YBT* IV, p. 24.

Ú-ur-si-si, cf. *Ur-si, TAPN,* p. 244; *Si-is-si, CPN,* p. 191.

ארשׁ, *erêšu,* to plant, produce, in *Ili-e-ri-iš, Ili-e-ri-šú.*

êrišu, gardener (cf. *Ìr-ri-šum, UDT,* p. 83), in *E-ri-šum, I-ri-si-im, I-ri-šum.*

erištu, product (cf. *E-ri-iš-ti-Addu, CPN,* p. 161), in *E-ri-iš-tî.*

Ir-tim, cf. *Ir; irte, SPN,* p. 90.

E-ra-tî, cf. *A-ra-di, TAPN,* p. 271; עֵרֶד, *Bi;* see also *Mâr-E-ra-tî.*

E-šú, Eg.(?) deity, in *E-šú-ba-ni,* and perhaps *Ḫa-bu-a-šú.*

aš-wa (cf. *ašwa, TAPN,* p. 272), in *Ba-at-a-na-aš-wa, Šá-ak-ri-aš-wa.*

A-šú-wa-an.

I-šú-ḫi-im, cf. *I-zi-ḫi-im.*

Išḫara, deity, in *ŠÚ-Iš-ḫa-ra.*

Aš-ku-tim, Aš-ku-ti-a, cf. *Ash-ku-du-um, RPN,* p. 67.

אשׁר, *ašru,* place, in *Ì-lí-aš-ra-ni* (cf. אַשְׂרִיאֵל, *Bi.*).

^{d}Ašur (written *^{d}A-šír, ^{d}A-šur, A-šír, A-šur*), deity, see names under *A-šír-, A-šur-,* and the fol., *A-dī-A-šur, A-aḫ-A-šur, A-mur-A-šur, A-mur-^{d}A-šur, A-*

na-aḫ-A-šur, *Bi-lá-aḫ-A-šír*, *Bi-la-ti-A-šír*, *Bûr-A-šur*, *Bu-ur-A-šur*, *Buzur-A-šír*, *Damqu-be-i-A-šír*, *Dan-A-šír*, *Dan-na-A-šír*, *Dan-dA-šur*, *E-din-A-šír*, *E-dī-in-A-šír*, *E-in-A-šur*, *En-bi-A-šur*, *En-um-A-šur*, *En-nam-A-šur*, *En-um-dA-šír*, *I-din-A-šur*, *I-na-A-šur*, *I-ku-bi-A-šír*, *In-ba-A-šur*, *I-nu-me-A-šur*, *Ir-A-šír*, *Ir-ma-A-šír*, *I-šar-ki-id-A-šur*, *Iš-ma-A-šír*, *I-ti-A-šír*, *Kúr-ub-A-šír*, *Ma-nu-um-ba-lim-A-šur*, *Ma-nu-um-kî-A-šur*, *Ma-nu-um-kî-dA-šur*, *Mâr-A-šur-ma-lik*, *Ni-ma-A-šur*, *Rabû-A-šur*, *Si-ma-at-A-šír*, *Šál-ma-A-šur*, *Šál-ma-dA-šur*, *Šá-lim-A-šur*, *Šá-at-A-šur*, *ŠÚ-A-šír*, *ŠÚ-dA-šír*, *Šú-ma-li-ba-A-šur*, *Ta-ki-el-A-šír*, *Ṭab-A-šur*, *Ṭâb-ba-A-šur*, *Ṭâb-zi-lá-A-šír*, *Ur-da-A-šur*, *Ú-zur-šá-A-šur*, *Zu-ta-A-šír*.

A-šú-ri-tim, the Asshurite.

A-šur-me-tî, cf. *A-šur-i-me-tî*.

Ištar (written *U.DAR*), deity, see names under *Ištar-*, and the fol., *A-aḫ-Ištar*, *A-mur-Ištar*, *Bi-lá-aḫ-Ištar*, *Bu-ur-Ištar*, *Buzur-Ištar*, *I-din-Ištar*, *I-ku-bi-Ištar*, *In-bi-Ištar*, *Is-me-Ištar*, *Kúr-ub-Ištar*, *Li-ib-tî-Ištar*, *Li-bi-it-Ištar*, *Li-bi-Ištar*, *Ma-nu-um-kî-Ištar*, *Mâr-Kúr-ub-Ištar*, *Ni-mar-Ištar*, *Nu-ur-Ištar*, *Šál-me-Ištar*, *Šá-ra-at-Ištar*, *ŠÚ-Ištar*, *Ú-zur-šá-Ištar*, *Ú-zur-si-Ištar*, *Zilli-Ištar*, *Zi-li-Ištar*.

A-ta-a, cf. *ata*, *TAPN*, p. 273; *A-at-ta-a*, *RPN*, p. 68; עֲדָה, *Bi.*; see also *Bu-uḫ-a-ta-a*.

A-ta-i-lá-li-iḫ-šú(?).

itti, with me, in *A-šír-i-ti*, *I-ti-A-šír*.

א$_4$תל, *etêlu*, to be great, be lord(?) (cf. עַתְלַי, *Bi.*), in *A-šír-li-du-ul*.

I-tî-lim, cf. *Im-tî-lim*.

a-tum, hypocoristic ending, in *Bi-lá-tum*.

A-ta-ni, cf. *ata*, *SPN*, p. 56.

א$_4$תק, *etêqu*, to support, assist, in *El-wa-da-ak*, *El-wa-da-ku*, *Ì-lí-wa-da-ku*.

A-ta-ta, cf. *A-da-da*.

בא$_4$ל, *bêl*, lord, in *Be-lá-nim*, *Bi-lá-tum*, *Be-lim-ba-ni*, *Be-lu-ba-ni*, *Be-li-a*, *Be-li-li*, *Be-lim-na-da*, *Al-be-li*, *A-šur-be-el-a-wa-tim*, *A-šur-be-li*, *A-šur-be-el-ma-al-ki-im*, *En-be-li*, *E-nu-be-lim*, *En-nam-be-lim*, *En-nu-um-be-lim*, *E-nu-dbe-lim*, *I-din-be-el*, *I-šar-be-li*, *Šá-lim-be-li*, *Šá-lim-bi-li*, *ŠÚ-be-lim*.

Ba-ba-zu-a, cf. *baba*, *SPN*, p. 58; *zuwa*, *SPN*, p. 253.

Ba-ba-lá, *Ba-ba-li*, *Ba-bi-li*, *Ba-ba-lim*, *Ba-be-lim*, cf. *Ba-bi-la-a-i*, *CPN*, p. 164;

papa-la, *SPN*, p. 174; see also *Ba-ba-la-nim*.

Bu-ba-li-a, cf. *buba-la*, *SPN*, p. 61.

Ba-be-ra-am, *Ba-bi-ru-um*, *Ba-bi-ri*, cf. *Babu*, diety, *TAPN*, p. 252.

Bu-bu-ra-nim.

Ba-bi-tî.

Ba-ga-ku-un, cf. *Ba-ga-ga*, *YBT* IV, p. 25; *baga* (Iran. god), *TAPN*, p. 274.

Ba-di-a, cf. *ba-ti*, *Bat-ti-ilu*, *CPN*, p. 168; *Ba-a-a-di-ilu*, *Ba-di-a*, *TAPN*, p. 49a; *bada*, *SPN*, p. 58.

Bu-du-du, see פּה; דוד.

Bu-da-tim, cf. *buta*, *SPN*, p. 63.

בוש, *ba-aš-tî*, for *ba-al-ti*, abundance (cf. *RPN*, p. 224, note 2), in *A-šur-ba-aš-tî*, *E-a-ba-aš-tî*, *Ištar-ba-aš-tî*.

Ba-zi-a, cf. *Bu-zi-a; Kambuzia*, *TAPN*, p. 274; *ba-zu*, *CPN*, p. 164; *Ba-za-a*, *LC*, p. 18, *HSS* IV, p. 26; *Ba-zi*, *HPN*, p. 84, *UDT*, p. 88.

Be-za, cf. בֵּצָי, *Bi*.

Bu-za, cf. *Bu-zu*, *Bu-zi-a; Bu-za*, *YBT* IV, p. 25; *Bu-zi-ia*, *YBT* V, p. 25; *Bu-zu*, *TbD*, p. 13; *Bu-u-za*, *GTK*, p. 74; בוזי, *Bi*.

Bu-zi, cf. above.

Bu-zu, *Bu-zi-a*, *Bu-zu-a*, cf. above; *Bu-zu-ú*, *LC*, p. 20.

Ba-za-za, cf. *Bu-za-zu*, *Bu-zi-a*, *Ba-zi-a*.

Bu-za-zu, cf. *Ba-zi-a* etc.; *Bu-za-zu*, *TAPN*, p. 274, LC, p. 20.

Bu-zu-zu, cf. above; *Pu*, *SPN*, p. 188; *zu-za*, *SPN*, p. 254.

Bu-zu-li-a, cf. *Bu-si-ili*, *TAPN*, p. 67; *Bu-us-su-lum*, *CPN*, p. 166.

Buzur-, see פזר.

Bu-zu-ta-a, cf. *Bu-zi-a;* בִּזְתָא, *Bi*.

bu-uḫ (cf. *bu-uḫ*, *CPN*, p. 164), in *Bu-uḫ-a-ta-a*.

Ba-ḫu-lu, cf. *Ba-aḫ-lu-ti*, *CPN*, p. 164.

Ba-ḫi-im, cf. *ba-ḫu*, *CPN*, p. 164; *Ba-ḫi-i*, *TAPN*, p. 274.

Bu-uk-da-šú.

Bu-ku-la-am.

ba-al, in *Ba-al-du-bu*, *Ba-al-ḫa-zi-a*.

Ba-lá-a, cf. *Ba'al*, *TAPN*, p. 252.

Bu-li-a, cf. *bu-li*, *CPN*, p. 165.

ba-al-du, in *Ba-al-du-šar*.

Be-lá-ḫa-a, *Bi-lá-ḫa-a*, *-bi-lá-aḫ*, see פלח.

Ba-al-ḫu-si-a, same as *Ba-al-ḫa-zi-a*.

בלל, *balâlu*, to water, make productive(?), in *Ištar-ba-li-el*, *Ištar-ba-li-lu*.

ba-lim, *ba-lu-um*, without, in *Ma-nu-um-ba-lim-A-šur*, *Ma-nu-ba-lu-um-A-na*.

Bu-li-na.

bi-la-ti (cf. *bêlûti*, lordship, *CPN*, p. 164), in *Bi-la-ti-A-šír*.

be-in (probably scribal error for *be-lí*), in *Šá-lim-be-in*.

Ba-na-ga, cf. *Bu-na-ak-ka*, *TAPN*, p. 275.

בנה, *banû*, to build, create, in *Ib-ni-^{d}Adad*, *Ib-ni-lí*, *Ib-ni-Sin*.

bânu, builder, creator, in *Ba-ni-a*, *Ba-ni-A-šír*, *^{d}Ab-ba-ni*, *^{d}Adad-ba-ni*, *A-mu-ur-ba-ni*, *^{d}Amurru-ba-ni*, *A-mu-ru-ba-ni*, *A-šír-ba-ni*, *Be-lim-ba-ni*, *El-ba-ni*, *^{d}En-lil-ba-ni*, *^{d}Ilabrat-ba-ni*, *Ili-ba-ni*, *Ištar-ba-ni*, *^{d}LÙ-ba-ni*, *Ni-tî-ba-ni*, *^{d}Sin-ba-ni*, *^{d}Šamaš-ba-ni*.

ba-ni (cf. *ba-ni*, Hittite, *CPN*, p. 165), in *E-šú-ba-ni*.

Ba-ni-ni, cf. *Ba-ni-ni-i*, *TAPN*, p. 52.

bûru, child, in *Bu-ur-A-šur*, *Bu-ur-Ištar*, *Bûr-Nu-nu*, *Bûr-si-lim*, *Bu-ur-Sin*, *Bu-ur-Šamaš*.

Ba-ru-ga, cf. *Barruqu*, *TAPN*, p. 276; בָּרוּךְ, *Bi*.

be-ir-wa (cf. *Bi-ri-a*, etc.), in *Be-ir-wa-aḫ-šú*.

Bar-wa-wa-šá.

Bi-ri-a, *Be-ru-a*, *Bi-ru-a*, *Be-ru-wa*, *Bi-ru-wa*, cf. *Bi-ri-a*, *CPN*, p. 166; *pru-wa*, *SPN*, p. 186; בֵּרִי, *Bi*.

Bu-ur-ki-a, cf. *Bur-qa-a-a*, *TAPN*, p. 66.

Bu-ra-ma, cf. *Bu-ra-me*, *CPN*, p. 167; *purma*, *SPN*, p. 189.

bu-ra (cf. *bûru*), in *Bu-ra-ma-ma*.

Ba-ra-nim.

Ba-ar-si-ba-lá.

Ba-ar-si-ak.

Bi-ra-tî.

bašû, to be, in *Šú-mu-um-li-ib-si*.

Bu-šú-ki-in, see פה; *šú;* כון.

Bu-šá-li, cf. *Bu-šá-lim*.

Bu-šá-lim, see פה; שלם.

Ba-šú-ri-e.

Bu-ta, cf. *Pu-ta*, *HSS* IV, p. 39; *Bu-tu-um*, *RPN*, p. 77; *buta*, *SPN*, p. 63; פוט, *Bi*.

Bu-ut-ki-im.

ba-at-a-na (cf. bata, *SPN*, p. 60) in *Ba-at-a-na-aš-wa*.

ga, pron. suff. 2 sg. m., in *A-šír-uš-ta-na-ad-ga*, *A-zu-e-el-ga*.

Ga-ba-zi, *Ga-áb-zi-a*.

Ga-áb-ri-a.

Ga-ba-tim.

Ga-ga, deity (cf. *Ga-ga*, *CPN*, p. 168, Clay *Traditions*, p. 104, *UMBS* XI(2), p. 149), in *Ga-ga-da-nim*.

Ga-gi-a, cf. *Ga-ki-i*.

Ga-di, cf. גַּדִּי, *Bi*.

Ga-du-du.

Ga-wa-a.

Ga-wa-lá, cf. *Ga-ma-li*, *CPN*, p. 77.

גור, *gîru*, guest (W. Sem., cf. Cooke, N. Sem. Inscr., p. 63; *Kar-ri-ia*, *CPN*, p. 180, *RPN*, p. 115; *gîru*, *TAPN*, p. 277; גֵּבָא, *Bi*.), in *Ga-ri-a*, *Gár-ri-a*.

Ga-zi-a, *Ga-zu-a*.
Ga-za-bi-id.
Ga-za-za.
Ga-ki-i, cf. *Ga-gi-a; Ga-gi-i, Ga-gu*, *TAPN*, p. 79; גוג (?), *Bi*.
Gi-lu-lu, cf. גלל, *TAPN*, p. 277; perhaps to be read *Zi-lu-lu*.
Ga-lu-lu-uš.
Ga-lu-me.
Ga-ni-a, *Ga-nu-a*.
Ga-ni-zi-a.
Ga-ni-si-im, cf. *Ga-ni-zi-a*.
Ga-ru-bu-a.
Ga-ra-wa, cf. *Gár-wa-a; kara-wa*, *SPN*, p. 96.
Gár-wa-a, *Ga-ar-wa-a*, *Ga-ru-wa-a*, cf. *Ga-ri-a*.
Ga-ar-na-lá-dī.
gár-tum (cf. קרד, *TAPN*, p. 304) in *Gár-tum-*[d]*Adad*.
Ga-si-im, cf. *Ka-si-i*, *CPN*, p. 180; *kaza*, *SPN*, p. 100.
Ga-a-tim, *Ga-ta-tim*, cf. *Ga-tì-im*.
Da-a-a, cf. *Da-a-a*, *YBT* IV, p. 25, *TrD*, p. 5, *HPN*, p. 111, *TbD*, p. 13.
du (cf. *Du-Te-šup*, *CPN*, p. 70), in *Du-Šá-lá*.
Du-ú-i-du-ú-i, cf. *Dui*, *ADB*, p. 74.
dubbu (cf. *dubbu*, *TAPN*, p. 278), in *Ba-al-du-bu*.
Di-ba-zi-a.
Dī-bu-lá.
Dagan (written *Da-ga-an*, *Da-gan*), deity, see names under *Da-gan-*, and *I-din-Da-ga-an*, *ŠÚ-Da-ga-an*.
du-ud, in *Du-ud-ḫa-li-a*, *Du-ud-ḫi-tì-šú*.
Du-du-li, perhaps דוד; אל.
דוד, *dâdu*, *dîdu*, *dûdu*, beloved one, in *Da-da*, *Da-da-a*, *Da-da-a-a*, *Da-da-nim*, *Da-tì-a*, *Da-tim*, *Dī-dī-a*, *Dī-dī-na-ri*, *Du-du*, *Du-du-a*, *Du-du-ú*, *Bu-du-du*.
Di-zi-a.
Du-uḫ-lí-iš, cf. *Du-uk-li*, *CTK*, p. 111.
Du-ḫu-si-li.
Da-ak-lí-iš, cf. *Du-uḫ-lí-iš*.
Da-ku-na, cf. *da*, *SPN*, p. 63; *kuna*, *SPN*, p. 123.
Dī-li-a, cf. דלי, *TAPN*, p. 279; *Du-li-ia*, *GTK*, p. 74.
du-lu-bi (cf. *talâmu*, to present, give; *Du-ul-lu-bu*, *CPN*, p. 170; *Dul-lu-bu*, *NBPN*, p. 54), in *A-šur-du-lu-bi*.
Du-ul-du-ma, cf. *duldi*, *CPN*, p. 170.
דלי, *dalû*, to draw out, save, in *Ištar-du-li-zu*.
דלל, *dalâlu*, to submit oneself, worship, in *A-da-làl* (cf. *A-da-la-li*, *CPN*, p. 151).
Da-lá-aš, *Da-lá-šú*.
Di-ma-a.
Du-i-me-im, cf. *Du-ú-i-du-ú-i*.
Du-ma-ḫi-ir, cf. *Ma-ma-ḫi-ir*.
Du-ma-na, cf. *du*, *CPN*, p. 169; *mana*, *TAPN*, p. 294.
דמק, *damâqu*, to be merciful, in *Dam-ga-a*, *Damqu-be-i-A-šír*, [d]*Adad-damiq*, *A-šír-damiq*, *Sin-damiq*, [d]*Šamaš-damiq*.
Da-me-si-e-it, cf. *Da-ma-su*, *TAPN*, p. 68.

Di-am-šú, cf. *τιαμος SPN*, p. 207.
Da-mu-tî, cf. *Da-mu-tum*, *CPN*, p. 170; *Da-am-ma-ti*, *TAPN*, p. 279.
Di-mu-tum, cf. above.
Da-na-dam.
דנן, *dannu*, strong, in *Da-na-a*, *Da-nim*, *Dan-A-šír*, *Dan-na-A-šír*, *Da-na-i-el*, *Da-nim-Ili*, *Da-nu-me-el*, *A-šír-da-ni*, *A-šír-dan*, *Ê-a-dan*, *Ga-ga-da-nim*, *Ga-ga-ta-nim*, *Î-lí-dan*, *Ili-dan-na*, *Ki-ki-da-ni-im.*
Du-nu-um-na.
da-ra (cf. *dara*, *SPN*, p. 64), in *Da-ra-ak-šú.*
Da-ar-ḫa-si-at.
Du-ru-uḫ-na.
Di-ri-ku-da, cf. *ture*, *SPN*, p. 220; *kuda*, *SPN*, p. 118.
Du-ra-am-, see דרא₃ם.
Du-tî-ki.
ובל, *abâlu*, to carry, support, in *A-šur-mu-ta-be-el*, *A-šur-mu-ta-bil*, *Ili-mu-ta-be-el*, *Ili-mu-ta-bi-el.*
Wa-da-ab-ra.
Wa-ad-du-Ili(?), cf. *Ma-ad-du-mu-tim-Ili*, *RPN*, p. 119.
Wa-wa-lá, *Wa-wa-li*, cf. *Wa-lá-wa-lá.*
Wa-wa-an-da.
Wa-za-wa, cf. *waza*, *SPN*, p. 240.
Wa-ak-li, *Wa-ak-lim*, cf. *A-ak-li-a; aklum.*
Wa-kúr-tum, possibly an official.
ולד, *waldu*, offspring(?), in *Wa-al-tî-lim.*
Wa-lá-wa-lá, *Wa-li-wa-li*, cf. *Wa-wa-lá.*
Wa-lá-aḫ-si-na.
Wa-li-si-id.
Wa-li-iš-ra.
וקר, *aqâru*, to be precious, in *A-ḫu-qar*, *A-ḫu-wa-qar.*
Wi-ir (cf. *Mâr*, lord, *TAPN*, p. 257), in *Buzur-Wi-ir.*
ורד, *wardum*, servant, in *Ir-ad-Ku-be*, *Ú-ra-ad-Ku-bi-im*, *Ur-da-A-šur.*
Wa-ri-zi, cf. *Ar-ri-zu*, *A-ri-ṣa-a*, *TAPN*, p. 30.
Wa-aš-ḫu-ru.
Wa-aš-na-ni.
Wa-tî-tum.
Zu, deity, perhaps same as *Sin*(*Zu-in*), in *A-mur-*^{d}*Zu*, *En-na-Zu*, *I-bi-Zu-a*, *Na-ra-am-Zu*, *Nu-ur-Zu*, *Zu-e-a*(?), *Zu-na-da*, *Zu-na-wi-ir*, *Zu-na-nim*(?).
zu, probably sometimes written for *ŠÚ*, cf. *Zu-a-li-a*, *Zu-e-a*(?), *Zu-e-ta-ta*, *Zu-ki-bi-im* (f. of *A-šur-ma-lik*, cf. *ŠÚ-Ku-bi-im*, f. of *A-šur-ma-lik*), *Zu-Ki-ki.*
Zu-a-li-a, cf. *Zu*(*-ú*)*-i-la*, *RPN*, p. 180.
Zu-e-ta-ta, cf. *zu* and *A-ta-ta.*
Za-bu-um, deity (cf. *RPN*, p. 218), in *I-din-Za-bu-um.*
Zu-ba, cf. *Zi-ba-a-a*, *TAPN*, p. 248; צובא, a city, *Bi.*
Za-ba-zi-a, *Za-ba-zu*, cf. זבד, *TAPN*, p. 281.
Zi-ga-a, in *Mâr-Zi-ga-a.*
Zu-ga-li-a, see סגל.

Zu-gu-ri-im.

Za-zi-a, *Za-az*, cf. *Za-si-ja*, *RPN*, p. 179; *Za-zi*, *BE* III(1), p. 89, *TbD*, p. 19; *TAPN*, p. 281; זָזָא, *Bi*; ᵈZa-za, *DmlPan*, p. 130.

Zi-zi-e, cf. *Zi-zi-im; Rab-zi-zi-e*, an official.

Zi-zi-im, cf. *Zi-zi*, *TAPN*, p. 249, *HPN*, p. 156, *HSS* III, p. 35, *DmlWTF*, p. 36; זִיזָא, *Bi*.

Zu-za-a, cf. above.

Zu-zu, *Zu-zu-a*, *Zu-zu-wa*, cf. *Zu-zu*, *TAPN*, p. 281; *Zu-u-zu*, *GTK*, p. 83.

Zu-zu-li.

Za-zu-ni(?).

Za-ḫa, *Za-ḫa-a*, cf. *Ṣi-ḫa-a*, *TAPN*, p. 303.

Zu-ḫu-za-a, cf. *Zu; Ḫu-za-a.*

Za-ḫa-an.

Zi-iḫ-ri-Î-lí, see צחר.

za-ki-im (cf. *za-ku*, *CPN*, p. 172, *TAPN*, p. 282), in *Za-ki-im*, *Za-ki-im-Ili.*

Zu-ku-a, cf. *Su-ka-a*, *TAPN*, p. 299; *Sú-ka*, *HPN*, p. 153.

Zu-ki-bi-im, cf. *zu; Zu-ku-ḫi-im.*

Zi-ku-ḫi-im, *Zu-ku-ḫi-im*, cf. above.

Zi-Ki-ki, *Zu-Ki-ki*, cf. *zu.*

Za-ak-li-a.

zikaru, man, male child, in *Zi-ku-ur-Î-*[*lí*], *Zi-kúr-Î-lí* (cf. *Zi-kir-Î-lí-šu*, *LC*, p. 52).

Za-li-a, cf. *Ṣa-li-a-a*, *TAPN*, p. 303; *zala*, *SPN*, p. 244; *Za-(al-)lum*, *RPN*, p. 178, סַלַּי, *Bi.*

zi-la-, see צלל.

Zi-li-a, cf. *Zi-li-ia*, *TAPN*, p. 248, *CPN*, p. 145; *zila*, *zula*, *SPN*, p. 253.

Zu-li-a, (cf. above), in *Zu-li-a-rabi.*

Zi-lu-lu, *Zu-li-li*, *Zu-lu-la-a*, cf. *ZU; Lu-lu; Zi-lu-lu-um-ga-mil*, *RPN*, p. 180.

Za-li-ti.

Zi-lu-tî-ri-el-ga.

Za-am-ru, cf. זִמְרִי, *Bi.*

zu-ra (cf. *zura*, *TAPN*, p. 282), in *A-be-zu-ra.*

Zu-ur-zu-ur.

Zu-ur-zi.

Zu-ur-zu-ni, perhaps for *Zu-ur-zu-in*, cf. *Zu-ur-zu-ur.*

zu-ta (cf. ᵈ*Zu-da*, *CPN*, p. 172; *Šú-ú-ta*, *TAPN*, p. 310), in *Zu-ta-A-šír.*

Zu-tî-a, cf. סוֹדִי, סוֹטַי, *Bi.*

ḫa-ba, *ḫa-bi-a*, *ḫa-bu* (cf. *Ḫa-ba-ia*, *CPN*, p. 173; *Ḫa-ab-ba*, *TrD*, p. 6; *Ḫab-ba*, *DmlWTF*, p. 37; *Ḫa-ba-a-a*, *UMBS*, XI(2), p. 149; חֲבָיָה, *Bi.*), in *Ḫa-ba*, *Ḫa-bi-a*, perhaps *Ḫa-bu-a-lá*, *Ḫa-bu-a-šú.*

Ḫu-be-da-am, cf. *Ḫu-bi-di*, *TAPN*, p. 89, *CTK*, p. 112.

Ḫi-ba-a-ni-a-im, cf. *Hipe*, Hittite goddess.

Ḫa-bu-ra (cf. *Ḫu-bur; Ḫa-bi-ra, GTK*, p. 75), in *ŠÚ-Ḫa-bu-ra.*
Ḫubur, deity, in *ŠÚ-Ḫu-bu-ur, ŠÚ-Ḫu-bur.*
Ḫa-ba-ta-li.
Ḫa-da-a-ni, Ḫa-da-a, Ḫa-du, Ḫa-du-wa, cf. *Adad, TAPN*, p. 250.
Ḫu-du-ur-lá.
ḫa-zi-a, in *Ba-al-ḫa-zi-a.*
Ḫu-za-a, cf. above.
Ḫa-za-al-bu-na, cf, חזל, gazelle, *TAPN*, p. 283; *buna*, child.
Ḫa-za-am-ri-im, perhaps, חזי, to see; עמר, worshipper.
ḫa-ḫa, (cf. *ḫa-ḫa, CPN*, p. 174; *Ḫa-ḫa, HPN*, p. 122), in *Ḫa-ḫa-lu-wa-an.*
ḫa-li-a, in *Du-ud-ḫa-li-a.*
Ḫa-lá (cf. *ᵈḪali, TAPN*, p. 255), in *Ḫa-lá-be-im.*
Ḫa-lá-da, cf. חֶלֶד, *Bi.*
Ḫa-al-ki-a.
Ḫa-lu-li, cf. *Ḫa-li-li, CPN*, p. 174.
Ḫa-li-ma.
Ḫi-ma-a, cf. *Ḫi-na-a.*
Ḫu-ma-da-šú.
Ḫa-ma-na-ni, cf. *ha-ma-nu, CPN*, p. 174.
Ḫa-ma-ra-a, cf. *Ḫa-mar-ri, CPN*, p. 174.
Ḫa-mu-ri-a, cf. above.
Ḫa-na-a, cf. *Ḫa-nu; Ḫa-ni-ia, CPN*, p. 175; *Ḫa-a-ni, TAPN*, p. 284; *Ḫa-na-a, CTK*, p. 112, *GTK*, p. 75.
hu-ni (cf. *UMBS* XI(2), p. 150), in *Ḫu-ni-a, Ili-ḫu-ni.*
Ḫa-na-zu.
Ḫi-na-ḫa.
חנן, *hinnu*, grace, (cf. חֵן), in *Ḫi-na-a.*
Ḫa-nu, Ḫa-nu-nu, Ḫa-na-nu-um, Ḫa-na-nim, cf. Hanno of Carthage.
Ḫa-na-na-bi-im, cf. *Ḫa-an-na-bu, CPN*, p. 175.
Ḫa-na-na-ri-im, perhaps, חנן; *ᵈNarum* (see *RPN*, p. 203).
חצר, *Ḫu-za-ru-um*, cf. *Ḫu-zi-ru-um, YBT* V, p. 27; *Ḫa-zi-rum, RPN*, p. 87; חֶצְרוֹ, *Bi.*
ḫi-ir, in *Ma-ma-ḫi-ir.*
Ḫa-ar-ḫa-ra-an.
Ḫa-ru-ḫu-ur.
חרץ, *ḫurâṣu*, gold (cf. *Ḫur-za-a-nim, ᶠHu-ra-za-tum, RPN*, p. 87; 187; חָרוּץ, *Bi.*), in *Ḫu-ra-zi, Ḫurazanim* (written *AZAG.GI.ZA.NIM*), *Ḫu-ra-za-nim.*
Ḫa-ar-šú-um.
Ḫu-ru-ta, cf. *Ḫu-ru-ta, TAPN*, p. 285.
Ḫu-šá, cf. *Ḫu-za-a; Ḫuš-a, BE*, III(1), p. 86.
Ḫa-šú-šá-ar-na, Ḫa-šú-šar-na.
ḫi-iš-ta, in *Ḫi-iš-ta-aḫ-šú, Ḫi-iš-ta-aḫ-šú-šar.*
Ḫa-tî, cf. *Ḫa-di-', TAPN*, p. 82.
Ḫa-ta-lá, cf. *Ḫa-ta-lum, RPN*, p. 86.
חתו, *ḫatânu*, to protect (cf. *Ḫa-ti-a-nu, TAPN*, p. 87), in *Ḫa-tî-ni.*

Ḫa-tî-a-ar, cf. *ḫa-tir*, *TAPN*, p. 286.
ḫi-tî-šú, in *Du-ud-ḫi-tî-šú*.
Ḫa-tî-tim.
Ḫu-ta-tim.
טוב, *ṭâbu*, good, see names under *Ṭâb-*, and the fol., *A-al-ta-bu-a*, *A-al-ṭâbu*, *A-šír-ṭâbu*, *ᵈŠamaš-ṭâbu*.
I-a-li-a, cf. *Ia'la*, *TAPN*, p. 91; יַעֲלָא, *Bi*.
I-šá-a, cf. יִשְׁעִי, יְשַׁעְיָה, *Bi*.
ישׁר, *ašâru*, to be right (cf. *Ja-sha-ru-um*, *RPN*, p. 114; יֵשֶׁר, *Bi*.), in *Iš-a-ra*, *I-šar-be-li*.
I-šar-ḫa-ri-im.
i-šar-ki-id, in *I-šar-ki-id-A-šur*.
Kubum, deity (cf. *Ku-ba-a*, *Ku-bi-a*, *CTK*, p. 114), in *Ku-bi-a*, *Ku-bi-din*, *I-din-Ku-bu-um*, *Ir-ad-Ku-be*, *Rabû-Ku-be-im*, *ŠÚ-Ku-be-im*, *Ta-ra-am-Ku-be*, *Ú-ra-ad-Ku-bi-im*.
Ku-bu-lim, perhaps *Kubum; Ilum*, cf. *Ku-bu-Ilu*, *CPN*, p. 100.
Ki-ib-si-im.
Ki-ga-ar-šá-an.
Ku-du.
Ki-da-ar, cf. קֵדָר, *Bi*.
Ku-da-ri-li, perhaps *Kudar; Ili*, cf. above; *Ku-du-ra-nu*, *CPN*, p. 178.
Ku-da-tum, cf. *kuda*, *SPN*, p. 118.
כון, *kânu*, to be firm, stand fast, in *I-ku-nu-um*, *I-ku-nim* (abbr.), *I-ku(n)-ba-šá*, *I-ku(n)-be-a*, *I-ku(n)-bi-a*, *I-ku(n)-bi-A-šír*, *I-ku(n)-bi-Ištar*.
kênu, true, in *Bu-šú-ki-in*, *Šar-rum-kênu*.
Ku-zi-a, *Ku-zi-im*, *Ku-za-am*, *Ku-zu*, cf. *Ku-za-a*, *TAPN*, p. 119; *Ku-uš-šú*, *CPN*, p. 102; *Qîsu*, *TAPN*, p. 184; קִישׁ, *Bi; kuza*, *SPN*, p. 129.
Ku-za-zu-um.
Ku-zi-zi-a.
Ki-iz-ḫa-nu-el.
Ku-za-ri, cf. *Ku-uz-za-ri*, *CTK*, p. 114.
Ku-za-tî-a.
כִּי, *kî*, like, in *A-šur-kî-na-ra-am*, *Ma-nu-um-kî-a-bi-a*, *Ma-nu-um-kî-A-šur*, *Ma-nu-kî-E-lí*, *Ma-nim-ki-i-e-li-a*, *Ma-nu-um-kî-Ištar*, *Ma-nu-kî-šú*, *Nu-ur-kî-Ì-lí*, *Nu-ur-kî-li*.
Kiki, deity (cf. *ᵈKu-ku*, *HPN*, p. 175; *Ki-ik-ki-a*, *GTK*, p. 77), in *Ki-ki-i*, *Ki-ki-da-ni-im*, *Zu-Ki-ki*(?).
Ku-ku-a, *Ku-ku-um*, cf. above.
Ku-ku-zi.
Ki-ak-lá-nu.
Ku-ku-lá-nim, (possibly to be read, *Mŭ-mŭ-lá-nim*, cf. A-šír-i-din, 5, 6 in Name List) cf. *ᵈKu-ku*, *HPN*, p. 175; *Kakkulanu*, *TAPN*, p. 289.
Ku-uk-ra-an cf. above.
Ki-kar-šá-an.
Ki-li, *Ki-li-a*.
Ku-la, *Ku-li-a*, cf. above; *kula*, *SPN*, p. 121.

Ku-ul-ku-lam, cf. *Ku-ul-ku-ul*, *CPN*, p. 179.
Ku-lu-uk-lu.
Ku-lá-ku-lá-rabi.
כלל, *kalâlu*, to be complete, in *El-ku-li.*
Ku-li-lim, cf. *Ku-li-lum*, *RPN*, p. 117.
כלם, *kalâmu*, to let see, reveal, in *A-šír-kal-la-ma.*
Ku-lu-ma-a, cf. *ku-lu-um*, *RPN*, p. 117.
Ki-lá-ri-tam.
Ku-um-ri-im, cf. *kumu-re*, *SPN*, p. 122.
ka-mu-šú (cf. *kamâšu*, to prostrate oneself), in *A-šír-ka-mu-šú.*
ki-na, in *Ki-na-aḫ-šú.*
Ku-na-ni-a, cf. *Ku-na-a-nu-um*, *YBT* V, p. 31.
Ku-ra, cf. *kura*, *SPN*, p. 124.
Ki-ri-im, cf. *Ku-ri-i*, *YBT* VI, p. 25.
כרב, *karâbu*, to incline towards, be gracious, see names under, *Kúr-ub-*, *Ku-ru-ub-*, and *Ili-kúr-ub*, *Mâr-Kúr-ub-Ištar.*
ku-ur-ku-ra, cf. *Ku-ra*; *dKur-kur*, *CPN*, p. 181.
Ku-ra-ra.
כשׂד, *kašâdu*, to conquer, (cf. *qaštu*, holy; *ka-ši-it*, *CPN*, p. 181), in *A-šur-ga-si-id*, *El-ga-si-id.*
Ku-uš-ku-zi-im, cf. *Kuš*, *TAPN*, p. 291; *kuza*, *SPN*, p. 129.
Ku-ta-a-a, cf. *Kud-da-ai*, *CPN*, p. 177; *Ku-ud-da-a*, *NBPN*, p. 91.

dLÙ, deity in *dLÙ-ba-ni.*
לבב, *libbu*, heart, in *Li-bi-Ištar* (cf. *Li-bi-it; Li-ib-bi-Ištar*, *RPN*, p. 117), *Šá-li-ba-a*, *Šú-ma-li-be-dAdad*, *Šú-ma-li-ba-A-šur*, *Šú-ma-li-be-A-šur*, *Šú-ma-li-be-I-li-a.*
lá-ba, Sem.(?) (cf. *la-ba*, *CPN*, p. 181; *Lab-bu*, *DmlPan*, p. 160), in *Ištar-lá-ba.*
La-bi-a, cf. *La-ba-'-u*, *TAPN*, p. 292.
Li-ba-a, my heart(?).
Laban, deity, in *ŠÚ-Lá-ba-an.*
Lá-bi-tì-im, cf. *fLa-bi-'-tum*, *CPN*, p. 182.
dLugal-Marda, in *UR-dLugal-Marda.*
lu-an, *lu-wa-an*, in *Ḫa-ḫa-lu-an*, *Ḫa-ḫa-lu-wa-an.*
Lu-zi-a.
Lu-zi-na, cf. *Lu-zi-na*, *UDT*, p. 93.
lá-ḫa-a (cf. *UMBS* XI(2), p. 151), in *Am-lá-ḫa-a.*
Lu-ḫa-du-ma-an, cf. *Ḫa-du-wa; ma-an.*
lá-aḫ-ra (cf. *La-ḫi-ra-a-a*, *TAPN*, p. 120), in *Lá-aḫ-ra-aḫ-šú.*
lu-ki, in *Ili-lu-ki.*
Lá-ki-ib, *Lá-ki-bu-um*, cf. *Laqipu*, *TAPN*, p. 120.
Lá-li-a, cf. *La-lim; la-lum*, *CPN*, p. 182, *RPN*, p. 117, *UMBS* XI(2), p. 151; *La-la-a*, *HSS* IV, p. 32, *HPN*, p. 128.
La-li-im, *La-lu-um*, cf. above.
Lu-lu, *Lu-lu-a*, *Lu-li-im*, cf.

Lu-li, *TAPN*, p. 122; *Lu-lu*, fullness, *CPN*, p. 182.

Li-lu-si-im, cf. *lila*, *TAPN*, p. 292.

Li-mur-šú-ma-an, cf. *ma-an*.

lamassu, protecting deity, in *Lá-ma-zi*, *La-ma-za-tum*, *A-šur-lá-ma-zi*, *A-šur-be-el-lá-ma-zi*, *Ištar-lá-ma-zi*.

Lá-ma-šá, cf. *Lá-ma-zi*; *La-ma-ša*, *HSS* IV, p. 32, *RPN*, p. 117.

lá-na-zi, scribal error for *lá-ma-zi*, in *A-šír-lá-na-zi*.

לפת, *liptu*, work, in *Li-ib-ta-nim*, *Li-ib-tî-Ištar*, *Li-bi-it-Ištar*.

lu-ar-ra, in *Lu-ar-ra-aḫ-šú*, *Lu-ar-ra-aḫ-šú-rabi*.

Lá-ta-ra-ak.

ma'du, fullness, abundance (cf. Heb. מְאֹד, force, might; imittu), in *El-me-tî*, *I-li-me-a-ta*.

Ma-ga-ni-ga.

Ma-da-wa-da, perhaps reduplication of element *ma-da*.

me-da-ku (cf. *wa-da-ku*), in *El-me-da-ku*.

Ma-za-a, cf. *Ma-zi*, *Ma-zu-im*; *Ma-za*, *CPN*, p. 183.

Ma-zu, *Ma-zu-im*, cf. *Ma-za-a*; *Ma-zu*, *HPN*, p. 136.

Mu-za, *Mu-zi-e*, cf. *Mu-zu*, *HSS* IV, p. 37, *HPN*, p. 138; *musa*, *SPN*, p. 158.

Ma-ḫa-i-a.

ma-ḫi-ra (cf. ^{d}*Ma.Ḫir*, *TAPN*, p. 257), in *Ma-ḫi-ra-aḫ-šú*.

Ma-ḫu-si.

Ma-ku-a, cf. *Ma-gu*, *HPN*, p. 135.

Ma-lá-a-a, cf. *mala*, *SPN*, p. 139.

Ma-lá-ba.

מלך, *malâku*, to reign, in *Ma-lik-Ili-šú*, ^{d}*Adad-ma-lik*, *A-šur-ma-lik*, *Ili-ma-lik*, *Mâr-A-šur-ma-lik*.

milku, counsel, in *A-šur-be-el-ma-al-ki-im*, *Da-gan-ma-al-ki-im*, *Ili-ma-lá-ak*.

Ma-lu-ku-lá-nim, cf. *Ku-ku-lá-nim*.

Ma-lá-aš.

Mama, deity (cf. ^{d}*Ma-ma*, *CPN*, p. 183; *Ma-a-ma*, *TbD*, p. 16; *Ma-ma*, *YBT* IV, p. 32), in *Ma-ma*, *Ma-ma-ḫi-ir*(?), *Bu-ra-Ma-ma*, *ŠÚ-Ma-ma*.

Me-me (cf. above), in *Me-me-ib-ri*.

Mu-mu-lá-nim, cf. *Mummu*, deity; cf. *Ku-ku-lá-nim*.

ma-an, cf. *A-ga-li-ú-ma-an*, *Ar-nu-ma-an*, *Li-mur-šú-ma-an*, *Lu-ḫa-du-ma-an*, *Si-im-nu-ma-an*, *Si-ta-ra-ma-an*, *Šá-ak-ri-ú-ma-an*, *Šú-be-ú-ma-an*.

Ma-ni-a, *Ma-nu-a*, cf. *Ma-nu-a*, *LgrTemps*, p. 102; *Ma-an-ni-ia*, *LC*, p. 34.

Ma-na-ma-na.

ma-nim, *ma-nu-um*, who, in *Ma-nu-ba-lu-um-A-na*, *Ma-nu-um-ba-lim-A-šur*, *Ma-nu-ki-a*, *Ma-nu-um-kî-a-bi-a*, *Ma-nu-um-kî-A-šur*, *Ma-nu-kî-E-lí*,

Ma-nim-ki-i-e-li-a, *Ma-nu-um-kî-Ištar*, *Ma-nu-kî-šú*, *Ma-nu-um-šú-um-šú*, *Ma-nu-šá-ni-šá*.

Ma-na-ki-li-a-ad.

Mu-ni-ki-im, cf. *Mu-ni-gim-dug*, *HPN*, p. 137.

Ma-na-na, cf. *Ma-na-ma-na*.

Me-na-nim.

maṣû, Perm., it is enough (cf. *maṣi*, *CPN*, p. 184), in *Ma-zi-Ì-lí*.

mâr, son, see names under *Mâr-*.

Me-ir, cf. above; *me-ḫir*, *TAPN*, p. 293; *Me-ra*, *HPN*, p. 137; מְחִיר, *Bi*.

Mur-šá-lim, perhaps scribal error for *Aḫ-šá-lim*.

me-šú (cf. Clay, *Empire*, p. 179, *CPN*, p. 185), in *Me-šú-rabi*.

Maš-ba-ni, scribal error for *Ili-ba-ni*.

me-šar, (cf. *me-šú*), in *Me-šar-rabi*.

מת, *mutu*, man (cf. מְתוּשָׁאֵל, *Bi*.), in *Mu-tî-Ili* (possibly to be read *Idin-Ili*).

Ma-ta-du-ú(?).

ma-tim (cf. *mat-ti*, *CPN*, p. 185), in *Ak-ta-ma-tim*.

נאד, *na'âdu*, to exalt, in *A-šír-na-da*, *Be-lim-na-da*, *Ili-na-da*, *Ištar-na-da*, *Sin-na-da*, *Zu-na-da*.

na'âdu III$_2$, in *A-šír-uš-ta-na-ad-ga*.

נאר$_2$, *nûru*, light, see names under *Nu-ur-*, and *Dī-dī-na-ri*.

Nu-a-e, *Nu-a-im*, cf. *Nu-ḫa-a*, *LC*, p. 38; *Nu-u-a-a*, *TAPN*, p. 176.

Na-ú-šá.

ni-ga (cf. *Ni-ga*, *UDT*, p. 95), in *Šú-be-a-ni-ga*.

Ni-ga-an, cf. above.

Nigin-gar, deity, in *Ur-Nigin-gar*.

Ni-bu-um, offspring, cf. *Ni-bu-um*, *YBT* V, p. 33.

נבא, *nabû*, to call, in *I-bi-Sin*, *I-bi-zu-a*.

na-ab (cf. נוב, to increase; *Na-bi-ili-shu*, *RPN*, p. 126), in *Na-be-li-šú*, *Na-áb-Sin*.

Na-ab-ra-ga.

Ni-bi-si-im, cf. *Na-áb-si-im*.

Na-áb-si-im, cf. *Nap-še*, *CPN*, p. 189; *napšu*, abundance; *Na-áb-Sin*.

נדן, *nadânu*, to give, see names under *E-dī-na-a* (cf. *Iddinaia*, *TAPN*, p. 94), *E-din-*, *E-dī-in-*, *I-din-*, *I-dī-in* (see Intro., p. 3), and the fol., *A-šur-i-din*, *A-šur-i-dī-in*, *Ku-bi-din*.

ni-wa, *nu-wa*, (cf. *Ni-ma-aḫ-šú*), in *Ni-wa-aḫ-šú-šar*, *Nu-wa-nu-wa*.

ni-wa-ri (cf. *nîru*, light), in *A-šur-ni-wa-ri*.

Ni-wa-šú, cf. *Ni-ma*.

Na-zi, cf. *na-zi*, *CPN*, p. 186; *nezi*, *SPN*, p. 168.

נזז, *nazâzu*, to stand, in *I-zi-za-am-Ili*.

נחם, (Heb.), to sigh, suffer (cf.

Na-ḫi-mi, RPN, p. 127; נחום, *Bi.*), in *Na-ḫu-ma*.

Na-ki-li-it.

Na-ki-iš-du-ar.

נמר, *namâru*, to be bright, light, in *Sin-na-wi-ir, Zu-na-wi-ir.*

ni-ma (cf. *Ni-ma-Ištar*), in *Ni-ma-aḫ-šú.*

ni-ma, ni-mar, in *Ni-ma-A-šur, Ni-ma-Ištar, Ni-mar-Ištar.*

nimri, panther, in *A-šur-ni-im-ri.*

Nana, deity, in *Na-na, Na-na-a, Na-na-a-a, Na-ni-a, Na-na-nim.*

Na-ni-ib, Na-ni-be-im.

Nunu, deity, in *Nu-nu, Nu-ú-nu, Bûr-Nu-nu* (cf. *Bûr-*^{d}*Nu-nu, YBT* V, p. 25), *ŠÚ-Nu-nu.*

נפח, *napâhu*, to rise, in *Na-ba-ḫi-e, Na-ba-ḫi-ma, Na-ba-ḫi-im*(?).

נצר, *naṣâru*, to protect, see names under *Ú-zur-*, and *Î-lí-uz-ra-ni, A-be-na-zi-ir.*

Na-ar-be-tim, cf. *Na-ar-bat-tum, TAPN*, p. 298.

Ni-ra-aḫ, deity, perhaps *NIN. IB;* cf. *MVAG* 1903, p. 239, *Nin-rag* equals *NIN. IB; ra-aḫ* in Capp. equals *rag*, cf. *Šál-me-ḫi-im, Šál-me-gim*), in *Ni-ra-aḫ-zu-lu-li, Buzur-Ni-ra-aḫ.*

ni-si-im (cf. *ni-šú*), in *A-šur-ni-si-im.*

našû, to lift up (cf. *Na-zi; Na-ši-ma, TAPN*, p. 298), in *Na-šú-a.*

Na-aš, scribal error for *A-na-aš.*

ni-šú, (perhaps to be read *lí-šú*, precative from *našû*, to lift up), in *A-šur-ni-šú.*

Ni-tî, deity(?) (cf. ^{d}*Nin-de, DmlPan*, p. 205; *Ni-ti-e, HSS* III, p. 26), in *Ni-tî, Ni-tî-ba-ni.*

si (cf. *si, CPN*, p. 189), in *A-ga-áb-si.*

Si-a-im, cf. *Si-ia-a, CPN*, p. 123.

si-e-ni, non-Sem. (cf. *Si-e-ni, TAPN*, p. 194; *Ar-ta-še-en-ni, Bu-ḫi-še-en-ni, I-ri-še-en-ni, Še-lu-ub-še-en-ni, CTK*, pp 110, 111, 113, 116), in *Áb-si-e-ni.*

Si-a-at.

סגל, *sukallu*, messenger (cf. *Su-ga-lí-a, TAPN*, p. 298; *Zu-ga-li-ia, HPN*, p. 156; *Zu-ka-lí-ja, RPN*, p. 180), in *Zu-ga-li-a, Zu-ga-lim.*

Si-wa-aš-me-i.

Si-li-a-ra, cf. *si-li, CPN*, p. 190; *a-ra, CPN*, p. 160.

סלם, *silmu*, grace, in *Bûr-si-lim.*

si-ma (perhaps for *si-ma-at*), in *Si-ma-Sin.*

Si-im-nu-ma-an, cf. *ma-an.*

simtu, ornament (cf. *zimat-matim, RPN*, p. 252), in *Si-ma-at-A-šír, Si-me-tî-Ili.*

Sin (written *Zu-in, Zu-en,* ^{d}*EN.ZU*), see names under *Sin-*, and the fol.,

Be-lá-aḫ-Sin, Bu-ur-Sin, Buzur-Sin, E-ni-Sin, En-na-Sin, I-bi-Sin, ᵈI-bi-ᵈSin, I-ni-Sin, I-din-Sin, I-din-ᵈSin, I-na-Sin, I-si-im-Sin, Iš-me-Sin, Na-áb-Sin, Si-ma-Sin, Šá-ra-Sin, Šarrum-Sin, Šarrum-ᵈSin, ŠÚ-Sin.

Si-nu-nu-tim.

סרק, *sarâqu*, to offer a libation (cf. *I-za-rí-ik*, *YBT* IV, p. 27, *UMBS* XI(2), p. 151; *I-zu-a-rí-ik*, *TbD*, p. 15), in *I-zu-ri-ik.*

si-šá, in *Si-šá-aḫ-šú-šar.*

sa-tu, (for *šadû*, mountain, cf. *šá-tu*), in *A-šír-sa-tu-e, Buzur-sa-tu-e, Ī-lí-sa-tu.*

Si-ta-ra-ma-an, cf. *ma-an.*

פה, *pû*, mouth, in *Bu-du-du, Bu-šá-lim, Bu-šú-ki-in, Damqu-be-i-A-šír, I-ku-ba-šá* (vowel attracted to *a* by following syllable), *I-ku-bi-a, I-ku-bi-A-šír, I-ku-bi-Ištar.*

פזר, *puzru*, security, concealment (written *BĀ.ŠÁ* and *MAN;* see Intro., p. 2), see names under *Buzur-*.

פלח, *palâḫu*, to fear, worship, in *Be-lá-ḫa-a, Be-lá-ḫa-nim, Bi-lá-aḫ-A-šír, Bi-lá-aḫ-Ištar, Be-lá-aḫ-Sin, ᵈAdad-be-lá-aḫ, Ili-be-lá-aḫ, Ištar-bi-lá-aḫ, Sin-bi-lá-aḫ.*

צחר, *ṣiḫru*, little one, in *Za-aḫ-ri-li, Zi-iḫ-ri-Ī-lí.*

צלל, *ṣillu*, shade, protection, in *Zi-lá-ᵈAdad, Zilli-Ištar, Ṭâb-zi-lá-A-šír.*

ṣulûlu, shade, protection, in *ᵈAdad-zu-lu-li, A-šur-zu-lu-li, Ni-ra-aḫ-zu-lu-li.*

קבא, *qabû*, to speak, call, in *ᵈAdad-iqbi, A-šír-iqbi.*

קיש, *qîštu*, present, in *Ištar-ki-iz-tim.*

qašdu, holy, perhaps in *A-šír-ga-si-id, El-ga-si-id*, but see כשד.

Ri-a-a, Eg.(?).

ri-a-ri, in *ᵈAdad-ri-a-ri.*

Ri-en-šá.

ר׳אם, *ra'mu*, to love, in *A-šur-du-ra-am, Du-ra-am-Ī-lí, Du-ra-me-el, Ta-ra-am-Ku-be, Ta-ra-am-šá-Ili.*

narâmu, darling, in *Na-ra-am-Zu, A-šur-kî-na-ra-am.*

Ri-ḫa-am.

ר׳אה, *rê'ûm*, shepherd, in *ᵈAdad-rê'ûm, A-šur-rê'ûm, Ili-rê'ûm, Sin-rê'ûm, ᵈŠamaš-rê'ûm.*

רבה, *rabû*, great (written *GAL, GAL.BA*), in *Rabû-A-šur, Rabû-Ku-be-im, ᵈAdad-rabi, A-šur-rabi, Ili-rabi, Ili-šú-rabi, Mâr-Rabû-Šá-li-a, Me-šar-rabi, Me-šú-rabi, Zu-li-a-rabi.*

ra-be-tim, in *ᵈAdad-ra-be-tim.*

רוצ, *rîṣu*, help, in *A-šur-ri-zi, A-šur-ri-zu-um.*

Ra-wa, deity(?) (cf. *ᵈRa, HPN*, p. 180, *UDT*, p. 100), in *I-na-Ra-wa.*

ריח, *rîḫtu*, rest (cf. *Ri-ḫa-te, TAPN*, p. 187; *Ri-ḫe-tum, NBPN,*

p. 174; *Ri-ḫat-^{d}Anu*, *BIN* II, p. 72), in *Ri-ḫa-ti-e*.

רמה, *ramû*, to loosen (cf. יִרְמְיָהוּ, *Bi.*), in *Ir-ma-A-šír*.

šá, *šá-at*, genitive particle, in *Šá-li-ba-a*, *Šá-at-A-šur*, *Šá-at-Ì-lí*, *Ta-ra-am-šá-Ili*, *Ú-zur-šá-A-šur*, *Ú-zur-šá-Ištar*, *Ú-zur-si-Ištar*.

šá, for *Šamaš*(?) (cf. *RPN*, p. 19 note 3), in *I-ku-ba-šá* (cf. *I-ku-bi-šá*, *RPN*, p. 98), *Ma-nu-šá-ni-šá*.

ŠÚ, probably genitive particle or *Gimil* (cf. *RPN*, p. 245 note 9), see names under *ŠÚ-*.

šú, pron. suff. 3 sg. masc., in *A-aḫ-šú* (cf. *YBT* V, p. 22), *Bu-šú-ki-in*, *I-lá-ni-šú*, *Ili-šú-rabi*, *Ištar-du-li-zu*, *Ištar-Ili-šú*, *Ma-lik-Ili-šú*, *Ma-nu-kî-šú*, *Ma-nu-um-šú-um-šú*, *Na-be-li-šú*.

šú-be-a, non-Sem., in *Šú-be-a-aḫ-šú-šar*, *Šú-be-a-aḫ-šú*, *Šú-be-a-ni-ga*, *Šú-be-ú-ma-an*.

Šá-bu-lí, cf. *Ša-bu-lu*, *TAPN*, p. 207.

Šú-bu-ul-tum, cf. *Shu-bu-ul-tum*, *RPN*, p. 194, *TAPN*, p. 307.

Šú-bu-nu-aḫ-šú, cf. *aḫ-šú*.

Šá-áb-ta, cf. *Šab-da*, *HPN*, p. 150; *Sa-ab-tum*, *RPN*, p. 140.

ŠÚ.GAN, deity (cf. *EL.ŠÚ.GAL*; *šukânu*, possession), in *Ì-lí-ŠÚ.GAN*.

Šú-ga-tim, cf. *Šú-ki-tim*; *Shu-ḫa-tum*, *RPN*, p. 194.

šadû, mountain, (cf. *šá-tu*, *sa-tu-e*), in *A-šír-šá-du-ni*.

šú-da-a (cf. *^{d}Šu-ud-da*, *CPN*, p. 207), in *Šú-da-a*, *I-li-šú-da-a*.

šú-du, (cf. above), in *Ì-lí-šú-du*.

Šá-du-uḫ-bel-a.

Šú-wa-ak-ru.

Šá-za-ga-ri-a.

Šá-zu-ḫa-ku.

Šú-zu-zu, cf. *zuza*, *SPN*, p. 254; perhaps *ŠÚ-Zu-zu*, cf. *^{d}Za-zu*, *TAPN*, p. 262.

Šá-aḫ-ga.

Šú-ḫu-ur, cf. *Šu-ḫu-ur-ni*, *Šu-ḫur*, *CPN*, p. 198; שְׁחַרְיָה, *Bi.*

šú-ḫa-ir (cf. above), in *Šú-ḫa-ir-^{d}Adad*.

Šú-ḫu-ur-be-a, cf. *Šú-ḫu-ur*.

Šá-ḫi-iš-ga-an, cf. *Ša-aḫ-si-ḫa-si-ḫa*, *CPN*, p. 198.

Šá-ki-zu.

šá-ak-ri, in *Šá-ak-ri-aš-wa*, *Šá-ak-ri-el-bi*, *Šá-ak-ri-ú-ma-an*.

Šá-ki-iš-ki-nim.

Šú-ki-tum, *Šú-ku-tum*, cf. *Šú-ga-tim*.

Šá-lá, deity, in *Du-Šá-lá*, *Rabû-Šá-li-a*.

Šú-li, *Šú-li-i*, *Šú-li-a*, cf. *zula*, *SPN*, p. 253; perhaps to be read *ŠÚ-I-li*.

Šá-li-ba-a, see *šá*; לבב; cf. *Še-li-bu*, *CPN*, p. 199.

Šá-li-a-ta, Šá-lu-wa-an-ta, Šá-lu-wa-ta.

שלם, *šalâmu*, to be safe, see names under *Šá-lim-, Šál-ma-, Šál-me-, Šá-al-ma-*, and the fol., *Áb-šá-lim, A-bu-šá-lim, Aḫ-šá-lim, Bu-šá-lim.*

šulmu, peace, in *Šú-ul-mu-um.*

שם, *šumu*, name, descendant (cf. *Šú-ma-a, NBPN*, p. 206), in *Šú-ma, Šú-ma-a, Šú-ma-bi-a, Šú-me-a-bi-a, Šum-ma-ḫu-um, Šú-ma-li-be-*^{d}*Adad, Šú-ma-li-ba-A-šur, Šú-ma-li-be-I-li-a, Šú-mu-um-li-ib-si, Ma-nu-um-šú-um-šú.*

שמא, *šemû*, to hear, in *I-si-im-Sin, Iš-ma-*^{d}*Adad, Iš-ma-A-šír, Is-me-Ištar, Iš-me-Sin.*

שמש, *šamšu*, sun, in *A-šír-šá-am-si, A-šír-šamši(-ši), A-šír-*^{d}*šamši(-ši).*

Šamaš, deity (written ^{d}*UD, UD*), see names under ^{d}*Šamaš-*, and the fol., *A-aḫ-*^{d}*Šamaš, A-mur-*^{d}*Šamaš, Bu-ur-Šamaš, Buzur-*^{d}*Šamaš, I-din-*^{d}*Šamaš.*

šú-in(?), (cf. *Sin*), in *I-dūr-Šú-in.*

šú-nu, pron suff. 3 plu., in *A-a-aḫ-šú-nu* (cf. *YBT* V, p. 22).

Šú-na-bar.

שנן, *šanânu*, to be like, in *Ma-nu-šá-ni-šá.*

שקל, *šaqâlu* I_2, in *A-šur-iš-ta-ki-el, A-šur-iš-ta-gal, A-šur-iš-tî-gal, Ī-lí-iš-ta-gal, Ī-lí-iš-ta-ki-el, Ī-lí-iš-tî-gal, Ī-lí-eš-tî-gal.*

šar (cf. *Šar, CPN*, p. 201), in *Ba-al-du-šar, Ḫi-iš-ta-aḫ-šú-šar, Ni-wa-aḫ-šú-šar, Si-šá-aḫ-šú-šar, Šú-be-a-aḫ-šú-šar.*

Ša-ra, deity, in *Šá-ra-Sin, En-nam-Šá-ra.*

Šú-ra, cf. *Ku-ra; sura, SPN*, p. 197.

Šá-ra-bu-nu-wa, perhaps *Šá-ra, CPN*, p. 201; *bu-nu-wa.*

Šá-ra-wa, cf. *sara-wa, SPN*, p. 190; *Šá-ra, Šá-ra-ma.*

šá-ra-za-na, deity(?), in *A-mur-šá-ra-za-na, Šá-ra-za-ma.*

Šá-ra-ma, cf. *Šá-ra-wa;* zerma, *SPN*, p. 249.

Šá-ar-ni-ga, Šá-ar-ni-ga-ar.

שרר, *šarrum*, king, see names under *Šarrum-*, and the fol., *E-a-šar, I-a-šar, I-a-šá-ri-im.*

šarratum, queen, in *Šá-ra-at-Ištar.*

Šá-šá-ma-a, cf. *Ša-aš-ma-a, TAPN*, p. 219; סַסְמַי, *Bi.*

Šá-tî-a, cf. *šá, šá-at; Ša-ti-ia, CPN*, p. 131.

šá-tu-e, (cf. *šadû, sa-tu*), in *Buzur-šá-tu-e.*

tappu, companion, in ^{d}*Šamaš-tab-ba-i.*

תור, *târu*, to return, be merciful, in *A-šur-du-ri, I-dūr-Ili, I-dūr-Šú-in.*

taiaru, compassion, in *A-šír-ta-a-a-ar*.

Ta-ki-e, cf. *ta-gu*, *ta-gi*, *CPN*, p. 203.

תכל, *takâlu*, to trust, in *ᵈAdad-ta-ak-lá-ku*, *A-šur-ta-ak-lá-ak-ku*, *A-šur-ta-ak-lá-ku*, *A-šur-ták-lá-ku*, *ᵈŠamaš-ta-ak-lá-ku*, *ᵈAdad-ta-ku-ul*, *Ta-ki-el-A-šur*.

tukultu, strength, assistance, in *A-šír-du-kúl-tì*, *A-šur-du-ku-ul-tì*, *Î-lí-du-kúl-tì*.

Ta-li-a, cf. *ta-al-li*, *CPN*, p. 204; Syriac *talitha*, maiden, *talya*, youth.

Ta-mu-ri-a.

Ta-ar-ḫu-nu, cf. *Tar-ḫu-un-da-ra-ba*, *CPN*, p. 137.

Ta-ra-ku, for *Ta-ra-am-Ku-be*.

Ta-ar-ma-na, *Tár-ma-na*.

Ta-ri-iš-ma-tum, perhaps ראש to rejoice, *ta-ri-iš*, and *ma-tum*, land, cf. *Da-ri-iš-ma-tum*, *TrD*, p. 5, *LC*, p. 49.

Ta-ta-a, cf. *Da-da*; *ta-at-ta* *CPN*, p. 205.

Tì-ta-a, cf. *Dī-dī-a*; *Teti*, *Ti-ti-i*, *TAPN*, p. 312.

Ta-ta-li-i.

LIST OF *LÎMU* EPONYMS

Like the Assyrians the Cappadocians designated their years by the names of *lîmu* officials. No Cappadocian lists of these officials have been found so that their sequence can not be determined. The following is a list of those mentioned incidentally in the dates of the business documents.

^{d}Adad-ba-ni, s. of *I-din-A-šir*.
^{d}Adad-ba-ni.
A-ḫu-wa-qar.
A-ku-tum.
A-lá-ḫu-um.
A-al-ṭâbu.
A-šur-damiq.
A-šur-i-din.
A-šur-i-me-tí.
A-šur-ma-lik.
A-šur-na-da.
A-šur-ṭâbu.
Buzur-Ni-ra-aḫ.
Bu-zu-ta-a.
Bu-zu-zu.
Di-ma-a.
En-na-Sin, s. of *Aḫ-me*.
En-na-Sin, s. of *ŠÚ-A-šur*.
En-na-Sin, s. of *ŠÚ-Ištar*.
Ib-ni-^{d}Adad.
I-din-a-bu-um, s. of *Na-ar-be-tim*.
I-din-a-bu-um.
I-din-a-ḫu-um.
I-din-A-šur, s. of *Ku-bi-din*.
I-du-a.
Ì-lí-dan.
Ili-rabi.
Ili-šú-rabi.
I-na-a.
I-na-Sin.
Iš-ma-A-šír, s. of *Ê-a-dan*.
Li-ib-ta-nim.
Lu-lu.
Ma-zi-Ì-lí.
Šál-ma-A-šur, s. of *Ku-ku-zi-a*.
Šú-da-a, s. of *En-na-nim*.
Šú-da-a.
ŠÚ-Ištar.
Sú-ra-ma.
ŠÚ-Sin, s. of *Ba-ba-lim*.
Ṭâb-ba-A-šur.

LIST OF *ḪAMUŠTUM* EPONYMS

Besides reckoning the years by the *lîmu* officials, the Cappadocians also designated a certain shorter period of time as the *ḫamuštum* of a particular individual. The officials named in this capacity are as follows:

A-ba-ba-a-a.
A-bu-um-Ili.
A-ku-za.
A-lá-ḫu-um.
A-mur-Ištar.
ᵈAmurru-ki....
A-mur-ᵈŠamaš.
A-šur-be-el-a-wa-tim.
A-šur-i-me-tî.
A-šur-iš-tî-gal.
A-šur-ma-lik, s. of *Lu-zi-na.*
A-šur-ma-lik, s. of *Zu-ga-li-a.*
A-šur-ma-lik.
A-šur-na-da.
A-šur-rabi.
A-šír-rê'ûm.
A-šur-ták-lá-ku, s. of *A-lá-ḫi-im.*
A-šur-ták-lá-ku.
A-šur-ṭâbu.
A-šur-zu-lu-li.
Bi-lá-aḫ-A-šur, s. of *Ga-di.*
Bu-ut-ki-im.
Bu-za-zu.
Buzur-sa-du-e.
Bu-zu-ta-a.
E-lá-ni.
El-ba-ni.
E-me-me.
En-na-ma-nim.
En-um-A-šír, s. of *Sin-na-da.*
En-na-Sin.
Ga-áb-ri-a.
Gár-wa-a.
Ga-si-im.
Ga-zi-a.
Ḫa-na-nim.
Ḫu-ra-za-nu-um.
I-din-a-be-im.
I-din-A-šur.
I-din-Ku-bi-im.
I-din-Sin.
I-dūr-Ili.
Î-lí-a-lim.
Î-lí-iš-tî-gal.
Im-tî-lim.
I-na-a, s. of *A-mu-ra-a.*
I-na-a.
Kúr-ub-Ištar, s. of *A-lá-ḫi-im.*
Kúr-ub-Ištar.
Lá-ki-ib.
Li-lu-si-im.
Lu-zi-na.
Ma-nu-ba-lim-A-šur.
Na-ra-am-Zu.
Šá-li-ba-a.
ᵈŠamaš-ba-ni.
ŠÚ-A-nim.
ŠÚ-Ištar.
ŠÚ-Ku-bi-im.
Šú-ma-li-ba-A-šur.
Ú-zu-ur-šá-A-šír.
Zu-ga-li-a, f. of *A-šír-ma-lik.*

LIST OF DEITIES CONTAINED IN NAMES

^{d}*Ab.*

Adad (^{d}*IM, A-du*).

Aia.

Am.

^{d}*Amurru* (*MAR.TU*, ^{d}*MAR.TU, A-mu-ru*).

Á-na, ^{d}*Á-na, Á-nim, Á-nu, E-na.*

A-šír, A-šur, ^{d}*A-šír*, ^{d}*A-sur.*

Bêl

Da-gan, Da-ga-an.

E-a, Ê-a, I-a.

El, Ilu (*AN, Al, A-lim, El, E-li, I-el, Î-lí, I-li, I-lim*).

^{d}*En-lil.*

E-šú.

Ga-ga.

Ḫu-bur.

^{d}*Ilabrat* (^{d}*NIN.ŠUBUR, I-lá-áb-ra-at*).

Iš-ḫa-ra.

Ištar (*U.DAR*).

Ki-ki.

Ku-bu-um.

Lá-ba-an.

^{d}*LU.*

Ma-ma.

Na-na.

Nigin-gar.

Ni-ra-aḫ.

Ni-tî.

Nu-nu.

Ra-wa(?).

Sin (*Zu-in, Zu-en*, ^{d}*EN.ZU*).

Šá-lá.

Šamaš (^{d}*UD, UD*).

Šá-ra.

ŠÚ.GAN.

Wi-ir.

Za-bu-um.

Zu.